# SUSTAINABILITY MANAGEMENT AND BUSINESS STRATEGY IN ASIA

# Japanese Management and International Studies
(ISSN: 2010-4448)

**Editor-in-Chief:** Yasuhiro Monden *(University of Tsukuba, Japan)*

*Published*

Vol. 16  *Sustainability Management and Business Strategy in Asia*
edited by Katsuhiko Kokubu & Yoshiyuki Nagasaka

Vol. 15  *Fixed Revenue Accounting: A New Management Accounting Framework*
edited by Kenichi Suzuki & Bruce Gurd

Vol. 14  *Holistic Business Process Management: Theory and Practice*
edited by Gunyung Lee, Masanobu Kosuga & Yoshiyuki Nagasaka

Vol. 13  *Management of Innovation Strategy in Japanese Companies*
edited by Kazuki Hamada & Shufuku Hiraoka

Vol. 12  *Lean Management of Global Supply Chain*
edited by Yasuhiro Monden & Yoshiteru Minagawa

Vol. 11  *Entrepreneurship in Asia: Social Enterprise, Network and Grassroots
Case Studies*
edited by Stephen Dun-Hou Tsai, Ted Yu-Chung Liu, Jersan Hu &
Shang-Jen Li

Vol. 10  *Management of Enterprise Crises in Japan*
edited by Yasuhiro Monden

Vol. 9  *Management of Service Businesses in Japan*
edited by Yasuhiro Monden, Noriyuki Imai, Takami Matsuo &
Naoya Yamaguchi

Vol. 8  *Management of an Inter-Firm Network*
edited by Yasuhiro Monden

Vol. 7  *Business Group Management in Japan*
edited by Kazuki Hamada

Vol. 6  *M&A for Value Creation in Japan*
edited by Yasuyoshi Kurokawa

Vol. 5  *Business Process Management of Japanese and Korean Companies*
edited by Gunyung Lee, Masanobu Kosuga, Yoshiyuki Nagasaka &
Byungkyu Sohn

For the complete list of titles in this series, please go to
http://www.worldscientific.com/series/jmis

# SUSTAINABILITY MANAGEMENT AND BUSINESS STRATEGY IN ASIA

*editors*

## Katsuhiko Kokubu
*Kobe University*

## Yoshiyuki Nagasaka
*Konan University*

 **World Scientific**

NEW JERSEY · LONDON · SINGAPORE · BEIJING · SHANGHAI · HONG KONG · TAIPEI · CHENNAI · TOKYO

*Published by*

World Scientific Publishing Co. Pte. Ltd.

5 Toh Tuck Link, Singapore 596224

*USA office:* 27 Warren Street, Suite 401-402, Hackensack, NJ 07601

*UK office:* 57 Shelton Street, Covent Garden, London WC2H 9HE

**Library of Congress Cataloging-in-Publication Data**

Names: Kokubu, Katsuhiko, 1962–  editor. | Nagasaka, Yoshiyuki, editor.

Title: Sustainability management and business strategy in Asia / edited by
  Katsuhiko Kokubu and Yoshiyuki Nagasaka.

Description: New Jersey : World Scientific, [2019] | Series: Japanese
  management and international studies, 2010-4448 ; Vol. 16

Identifiers: LCCN 2019011584 | ISBN 9789811200182

Subjects: LCSH: Management--Environmental aspects--Asia. |
  Sustainable development--Asia.

Classification: LCC HD30.255 .S869 2019 | DDC 658.4/012--dc23

LC record available at https://lccn.loc.gov/2019011584

**British Library Cataloguing-in-Publication Data**

A catalogue record for this book is available from the British Library.

For any available supplementary material, please visit
https://www.worldscientific.com/worldscibooks/10.1142/11274#t=suppl

Desk Editor: Lum Pui Yee

Typeset by Stallion Press
Email: enquiries@stallionpress.com

# Contents

*Preface*                                                                    ix

*About the Editors*                                                          xi

**Part 1    Japanese Sustainability Management and Disclosure      1**

Chapter 1    The Role of Indicators in Integrating Process of
             Sustainability into Corporate Activities: Case Studies
             of Japanese Companies                                            3
             *Hirotsugu Kitada and Katsuhiko Kokubu*

Chapter 2    Two Way Processes of Environmental Management
             Control Systems — Attention to Inside and Outside
             of Companies                                                    15
             *Takashi Ando*

Chapter 3    Do Sustainability Management Control Systems
             Mediate the Relationship between Corporate
             Governance and CSR Performance? Evidence
             from Japan                                                      33
             *Jaehong Kim and Katsuhiko Kokubu*

Chapter 4    Legitimacy through Corporate Social Responsibility
             Rhetoric: An Analysis of Institutional Context
             and Language                                                    49
             *Yuriko Nakao and Katsuhiko Kokubu*

**Part 2   MFCA Development**     **63**

Chapter 5    Development and Possibilities of MFCA as a Tool
of Sustainability Management: In View of
Japanese, German, and some Asian Experiences     65
*Michiyasu Nakajima*

Chapter 6    How Does Material Flow Cost Accounting Continue
in Practice?: The Effective Policy from a Questionnaire
Survey     81
*Tatsumasa Tennojiya, Akira Higashida,
Hirotsugu Kitada and Jaehong Kim*

Chapter 7    Toward Sustainable Production: The Role of
Emotion in Material Flow Cost Accounting
Practices     95
*Kana Okada, Naoko Komori and Katsuhiko Kokubu*

Chapter 8    Material Flow Time Costing: New Management
Accounting Concept Consistent with Toyota
Production System and Material Flow
Cost Accounting     113
*Noriyuki Imai*

**Part 3   Sustainability Management in Asia**     **129**

Chapter 9    Comprehensive Environmental Management
Control System and Stakeholder Influences:
Evidence from Thailand     131
*Katsuhiko Kokubu, Qi Wu, Kimitaka Nishitani,
Jittima Tongurai and Pakpong Pochanart*

Chapter 10   Corporate Social and Environmental Reporting
Research in Asia: A Structured Literature Review     149
*Trong Q. Trinh*

Chapter 11   Which Factors Influence Sustainability Reporting
in Indonesia? A Literature Review     167
*Nurhayati Soleha*

**Part 4   Advanced Topics**                                              **187**

Chapter 12   Pricing Strategy and Cost Compensation of the
Platforms of a Two-sided Market — With a Case
Study of Amazon Online Shopping                              189
*Yasuhiro Monden*

Chapter 13   Environmental Effect and Economic Analysis of
Environmentally Conscious Capital
Investment — Case of Small Chinese Steel
Company A                                                              203
*Xuechao Meng and Shufuku Hiraoka*

Chapter 14   Environmental Management to Improve Production
Quantity per Unit of Energy: Case Study of a
Japanese Manufacturing Company                        221
*Kenji Hirayama and Yoshiyuki Nagasaka*

*Index*                                                                          239

# Preface

Global environmental problems are the biggest issues of this century. There is a need for drastic responses to problems that hinder global sustainability, such as climate change, resource depletion, and ecosystem destruction. The response of Asian countries is particularly important. Asian GDP is currently the largest in the world, and the Asian Development Bank estimates that it will reach 50% of the global GDP by 2050. In order to solve the global environmental problems and achieve sustainable development, efforts in the Asian region are essential.

Japan has so far led Asian countries in environmental matters. In particular, Japanese companies have been working on sustainability management since the publication of the Kyoto Protocol in 1997 and have produced excellent results. Sustainability management of Japanese companies is spreading to Asia through subsidiaries and business partnerships, and this trend will be further accelerated in the future. Under such circumstances, a broad understanding of the theory and practice of Japanese companies' sustainability management is highly significant for Asian countries and other countries via Asia.

The purpose of this book is to clarify the current state of sustainability management of Japanese companies, to study some effective management methods used therein, and to provide useful suggestions to Asian countries.

Part 1 examines the current state of sustainability management and information disclosure of Japanese companies through case studies, questionnaire surveys, and text analysis. The strength of sustainability management in Japanese companies is that they are systematically operated as part of the corporate management model. In Part 1, we analyze these characteristics from various aspects.

In Part 2, material flow cost accounting (MFCA), which is a sustainability management method developed in Japan, is analyzed from various perspectives. MFCA is an environmental management accounting method that was originally created in Germany and later developed in Japan. International standard ISO 14051 was issued in 2011, and MFCA has recently been introduced in Asian countries where interest is growing. Part 2 analyzes the possibility of sustainability management using MFCA, focusing on case studies of Japanese companies.

In Part 3, we consider sustainability management in Asia. Based on questionnaire and literature surveys, we clarify the current status of sustainability management in three Southeast Asian countries — Thailand, Vietnam, and Indonesia. In order to develop sustainability management in Asia, it is necessary to clearly understand the current state of Asian countries. In this part, we analyze the three countries that are expected to become the center of Asian economic development in the future.

In Part 4, we discuss some issues as advanced topics. Since the area of sustainability management is diverse, various decision-making issues are involved. Part 4 aims to examine some advanced topics related to sustainability management.

Through this book, we hope to deepen the understanding of Japanese companies regarding the theory and practice of sustainability management in Asian countries. Editing of this book was supported by the Environment Research and Technology Development Fund (S-16) of the Environmental Restoration and Conservation Agency, Japan.

August 18, 2019<br>
Katsuhiko Kokubu<br>
Yoshiyuki Nagasaka

# About the Editors

**Katsuhiko Kokubu** is a Professor of Social and Environmental Accounting at Kobe University Graduate School of Business Administration. He completed his PhD in Business Administration at Osaka City University. After serving as an Associate Professor at Osaka City University, Professor Kokubu moved to Kobe University in 1995. He has been Vice President of Kobe University since 2019. Professor Kokubu is a leading scholar of sustainable management and accounting and has been heading the international standardization of material flow cost accounting (MFCA) as a convener for ISO/TC207/WG8. He has published 29 books (one has been translated into Chinese and two into Korean) and more than 200 papers (in English and Japanese) in leading journals including *Journal of Cleaner Production*, *Environmental and Resource Economics*, *Business Strategy and the Environment*, *Accounting, Auditing and Accountability Journal*, and *Accounting, Organizations and Society*.

**Yoshiyuki Nagasaka** is a Professor in the Faculty of Business Administration, Konan University. He received his BS, MS, and PhD degrees in engineering from Osaka University in 1981, 1983, and 1992, respectively. In 1974, he joined Komatsu Ltd. as a researcher. From 1987 to 1989, he studied at the University of British Columbia, Canada. From 1994 to 2001, he was an Associate Professor in the

Faculty of Department of Business Administration, Osaka Sangyo University. He moved to Konan University in 2001. He is the President of Konan University from 2014 to 2020. His research interests include business process management, information technology, and cost management. He is now the Vice Chairman for the Japan Society of Organization and Accounting. He has published many articles and books in English and Japanese. His recent publications include *Holistic Business Process Management* published by World Scientific in 2017.

# Part 1

# Japanese Sustainability Management and Disclosure

# Chapter 1

# The Role of Indicators in Integrating Process of Sustainability into Corporate Activities: Case Studies of Japanese Companies

Hirotsugu Kitada* and Katsuhiko Kokubu†

*Faculty of Business Administration
Hosei University, Chiyoda, Tokyo, Japan
†Graduate School of Business Administration
Kobe University, Kobe, Hyogo Prefective, Japan

## 1. Introduction

Amid an increase in information disclosure processes that consider the views of investors, companies have been embedding sustainability into their business. Rather than just reporting on the relation between sustainability and business activities, firms have also been using key performance indicators (KPIs) to report on targets and results. Decisions on the kind of management indicators selected and the kind of criteria used to select management targets are linked to the kind of relationship the company seeks to build with its society and environment.

At the strategic level — such as in external reporting — attempts have been made to integrate sustainability into corporate activities, but translating this into organizational activities requires further integration at the management system level (Gond *et al.*, 2012). In this process, the use of

KPIs is expected to play an important role within management systems. As well as being the foundation of management control systems (MCS), KPIs are expected to play a role in external reporting.

However, studies suggest that sustainability indicators are not used in a uniform manner. When management systems use indicators for environmental control, improvements in environmental performance have indirect impacts on economic performance (Henri & Jounault, 2010), and the use of indicators may promote the integration process. On the other hand, these frameworks also reflect the demands of external stakeholders in organizational activities (Rodrigue, Magnan & Boulianne, 2013), regulate the organization's internal and external boundaries (Bouten & Hoozee, 2013), and acknowledge social responsibility.

Sustainability indicators thus have a multifaceted nature. Against this background, this study investigates the role of indicators in integration management processes. Specifically, we use case studies on three Japanese companies to analyze each of their management processes.

Our findings are as follows. First, regarding the integration of sustainability into corporate activities, some companies focus on indicator-based control while others prioritize control through their organizational culture. While their objective (i.e., integration) may be the same, companies use different approaches. Second, differences in the approach to management control influence how the demands of stakeholders — particularly investors and rating agencies — are received. Third, the roles environmental control indicators play in the integration process differ depending on which stakeholders are prioritized in the sustainability strategy.

Through these analyses, this study makes two important contributions to the literature. First, it provides a comparative study of companies applying different sustainability management approaches to attain the same integration goal. Second, it shows that indicators are used in different ways depending on whether the interaction between the environment and economics is understood in relation to capital markets or to product markets.

The rest of this chapter is structured as follows. Section 2 reviews the literature to locate the study within the current research. Section 3 describes the study's methodology. Case study analyses are provided in

Section 4. The case studies are discussed in Section 5. Finally, Section 6 concludes the chapter.

## 2. MCS and Integration Management

Recent studies have shown that, when management systems use indicators for environmental control, improvements in environmental performance have indirect impacts on economic performance (e.g., Henri & Journeault, 2010; Henri, Boiral & Roy, 2014). These studies have also shown that the use of systems for environmental control does not have a direct impact on the economic performance. This suggests that companies can link the environment and economics by using management systems based on sustainability indicators, and thereby improve their performance.

A rich body of work in the fields of strategy and business administration has been accumulated concerning the relation between corporate social responsibility (CSR) activities and financial performance. A meta-analysis of these studies shows a positive correlation between the two (e.g., Orlitzky, Schmidt & Rynes, 2003). However, not all companies are able to link their CSR activities to financial performance, and companies that have the ability differ in their capacity to do so (Barnett & Salomon, 2012). One important competence is environmental management control. Since its effectiveness is context-dependent, it is important to clarify the mechanisms by which indicators link the environment to economics.

Further, internal sustainable management efforts tend to be less advanced than external information disclosure efforts, which has a negative impact on investors' evaluations (Hawn & Ioannou, 2016). Amid the growing influence of investors on sustainability activities through integrated reporting, the kind of influence their demands have on internal management is also an important question.

The selection and use of sustainability indicators also function to incorporate social demands into the organization. Establishing environmental management indicators clearly defines stakeholders' demands and engages with them within the organization (Rodrigue, Magnan & Boulianne, 2013). While external reporting and indicator-based internal management influence each other, they also promote and restrict sustainability activities (Bouten & Hoozee, 2013). Therefore, an analysis of the role of indicators in the integration process needs to take into account the role of indicators in mediating social issues.

## 3. Materials and Methods

We conducted interviews with three Japanese companies (who are pseudonymous in this study) to discover how indicators are used within their integration management processes. The cases were selected based on the book by Yin (2003). To analyze the companies' role within integration management processes, we selected companies that had clear environmental elements within their corporate strategy and that had sought to contribute to sustainability through their products and services.

An overview of each of the companies is provided in Table 1. The companies operate in the manufacturing sector. Our interviewees included not only staff in the environmental department but also managers in the finance and corporate planning departments. The interviews were recorded and transcribed. Where necessary, we also refer to internal and public materials, such as lists of the control indicators in use.

**Table 1.** List of interviewees.

| Name of corporation | Industry | Interviewee |
|---|---|---|
| Alpha | Precision manufacturing | • Manager for social and environmental issues<br>• Staff in the social and environmental department<br>• CSR manager<br>• PR manager |
| Beta | Machine tools | • High-level manager in the corporate planning department<br>• High-level CSR manager<br>• Staff in the corporate communication department |
| Gamma | Housing manufacturing | • CFO<br>• CSR officer<br>• High-level environmental manager<br>• High-level PR manager |

## 4. Case Study Analysis

### 4.1 *Alpha case study*

Alpha company is engaged in several business areas, such as multifunction devices, healthcare devices, and industrial materials. It recognizes the role of sustainable management in increasing sales, reducing costs, and raising brand value. It therefore values CDP and other rating agencies, indexes, and external commendations. Alpha has a high level of CSR orientation and takes a proactive approach to sustainable management.

Examples of the strategic elements of Alpha's engagement with sustainable management include its green products, green marketing, and green factory. It also proactively uses non-financial indicators to promote integration management in each of these processes. Let us now analyze the issue from the perspective of products and business processes.

First, in its product-related activities, Alpha sets out numerical targets for the proportion of sales represented by green products, which are managed at the level of management control. At the strategic level, the corresponding indicators are incorporated into the firm's environmental management targets and are reported externally. In other words, Alpha's use of indicators has produced an interaction between the environment and economics. In its actual operations, Alpha has developed certification standards for its green products, which are reflected in its product development.

However, Alpha has not been able to clearly sketch out the relation between green products and profitability. Rather, these indicators have been used to respond to demands from external rating agencies, and efforts to promote integration have been informed by the views of their stakeholders. In this sense, it could be argued that Alpha's integration between sustainability and corporate activities at the product level has a high level of CSR orientation.

Second, in its business processes, Alpha has attempted to integrate sustainability with its corporate activities through optimization. Through its green marketing, it promotes environment-friendly activities in its logistics, packaging, sales, and services; in its green factories, it evaluates and certifies the environmental impact of its production sites. These activities both aim to reduce the company's environmental burden while cutting costs by making their processes more efficient.

At the management control level, these activities are, by definition, elements of cost management, and their environmental contribution is limited to calculating and reporting on the results afterward. Since environmental management has traditionally been associated with additional costs for the company, Alpha has been able to change its mind-set by emphasizing the costs that can be saved by optimizing the use of resources and energy conservation. However, since it is difficult to separate cost-cutting due to environmental measures from other cost reductions from the outset, the environmental contribution ends up being evaluated after the event.

## 4.2  *Beta case study*

Beta company is engaged in a range of business activities involving agricultural machinery, engines, construction machinery, water treatment facilities, and other markets. It began to make proactive environmental efforts at an early stage in the 1990s. Since its products are in areas closely related to social and environmental issues, such as water, agriculture, and energy, the company recognized the relation between improving and selling its products and solutions to local and social issues.

For example, manufacturing and selling agricultural machinery in Thailand, Vietnam, and other parts of Southeast Asia was understood to improve local productivity as well as generate employment and contribute significantly to sustainable development. In recent years, economic development and urban migration in Southeast Asia have led to the modernization of agriculture and a greater need for machinery and equipment. Beta's products promote more efficient food productivity, and responding to customer needs is also seen as contributing to solving social issues.

The intersection between business activities generated through products and services and sustainability is easy to break down into strategies and operations. Thus, Beta uses ordinary financial indicators rather than setting out special indicators for integration management at the management control level. However, to complement its indicator-based MCS, Beta incorporates environmental considerations into its organizational culture and other informal management frameworks.

Beta deals in a range of products, such as agricultural machinery, engines, construction machinery, and water treatment facilities. Its customers thus vary widely, from individual farmers to construction and automobile businesses, to the government, each relying on different commercial practices, contract terms, and product life cycles. Various organizational cultures have therefore been formed at each site. Given this state of affairs, Beta has been reluctant to apply non-financial indicators for its company-wide management.

On the other hand, its internal management places importance on developing interpersonal networks, with the organizational culture positioned as underpinning human relations. The emphasis on the cultural aspects of organizational control is also applied to sustainable management. Rather than using indicators to manage the environment or society, such approaches are reflected in the culture of the organization.

## 4.3 *Gamma case study*

gamma company operates in the housing sector. It began to record a deficit during the 2008 financial crisis, but its subsequent strategies have come to recognize the importance of an environmental strategy. The environmental impact of Gamma's products appeals to its highly educated customers, and efficient utility costs and its eligibility for government subsidies also help differentiate it from other companies. Customer needs have thus influenced the direction of its integration management, with Gamma developing strongly customer-oriented eco-products.

Being able to link products and services to social or environmental issues makes it easier for a company to try to integrate sustainability and corporate activities at the strategic level. Gamma's environment-friendly homes have received much attention since the change in social attitudes to renewable energy occurred following the 2011 earthquake and tsunami. Traditionally, Gamma has provided high-quality housing at high prices, targeting highly educated, high-earning customers. This customer bracket is particularly sensitive to environmental issues, which makes Gamma's products a good match for their needs. Gamma's environment-friendly housing accounts for at least 80% of sales.

Gamma also started using solar power and Ene-Farm in its environment-friendly housing before other companies and has been able to receive government subsidies on terms more favorable than those its competitor products have been offered. In this sense, rather than being oriented simply toward realizing economic and environmental factors through its products, Gamma has incorporated the environment into its development and commercialization processes as a way of differentiating itself from its competitors. These products are difficult for other companies to copy and form into a sustainable core competence (Chen, 2008), enabling Gamma to use its product image and government projects to differentiate itself from other companies to generate a competitive edge.

Because Gamma has integrated the environment and corporate activities at the product and strategic levels in this way, it uses ordinary financial information for management control purposes. Like Beta, Gamma emphasizes the embedding of a sustainability approach within its organizational culture.

However, Gamma does not use non-financial environmental indicators to promote the integration between business and sustainability. Gamma eliminated the environmental elements that lack customer appeal from its strongly customer-oriented integration management. Biodiversity is a representative example of such a category. Unlike energy conservation at home, burdening the consumer with additional costs would not necessarily contribute significantly to differences in quality or function.

Gama uses non-financial indicators to manage these factors. Instead of promoting integration between the product and strategic management, Gamma controls other environmental elements that appeal to investors and other stakeholders. These indicators complement Gamma's sustainability management by covering non-profitable aspects of environmental concerns.

## 5. Discussion

This study was designed to investigate the role of indicators in integration management processes. Specifically, we use case studies of three Japanese companies to analyze each of their management processes. The findings yield valuable insights into the effects of using sustainability indicators in combination with social, environmental, and economic activities.

First, among the processes applied within the three companies to integrate sustainability into their corporate activities, some have focused on indicator-based control and others have focused on control through their organizational culture. While their aim (i.e., integration) might be the same, the companies use different approaches. The companies differ in their capacity to link their CSR performance to financial performance (Barnett & Salomon, 2012), and this difference in competence also influences how effectively the indicators are used in the integration process. Alpha, recognizing that its products do not contribute to sustainability as such, developed non-financial indicators related to sustainability and oriented its organizational activities along these lines. By contrast, Beta and Gamma were aware that the environment was integrated into their corporate activities at both the product and strategic levels, which enabled them to manage their organizations through an MCS comprising ordinary financial indicators. Incorporating sustainability into their informal systems, such as in their company's vision and culture, also complemented the use of these indicators (Epstein, Buhovac & Yuthas, 2015).

Second, differences in management control also impact how the demands of investors and rating agencies are received. Establishing and reporting on internal management systems relating to sustainability activities generate useful information from the point of view of investors and rating agencies (Hawn & Ioannou, 2016). Alpha developed an eco-product certification system to reflect the demands of investors and rating agencies, promoting the integration of the environment with corporate activities at the product level. It then used indicators to control its progress and disclosed the information externally. As accountability in external information disclosure was consistent with accountability for internal management purposes, the company was able to build on this link to advance its sustainability activities.

For Beta and Gamma, on the other hand, the aim of externally disclosing non-financial information was to take into account the demands of investors and rating agencies and then legitimatize their organization. However, this was decoupled from their internal integration management. With the environment and economics integrated at the product and strategic levels, Beta and Gamma designed their management systems in relation to their customers. Thus, their accountability frameworks for information disclosure to investors were not necessarily consistent with their internal management frameworks.

Third, our findings suggest that the role of environmental control indicators in the integration process differs depending on which stakeholders are prioritized in the sustainability strategy. Henri and Journeault (2010) showed that the use of environmental control indicators had an impact on business results through improved environmental performance. As our case studies show, however, indicator-based control is effective in integration process when sustainability management systems take into account the views of investors, but the use of indicators is not necessarily effective when customers are the focus; in such a case, the alternative — whereby control is based on organizational culture — has a greater effect.

Beta and Gamma took customer needs into account in their sustainability management. For these companies, the role of sustainability indicators was to complement the sustainability elements that tended to be neglected in their product development. When sustainability is promoted within product development, the latter concept often takes priority, and any environmental elements that do not fit tend to be neglected. External stakeholders therefore need to be the judge of whether the content of activities and standards are socially appropriate. Sustainability indicators that are disconnected from the integration process can still function effectively in processes that incorporate the demands of stakeholders (Rodrigue, Magnan & Boulianne, 2013).

Using sustainability indicators as control indicators and determining targets serve to incorporate external perspectives into the organization (Rodrigue, Magnan & Boulianne, 2013; Bouten & Hoozee, 2013; Contrafatto & Burns, 2013). However, management based on these indicators can generate conflict between economics and the environment, particularly in the short term. The use of indicators can thus also restrict corporate activities (Burns & Stalker, 1961).

## 6. Conclusion

This chapter reports on three case studies of Japanese companies. We analyzed their integration management processes and investigated the role of indicators. We focused on the use of indicators in the integration process and report several findings. First, in integrating sustainability into their corporate activities, some companies focus on indicator-based controls, while others prioritize control through their organizational culture. While their purpose (i.e., integration) is the same, companies use different approaches. Second, the differing approaches to management control impact how stakeholder demands — particularly demands from investors and rating agencies — are received. Third, the role that indicators play in environmental control in the integration process differs depending on how the firm prioritizes its stakeholders in its sustainability strategy.

Through these analyses, this chapter makes two contributions to the literature. First, it provides a comparative study of companies that apply different sustainability management approaches to attain the same integration goal. Second, it shows that companies use indicators differently, depending on whether they understand the interaction between the environment and economics in relation to capital markets or product markets.

Our findings, particularly the evidence on the differences in integration process depending on stakeholder prioritization, have implications for sustainability managers who design the MCS for companies to achieve their sustainability strategies. Furthermore, our evidence is important for rating agencies that focus on sustainability issues, as they concentrate on evaluating the corporate internal management capability to assess sustainability performance. Although these assessments mainly address formal sustainability management systems, some companies can integrate sustainable development using mainly informal management systems, such as the cultural aspects of organizational controls.

## Acknowledgments

This work was supported by JSPS KAKENHI Grant Numbers JP18H03824, JP16H03679, and JP18K12902.

## References

Barnett, M. L. and Salomon, R. M. (2012). Does it pay to be really good? Addressing the shape of the relationship between social and financial performance. *Strategic Management Journal 33*(11), 1304–1320.

Burns, T. E. and Stalker, G. M. (1961). *The Management of Innovation*. Rochester, NY: Social Science Research Network.

Bouten, L. and Hoozée, S. (2013). On the interplay between environmental reporting and management accounting change. *Management Accounting Research 24*(4), 333–348.

Chen, Y. S. (2008). The driver of green innovation and green image–green core competence. *Journal of Business Ethics 81*(3), 531–543.

Gond, J. P., Grubnic, S., Herzig, C. and Moon, J. (2012). Configuring management control systems: Theorizing the integration of strategy and sustainability. *Management Accounting Research 23*(3), 205–223.

Epstein, M. J., Buhovac, A. R. and Yuthas, K. (2015). Managing social, environmental and financial performance simultaneously. *Long Range Planning 48*(1), 35–45.

Henri, J. F. and Journeault, M. (2010). Eco-control: The influence of management control systems on environmental and economic performance. *Accounting, Organizations and Society 35*(1), 63–80.

Henri, J. F., Boiral, O. and Roy, M. J. (2014). The tracking of environmental costs: Motivations and impacts. *European Accounting Review 23*(4), 647–669.

Hawn, O. and Ioannou, I. (2016). Mind the gap: The interplay between external and internal actions in the case of corporate social responsibility. *Strategic Management Journal 37*(13), 2569–2588.

Orlitzky, M., Schmidt, F. L. and Rynes, S. L. (2003). Corporate social and financial performance: A meta-analysis. *Organization Studies 24*(3), 403–441.

Rodrigue, M., Magnan, M. and Boulianne, E. (2013). Stakeholders' influence on environmental strategy and performance indicators: A managerial perspective. *Management Accounting Research 24*(4), 301–316.

Yin, R. K. (2003). *Applications of Case Study Research*, 4th edn. Applied Social Research Methods. Thousand Oaks: Sage Publications.

# Chapter 2

# Two Way Processes of Environmental Management Control Systems — Attention to Inside and Outside of Companies

Takashi Ando

*Chiba University of Commerce, 1-3-1 Kounodai, Ichikawa*
*Chiba Prefecture 272-8512, Japan*

## 1. Introduction

In recent years, interest in environmental management control research has increased in two accounting-related areas, namely management accounting and environmental accounting. Environmental management control has been a topic of debate since emerging from the environmental accounting field as eco-controlling (Öko-controlling) in the 1990s. Notable research on environmental management control in the management accounting field began to appear after the 2000s, indicating that the concept is not new in either field. However, a likely reason for increasing attention in recent years is the shifting focus of discussions. Before 2010, most centered on system design; however, after 2010, focus shifted to system use (Ando, 2015).

Environmental management control aims to achieve both environmental *and* economic development goals. Anthony (1988, p. 10) defines a management control system as follows:

"Management control is the process by which managers influence other members of the organisation to implement the organisation's strategies" (Anthony, 1988).

In this chapter, I add two concepts to Anthony's definition to define environmental management control: *Environmental Strategy* not only aims toward an economical goal but also toward both environmental and economical goals. In addition, environmental management control not only implements but also creates environmental strategies. With these two additional points, environmental management control is defined here as *a management process by which managers influence other members of the organization to implement and create the organization's environmental strategy*. The *environment* and *economy*, elements of strategy, are not subordinates to each other. We must acknowledge the equal importance of both.

The purpose of this chapter is to elucidate the process and features of environmental management control systems (EMCS) inside and outside of companies. The internal process includes (1) formulation of goals and policies, (2) collection of information, (3) supporting decisions, (4) implementation and controls, and (5) internal and external communication by previous researches. Then I compared EMCs to management control systems (MCS) using a case study. I find that the most characteristic point of EMCs is the last stage, "communication." Due to the lack of sufficient descriptions about environmental communication in previous studies, I try to be clear about this point using a case study.

The chapter is structured as follows. In Section 2, I formulate an environmental management control process based on prior research. Then, I compare traditional and environmental management control to elucidate the characteristics of environmental management control. I clarify that compared to traditional management control and indicate an important characteristic of environmental management control, which is the emphasis on communication with extended stakeholders. In Section 3, after clarifying the characteristics (aims, methods, and organizational results) of environmental communication, I discuss its significance. Then I introduce an actual case which promotes environmental management control by environmental communication for deeper understanding. Finally, I state the conclusions and our future challenges in Section 5.

## 2. The Processes of EMCS

In this section, I first discuss traditional management control to clarify the characteristics of environmental management control. Here, I examine Anthony (1988) as a good basis for the understanding of traditional concepts on this subject.

### 2.1 *The internal process of EMCS*

At first, we discuss the internal process of MCS and find the characteristics of its concept. In order to clearly understand the characteristics of EMCs, we are going to confirm the basic process of management control. Then we review the process of EMCs by looking at previous research, comparing the two concepts. This will finally make clear the characteristics of EMC.

#### 2.1.1 *The process of management control systems*

Anthony (1988) explains management control as a five-stage business process, namely planning, budgeting, execution, evaluation, and rewards (see Fig. 1).

Planning and strategic planning are different concepts. A strategy comprises two aspects, namely formulation and action. Strategic planning relates

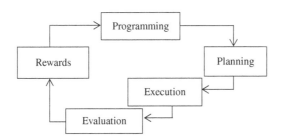

**Fig. 1.** Anthony's (1988) management control process.

*Source*: Extracted from Yokota (1998, p. 53).

to the former and planning to the latter. A characteristic difference for Anthony (1988) is that strategic planning is unsystematic, while planning is systematic. Budgeting is a more specific expression of planning. A budget is a plan, usually expressed in monetary terms and usually for a period of one future year (Anthony, 1988, p. 87). Anthony (1988) emphasizes the importance of the next step, performance evaluation, which is important because (1) evaluation becomes a powerful source of motivation for managers, and (2) evaluating decisions and the results of recent activities provide the foundation on which plans for the following term can be reconsidered. Anthony (1988) notes that rewards comprise subjective and objective elements, and the higher the management position, the greater the influence by the former. Rewards and performance evaluation serve an important function in motivating the subject in relation to work responsibilities. In this section, I reviewed the traditional management control process. In Section 2.1.2, I develop an environmental management control process based on prior research.

### 2.1.2  *The internal process of EMCS*

Originating in Germany and its surroundings, environmental management control first emerged as *Öko-Controlling* (eco-controlling). As far as I could determine through a review of the research, Schaltegger and Sturm (1998) were the first to publish on the subject systematically. Aiming to popularize the concept, their book included case studies on the eco-controlling system, which was emerging in Germanic regions at the time. Their book provides the fundamentals for designing a traditional EMC. Nearly two decades later, its content remains rich with practical insights. Therefore, Schaltegger and Sturm (1998) serve as the focus of the review on the environmental management control process, with Schaltegger and Burritt (2000) supplementing the argument.

Schaltegger and Sturm (1998) argued that an EMC should not be based on environmental issues, but on existing financial control systems. In addition, as the purpose of financial control is the pursuit of economic efficiency and effectiveness, environmental management control should pursue economic and environmental efficiency and effectiveness as a purpose. This characteristic is clear in Fig. 2.

Schaltegger and Burritt (2000) explain that when using the matrix in Fig. 2, it is important to move all segments of the quadrant toward the

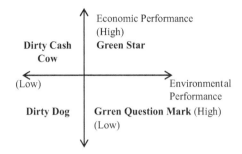

**Fig. 2.**  Eco-efficiency portfolio matrix.

*Source*: Designed by the author based on Schaltegger and Burritt (2000, p. 391).

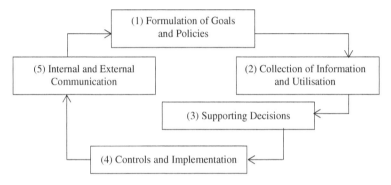

**Fig. 3.**  The Implementing Process of Environmental Management Control Systems.

*Source*: Designed by the author based on Schaltegger and Sturm (1998) and Schaltegger and Burritt (2000).

"green star" status. In other words, to move toward the segment that achieves high environmental and economic performance. In addition, it is understood from this matrix that environmental management control is MCs with both environmental and economic purpose. Considering the results of Schaltegger and Sturm (1998) and Schaltegger and Burritt (2000), environmental management control is a five-step process, as seen in Fig. 3 — (1) formulation of goals and policies, (2) collection of information, (3) supporting decisions, (4) implementation and controls, and (5) internal and external communication.

In *Stage* 1, it is necessary that clear goals and policies are formulated. This is an important stage, as formulated goals and policies determine the fundamental direction of the EMCS (Schaltegger and Sturm, 1998).

In *Stage* 2, information is collected and utilized. Two previous studies highlight the necessity of collecting information from various sources (e.g., from environmental accounting and environmental reports) during development. Essentially, the foundation of environmental management control is information management (Schaltegger and Burritt, 2000). Specifically, using analytical data based on Material Flow Cost Accounting, which is discussed later, and environmental management accounting information measured with performance drivers as seen in a sustainability-balanced score card (SBSC) contributes to development during this stage.

In *Stage* 3, support for decisions is sought. Here, an environmental version of the BCG matrix in Fig. 2 is effective. Using this matrix makes it easier to make strategic decisions based on an evaluation of the economic and environmental impact of a product, strategic business unit, and various industries.

*Stage* 4 is the controls and implementation phase. During this stage, an environmental performance evaluation system and accompanying reward system is developed. This is the backbone of the EMCS.

*Stage* 5 is the final stage of the process, refers to the corporation's internal and external communication. Schaltegger and his co-authors repeatedly emphasize the importance of widely sharing information on the corporation's engagement in environmental issues, both internally and externally.

### 2.1.3 *The importance of communication in EMCS*

The arguments in the Sections 2.1.1 and 2.1.2 confirm that the biggest difference between traditional management control and environmental management control is the emphasis on communication in Stage 5 (as seen when comparing Figs. 1 and 3). However, why is environmental communication important enough to be emphasized as the final stage of environmental management control? Simons (1995), who discusses in detail the importance and methods of control with an emphasis on communication, states that the purpose of communication is to reduce environmental uncertainty.

However, I think the purpose of environmental communication is not only to reduce uncertainty. In Section 2.2, I discuss the purpose and features of EMCs (focusing especially on environmental communication).

## 2.2 *The external process of EMCs*

The importance of environmental communication based on environmental management control theory has been advocated since the last half of the 1990s. However, it was only after 2010 that researchers began probing specifics to develop a body of research on the subject. This section refers to Arjaliès and Mundy (2013) as a representative case of research after 2010, emphasizing environmental communication in environmental management control use. Through this review, I examine the functional purpose of environmental communication in environmental management control.

### 2.2.1 *Characteristics of environmental communication*

Arjaliès and Mundy (2013) surveyed France's largest publicly listed corporations — members of the CAC 40 — to determine how they utilized an MC to implement corporate social responsibility (CSR) strategies. Their research aimed to clear the problem "How do organizations use management control systems to manage CSR strategy?" For this purpose, they created a questionnaire based on prior research, and employed Simons' (1995) Levers of Control (LoC) theory as a framework. The advantage of this theory is that it targets the highly uncertain market environment where strategy formation is not given. In addition, Simons (1995) asserts the importance of using four different control levers based on market characteristics and the product life cycle. Arjaliès and Mundy (2013) substantiate their use of Simons (1995) as their analytical tool based on (1) its usefulness in conditions where new opinions from stakeholders are sought and in encouraging strategic change, (2) it being an analytical tool that is useful in dealing with strategic uncertainty, and (3) its ability to motivate managers as multifaceted performance evaluation indicators. Respondents to the questionnaire were the managers of CSR Departments (CSRD). Furthermore, the response rate for the survey was high at 87.5%. The results were tabulated similar to that in Table 1.

Figure 4 shows how, for what purpose, and the effectiveness of the four control levers (Simons, 1995) in CSR strategy management. Here, CSR strategy management is (1) *the execution of intended strategy*, (2) *gathering up-to-date information from the ground up and incorporating emergent*

**Table 1.** How to use the levers of control for CSR strategy.

| | Diagnostic process to manage critical performance variables | Interactive process to manage strategic uncertainties and opportunities |
|---|---|---|
| Purpose | to define and measure key performance indicators for CSR strategy against internal and external targets; to identify the gaps between achievements to date and past plans | to reveal and dabate emergent strategies and identify opportunities for innovation in relation to CSR activities |
| How leveraged | senior managers/CSRDs use reports to manage the activities of operational departments in relation to the performance of critical CSR activities | through regular and formal discussions between CSRD/senior managers and operational managers |
| Example of MCS | used to provide information on performance: EMS, standerdized CSR reporting processes (GRI, Global Compact); competitive benchmarking | used interactively:regular meetings between CSRD and operational managers; intranet systems for communities of practitoners; exchange of best practices to share innovations |

| | Belief systems to communicate core values | Boundary process to manage risks |
|---|---|---|
| Purpose | to establish a shared vision of CSR;to unite employees around a set of organizational values;to inspire employees to seek opprtunities | to set strategic limits and business conduct boundaries around CSR plans and activities |
| How leveraged | formal and explicit statements of intentions with respect to CSR mission and values | formal and explicit statements of appropriate and inappropriate areas for consideration in CSR strategy and of acceptable and proscribed behaviours |
| Example of MCS | use to communicate values and purpose:CSR strategic plans; organizational-wide conferences; 'Values Chart', mission statements; training sessions; communication tools such as intranet | used to provide boundaries: external documentation on legal and voluntary regulations e.g. NRE,GRI tha help to identify key strategic priorities (e.g. reduction in $CO_2$ emissions); guidelines on approved activities; ethic guides,code of conduct, anti-bribery guidelines; guidelines on best or recommended practices; job descriptions (e.g.purchasers); communities of best practice |

*Source*: Extracted and modified from Arjaliès and Mundy (2013, p. 296).

*strategies*. Anthony (1988) initially intended the theory for system design. However, if we try to effectively utilize the system Anthony (1985) proposed, then according to the LOC framework (Simons, 1995), it would be effective to mobilize the diagnostic control lever to achieve the aforementioned (1).

However, in this chapter, we attend another purpose, namely system utilization to create new strategies. Especially Arjaliès and Mundy (2013) elucidate concrete ways of utilization by focusing on environmental communication. Specific examples of the means of communication are strategic planning of documents, organization-wide conferences, company intranet, and physical artefacts such as posters. Through such communications, corporate members evaluate their own strengths and weaknesses in implementing a new strategy and realize the necessity of concrete action that conforms to the CSR strategy.

Through such communication what organizational results do we get? The answer to this question is the result of interactive use. The interactive process promotes communication between upper managers, employees, suppliers, and other stakeholders to share information and ideas. Through such activities, organizations enhance their legitimacy and reputation. Indeed, many corporations in the automotive and chemical industries aspire toward a more interactive use such as communication. The following is an excerpt from a supplementary interview Arjaliès and Mundy (2013) conducted with the corporations in their study: *We believe CSR is a tool to stimulate innovation via relationships with our stakeholders, whoever they are*. Finally, we can find the feature that Arjaliès and Mundy (2013) defined — environmental management control as a method of implementing CSR strategy and as a process of the corporation's internal and external communication.

## 2.2.2 *Significance of environmental communication*

According to Simons (1995), the purpose of communication in management control theory within the management accounting field is to reduce environmental uncertainty. In turn, it should be noted that compared to Simons (1995), the target and reach of communication has dramatically increased. Even Arjaliès and Mundy (2013) noted the appearance of stakeholders from a wider circle beyond economic interests, such as environmental conservation groups and NGOs. I believe that this highlights

the significance of environmental communication, as evident in the aforementioned quote by Arjaliès and Mundy (2013), who use the word "whoever." Likely, this points to entities with interests in addition to economic
ones with whom the company has a relationship.

   In other words, this could mean that corporations have begun to aban-
don their perceptions of being economic entities and have shifted their
vision, now sharing and strengthening their identities as active, living
entities as inhabitants of this planet. In recent years, in the environmental
accounting field, there has been a shift from CSR to Creating Shared
Value (CSV) (Porter & Kramer, 2011). Porter and Kramer (2011) define
CSV as "Policies and operating practices that enhance the competitiveness of a company while simultaneously advancing the economic and
social conditions in the communities in which it operates" (Porter &
Kramer, 2011, p. 6). According to Kokubu (2015), CSV is "a strategy
where a corporation tries to increase the common value of the ever-wider
circle of stakeholders that surround the corporation and in doing so, aims
for its own growth" (Kokubu, 2015, p. 27). In this way, we see that what
was envisioned in past management accounting is now extended into the
environmental accounting field, including its targeted stakeholders, time-
line, and an expanded area of activities. For this reason, the theory is gaining attention and many are following its development.

   In other words, the purpose of the environmental communication does not
merely only reduce environmental uncertainty. It brings radical innovation
through association with the main constituent inside and outside the company
which did not matter before and it positively and finally brings about CSV.
However, it is difficult to get a realistic understanding because I examined the
past discussion mainly by reviewing documents. Therefore, in Section 3, I'll
introduce a case of the cooperation between Panasonic Corporation (home-
appliance maker in Japan) and Greenpeace Japan (the environmental NGO).
Through it, let's formulate the external process of EMC.

   Simons (1995) says the aim of communication in standard management
control is to reduce environmental uncertainly. When companies tackle
environmental uncertainly, it is convenient to use interactive control systems (Simons 1995). But environmental management control can use
communication to create CSV. The main targets of standard management
control are economic interests, but environmental management control's
aim is wider (economic, social and ecological). Finally standard management control results in emergence of a new strategy through innovation,

**Table 2.** Differences in Standard Management Control and Environmental Management Control.

|  | **Standard Management Control** | **Environmental Management Control** |
|---|---|---|
| Purpose | Reduce environmental uncertainty | Create a common social value and shared purpose |
| Target | Stakeholders have an economic interest | Stakeholders have economic and environmental interest |
| Results | Emergence of a new strategy through innovation, or adaptation to the environment through such innovations | Generates radical innovations that standard management control is difficult to produce |

or adaptation to the environment through such innovations (Simons 1995), but environmental them tend to result in radical innovations that are difficult to produce by standard management control. A main reason of resulting in radical innovation by environmental management controls is open innovation tends to lead to such orientation. Open innovation is the result of cooperation with strangers that they are difficult to meet before. Especially environmental management controls' scope is not only economical goals but also social and ecological goals, so they tend to create a lot of goals and value. Differences in standard management control and environmental management control are summarized in Table 2.

## 3. Case Study (Cooperation of Panasonic Corporation and Greenpeace Japan)

In this chapter, we argue about the importance of environmental communication in the evolution of environmental management control. Then let's see the actual example, so we can understand this theory more deeply. This case is the interaction between Panasonic Corporation (previously known as Matsushita Refrigeration Company) and NGO Greenpeace Japan.[1] Panasonic is mainly a home appliance company and Greenpeace is an international environmental NGO. In general, companies and NGOs had entirely different aims and performance evaluation systems. But in this chapter, I'll introduce an example of organizations as different as water and oil that cooperated in the commercialization of non-Freon refrigerating machines in three periods — Introduction, Evolution, and Results.

---

[1]This section's information is based on Sasaki (2009) and Aihara (2009).

## 3.1  *Introduction*

Greenpeace Japan, founded in 1979, has about 6,000 supporters and their total equity was about 196 million yen (on 31 December 2015). The beginning of their activities can be traced to the time when 13 journalists and students opposed a nuclear test in the USA. There are two main features of their activities — (1) policies mainly involving direct action, and (2) the evolution of their activities were mainly based on donations from their supporters, and a policy of no donations at all from governments or corporations. There are about three million Greenpeace supporters in the world, and 6,000 supporters in Japan. Their range of activities is very wide. For example, they support nuclear abolition, disarmament, forest preservation, preservation of oceanographic ecology, and oppose genetic modification. However, in their early years, their main activity was drawing attention to global warming. Their main target in the early stages of their environmental activism was to get people to change from using chlorofluorocarbon substitute (CFC) to alternative chlorofluorocarbon substitute (alternative CFCs). Even now non-Freon refrigerating machines are popular with everyone, and it has the majority of the market share. However in the early 2000s, this machine had not yet been developed. Panasonic was the first developer of this type of refrigerator in February 2002. Non-Freon refrigerating machines are said to be environmentally friendly. This type of refrigerator has a global warming factor of 3, but the standard type of refrigerator has a factor of 1300. Panasonic planned to get a competitive advantage by developing a product that was environmentally friendly and saved energy. In the background of this new machine, there was a cooperative and conflictive relationship between the maker of the refrigerator and the NGO.

In the first place, the technology of non-Freon refrigerating machine was developed in Germany. Before 1994, all German companies had changed from Freon to non-Freon-type refrigerators. Greenpeace and Folon Corporation were the first developers of this type of refrigerators in the country. So Greenpeace Japan wished to co-develop with Folon Corporation to penetrate non-Freon-type refrigerators in Japan. So Greenpeace Japan formulated their strategy where (1) proposed makers create alternative Freon-type refrigerators, (2) making public opinion more aware of the environment, and (3) strengthened the international and domestic rules and so on.

On the other hand, Panasonic was aggressively trying to develop on its own. By, for example, (1) changing chlorofluorocarbon substitute (in 1993), (2) developing insular non-CFC (in 1994), and (3) creating inverter refrigerators (in 1996) and so on. Greenpeace Japan appreciated Panasonic's activity. Greenpeace Japan visited Matsushita's laboratory, where they exchanged their ideas on developing and penetrating non-Freon-type refrigerators and dispatched a member of Greenpeace Japan for employee environmental education. At this stage, their partnership was very friendly and cooperative.

In summary, Panasonic aimed to maintain strategic positioning as an "environmental frontier company" and the non-Freon refrigerating machine was the ideal environmentally conscious product. And Panasonic wished to keep a good relationship with Greenpeace Japan. On the other hand, Greenpeace Japan wished to reduce the time it took to produce non-Freon refrigerators in Japan. Therefore, they focused on Panasonic, because they had the top market share, and the basic technology of this product.

Then Greenpeace Japan pressurized Panasonic for early commercialization. For example, they continued developing grass-root campaigns (e.g., (a) visiting Panasonic with the signatures of 12,000 consumers (June, 1999), (b) telephone campaign and the penguin campaign in the Osaka electronics quarter, (c) the comparison of refrigerators displayed in the eco-product exhibition). And they announced public statements such as "I wished Panasonic had made non-Freon refrigerating machine earlier!", "When can we buy non-Freon refrigerating machine!?" and "Panasonic is warming the earth by producing a chlorofluorocarbon alternative machine that warms the earth!!" Then they continued calling for clarification at the time of release. Panasonic says "That time was a true period of conflict."

## 3.2 *Evolution* (*January 1999–January 2002*)

Panasonic started an organizing committee to take measures to meet Greenpeace Japan. For example, Panasonic visited Greenpeace Japan and explained the basic way of thinking about the non-Freon refrigerator, and they corresponded by organizing a postcard campaign to answer to the Greenpeace International Secretary General.

In addition, they began to create voluntary safety standards in October, 1999 with the goal of finishing them by January 2001. The Japan Electrical Manufacturer's Association (JEMA), began the implementation of independent safety standards which were to be used across the whole industry.

And Panasonic answered to Greenpeace Japan by saying it intended "to commercialize non-Freon by the end of 2002". And Greenpeace Japan introduced a technique which allowed for the realization of commodification gratis from Germany. It also supported Panasonic in various ways. Panasonic finally shipped non-Freon refrigerators on 1 February 2002.

Looking back at the situation during the time Mr. Takahiro Mori of Panasonic (the General Manager of the Corporate Communication division) states, "I took a big hint to find a problem in the Greenpeace Japan", and Masafumi Kimura (Corporate Communication Secretary General) states, "Environmental NGOs have a responsibility to propose and criticize equally. And a sustainable company is necessary for sustainable society."

### 3.3 *Results (After February 2002)*

The unit sales of refrigerators in 2001 of Panasonic was 880,000 and the market share decreased to 18.3%. It improved to 115 million in 2002, and 111 million and 22.3% market share in 2003. Besides, Panasonic impressed many environmentally-conscious people, and completely changed the flow of the whole industry. Moreover, 95% of home refrigerators in the country were non-Freon type at the end of 2003.

## 4. A Case Analysis

In Section 3, we saw how Panasonic changed the development of its refrigerator products to the non-Freon type and how its relationship worked with the NGO. I can summarize the process of the outside communication of the environmental management control in Fig. 4.

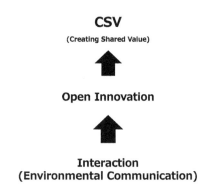

**Fig. 4.** Co-creation Process of External Environmental Management Control Systems.

I will divide the communication into two phases for the construction stage of the relationship. This external communication (external environmental management control system) process is a co-creation process of a company and NGO. At first Panasonic and the Greenpeace Japan succeed in building friendly relations. Actually, the environmental NGO appreciated the action for advanced environmental problem of Panasonic. Then the environmental NGO went offensive by (1) dispatching a lecturer for environmental education, and (2) visiting Panasonic for development and spread of non-Freon-type refrigerators. For the environmental consideration product to be realized quickly, the company tried to influence the public opinion, as well as other approaches, including the strategic bridging of environmental technology that was free of charge in the company. The company set up a new post within the (1) company and applied pressure in the (2) trade group making the system of measures transversely in the company; the company builds the relationship that they previously did not have. And Panasonic sold the non-Freon-type refrigerator which greatly changed the direction of the electric Industry on 1st February, 2002.

According to Chesbrough (2006), open innovation is "a paradigm that assumes that firms can and should use external ideas as well as internal ideas, and internal and external paths to market, as the firms look to advance their technology." (Chesbrough, 2006) Open innovation accesses a market through a channel other than the existing company to commercialize ideas and creates added value. In the past, Japanese companies in particular often accumulated the source of the comparative advantage in a company. In other words, it was "closed." However, in recent years, the boundary of the organization lowered and came to take in the useful assets across a border for the company. Panasonic in this case and the cooperation activity of Greenpeace are rightly equivalent to this open innovation. Conventionally, the environmental NGO displayed intense opposition to a company. They were like "water and the oil" so to speak. However, recently companies cannot divide into such discord as in the past and they now succeed in bringing epoch-making innovation. I am concerned with the individual and the organization of the company outside having useful assets for the company.

Finally, Panasonic greatly enhanced to the popularity of being an "environment consideration company" by the sale of the non-Freon-type refrigerator which greatly changed the direction of the industry. And through this, Panasonic made more profit than ever before. It is CSV that Porter and Kramer (2011) talked about. Recently, companies are building a relationship with various stakeholders from a longer term point of view. And they begin to make much of improving value to society. Porter and Kramer (2011) define CSV as "policies and operating practices that enhance the competitiveness of a company while simultaneously advancing the economic and social conditions in the communities in which it operates." (Porter & Kramer, 2011, p. 66) And Kokubu (2015) interprets it as a "strategy to aim at the growth of the company by raising the common value with the enlarged stakeholder main constituent surrounding the company" (Kokubu, 2015, p. 27). In fact, the action to get profit only for the company will not last long, if a company aims at growth continuously for a long term. In short, companies have a role of a social member, so to some extent they need to be conscious of the public while acquiring their own profit. In the case of Panasonic, it succeeds in reaching such an aim as a result of developing and producing environment-conscious products.

## 5. Conclusion and Our Future Challenges

This chapter elucidates the process of EMCs inside and outside of companies. The internal processes have been clear — (1) formulation of goals and policies, (2) collection of information and utilization, (3) supporting decisions, (4) controls and implementation, and (5) internal and external communication by previous researches. Then I compared EMCs to MCs; I find that the most characteristic point of EMC is the last stage "communication." Due to the lack of sufficient descriptions about environmental communication in previous studies, I try to be clear about this point by using a case study. In this case, which involves Panasonic Corporation (previously known as Matsushita Refrigeration Company) and NGO Greenpeace Japan, the outside processes are (1) interaction, (2) open innovation, and (3) CSV. The main contribution of this study is the external way of EMC of the companies.

But I think the most important feature of Environmental Management Control is in the internal process. In traditional management control study, the communication style is debate and dialogue (Simons, 1995, the latter style is called "communication" in this chapter). But why is it the only effective communication in Environmental Management Control? I think almost everyone knows well that the environmental problem is very important. Since it is not so difficult, we can mutually agree by polite communication. I think this polite communication is better in a face-to-face style. This communication style, which we can arrange case by case, focuses on how to talk and what topics the listeners are likely to be interested in. I think there is "sensitivity" (Roberts 2003) in the assumption here. We should first collect the ideas found in this chapter's studies first. And we can analyze and feel why employees tackle environmental activities in their workplaces. That is the most important of our future challenges for deeper and wider evolution of Environmental Management Control Systems. Figure 5 shows shown this paper's essential points, especially in this section. Referring to previous studies, the traditional environmental management control systems' process is only an internal one. In addition, by an analysis of Japanese advanced case study (Panasonic Co.), I find another external process of environmental management control systems. But I find another one external process. External process is (5) environmental communication (external communication), (6) open innovation, (7) CSV. The most important future task of this research field is inquiring the source of motivation to the environment. Managers need to understand why and when employees tackle the environment earnestly, because they need to influence them to the organization's environmental strategies.

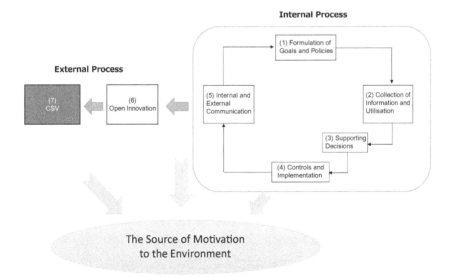

**Fig. 5.**   Two-way processes of EMCs and our future challenges.

# References

Aihara, M. (2009). A case study of strategic co-operation of NPO, Government and Company — Introduction of non-Freon refrigerator into Japanese Market. *Economic Studies 59*(1), 67–102 (in Japanese).

Ando, T. (2015). The significance and prospects of environmental management control research. *Cost Accounting Research 39*(2), 44–54 (in Japanese).

Anthony, R. N. (1988). *The Management Control Function*. Brighton, MA: The Harvard Business School Press.

Arjaliès, D. L. and Mundy, J. (2013). The use of Management Control Systems to manage CSR Strategy — A levers of control perspective. *Management Accounting Research 24*(4), 284–300.

Chesbrough, H. (2006). *Open Innovation — The New Imperative for Creating and Profiting from Technology*. Harvard Business Press.

Kokubu, K. (2015). Corporate Management and CSR. In Washida, T. and Aoyagi, M. (eds.) *The New Horizon of Environmental Policy*, Vol. 8, Environmentally Responsible People and Organizations. Tokyo Prefecture, Japan: Iwanami Shoten, pp. 13–33 (in Japanese).

Porter, M. E. and Kramer, M. R. (2011). Creating shared value. *Harvard Business Review 89*(1–2), 62–77.

Roberts, J. (2003). The manufacture of corporate social responsibility — Constructing corporate sensitivity. *Organization 10*(2), 249–265.

Sasaki, T. (2009). *The Co-operation Company and NPO — A Development of non-Freon Refrigerator by the Co-operation Matsushita and Greenpeace, Social Management leaning by the cases*. Bunshindo Publishing, pp. 11–29 (in Japanese).

Schaltegger, S. and Burritt, R. (2000). *Contemporary Environmental Accounting: Issues, Concepts and Practice*. Greenleaf Publishing.

Schaltegger, S. and Sturm, A. (1998). Eco Efficiency by Eco-Controlling: On the Implementation of EMAS and ISO14001. Hochschulverlag AG, ETHZ/ Swiss Federal Institute of Technology.

Simons, R. (1995). *Levers of Control: How Managers Use Innovative Control Systems to Drive Strategic Renewal*. Harvard Business School Press.

Yokota, E. (1998). *The Management and Psychology of Flat Organizations: Management Control in the Age of Change*. Tokyo Prefecture, Japan: Keio University Press (in Japanese).

Chapter 3

# Do Sustainability Management Control Systems Mediate the Relationship between Corporate Governance and CSR Performance? Evidence from Japan

Jaehong Kim* and Katsuhiko Kokubu[†]

*Department of Economics, Kanto Gakuen University, Ōta, Gunma, Japan
[†]The Graduate School of Business Administration, Kobe University
Kobe, Hyōgo, Japan

## 1. Introduction

Management Control Systems (MCS) constitute a means to effectively control an organization's structure to provide useful information for managers' decision-making and performance evaluation. In a rapidly changing business environment, managers use MCS to achieve strategies and ultimately improve organizational performance. In the field of management accounting, since the study of Simons (1995) with regard to Levers of Control (LOC), many other studies have discussed the role, use, and effect of MCS. Similarly, as interest in various stakeholders' environmental and social issues increases, companies are formulating corporate social responsibility (CSR) strategy and using various control systems to promote the participation of employees in CSR management.

Previous research has emphasized that, to execute CSR strategy and conduct related activities, Sustainability Management Control Systems

(SMCS) need to be understood as a comprehensive package. Various studies on SMCS have been conducted, including studies on the antecedents of using SMCS and the influence of using SMCS in organizational performance. The antecedents, such as industry, company size, environmental uncertainty, stakeholders' pressure, and managers' commitment toward using SMCS, can contribute to the improvement of organizational performance (Henri & Journeault, 2010; Journeault, 2016; Pondeville, Swaen & Rongé, 2013; Wijethilake, Munir & Appuhami, 2018).

Previous studies have also shown that corporate governance affects MCS, with regard to aspects such as corporate management and the decision-making systems (Merchant & Van der Stede, 2007). Similarly, corporate governance influences SMCS with regard to CSR strategy. This is an important finding, because understanding corporate governance in relation to CSR has become increasingly important, but little is known about the relationship between corporate governance and SMCS. Therefore, drawing on Simons' (1995) LOC, this chapter clarifies the mediating effect of SMCS on the relationship between corporate governance and CSR performance.

The rest of this chapter is organized as follows. Section 2 reviews previous research and develops a set of hypotheses. Section 3 describes the method of analysis. This is followed by a presentation of the results. Section 5 discusses the results and concludes the chapter by presenting the theoretical contributions and practical implications.

## 2. Theory and Hypotheses Development

### 2.1 *SMCS as a package*

Simons (1995) defined MCS as comprising formalized procedures and systems that use information to maintain or alter patterns in organizational activities. Simons' (1995) LOC framework includes four control systems — beliefs system, boundary system, diagnostic control system, and interactive control system — to analyze how organizations leverage their MCS in order to implement business strategies. The four levers of control are realized when they are mobilized together, such that they facilitate the attainment of an organization's strategic objectives. In particular, the framework highlights the interrelationship between the control systems. Simons' (1995) LOC framework is a suitable model to analyze SMCS as a cohesive package of several control systems with each playing different roles, rather than treating each control system as autonomous. Further, the LOC framework is the most cited model in a variety of frameworks. Though several frameworks on MCS have been presented, this chapter employs Simons' (1995) LOC framework for analysis.

In the context of SMCS, the beliefs system includes vision and mission statements, credos, and a statement of purpose that integrates CSR aspects. The boundary system includes CSR checklists, codes of conduct, and operational guidelines. The diagnostic control system represents a feedback system that monitors organizational outcomes and corrects deviations from the present CSR goal and intended CSR strategy. The interactive control system represents the formal CSR information system used by top managers to regularly make decisions concerning the CSR activities of subordinates.

With regard to the antecedents of SMCS, previous research has analyzed several factors, such as industry, company size, environmental uncertainty, stakeholders' pressure, and manager's commitment to the environment and CSR. In particular, managers, who are influenced by stakeholders such as the board of directors and shareholders, use SMCS to promote employees' participation in CSR management. In other words, corporate governance involving the board of directors and shareholders is also considered as an antecedent in using SMCS.

## 2.2 Corporate governance and SMCS

Williamson (1996) refers to governance as "the means by which order is accomplished in a relation in which potential conflict threats to undo or upset opportunities to realize mutual gains" (Williamson, 1996, p. 12). At the firm level, corporate governance is a mechanism used for controlling the agency relationship between investors (principals) and executives (agents), including aspects such as the independence of the board of directors, the auditing organization, and incentives of executives (Bushman & Smith, 2001). Research on various forms of corporate governance has been conducted. Among these, numerous studies analyzed the mechanism of corporate governance to improve organizational performance (Black, Jang & Kim, 2006; Larcker, Richardson & Tuna, 2007). Meanwhile, studies that analyzed the relationship between corporate governance and the quality of financial information showed that corporate governance improves the quality of financial information and prevents serious lapses in the financial reporting process (Hoitash, Hoitash & Bedard, 2009).

The common finding of these previous studies is that corporate governance instils discipline in managers and enables them to make rational decisions. In addition, corporate governance facilitates communication among stakeholders, allowing companies to ensure transparency in management practices and alleviate information asymmetry among stakeholders. Therefore, for companies to respond appropriately to the business environment and execute CSR activities effectively and efficiently, corporate governance could promote the appropriate utilization of SMCS and make it possible to maximize the effect of SMCS.

This chapter analyzes how corporate governance affects SMCS as a package composed of a beliefs system, boundary system, diagnostic control system, and interactive control system. The beliefs system and the boundary system each set CSR targets and restrict the range of action of employees to CSR activities so that when a company carries out CSR management, corporate governance affects the beliefs system and the boundary system which are the basis of CSR activities. The diagnostic control system is a means of mechanical control aimed at monitoring the progress of CSR activities in order to effectively execute CSR strategy. Stakeholders such as the board of directors and shareholders expect rational decision-making from managers. As such, managers use the diagnostic control system to accurately grasp the achievement of the CSR strategy. Finally, the interactive control system is a means of organic control that helps employees adapt to an uncertain corporate environment, enables communication between employees, and promotes organization learning regarding CSR activities. Similarly, managers use the interactive control system to respond appropriately to the corporate environment, to achieve CSR strategy, and to promote the participation of employees in CSR activities. Previous research has not analyzed the relationship between corporate governance and SMCS. However, as discussed above, this chapter assumes that corporate governance maximizes the effect of SMCS by inducing managers to use SMCS, and formulates hypothesis 1 as follows:

**Hypothesis 1:** Corporate governance affects the use of SMCS.

## 2.3 *SMCS and CSR performance*

SMCS improve the CSR performance, including environmental performance and social performance. Previous research has shown that the use of Environmental Management Control Systems (EMCS) and eco-control to implement environmental management affects the environmental performance of the company. Henri and Journeault (2010) analyzed the impact of eco-control on firm's environmental performance and financial performance. They found that eco-control does not directly affect financial performance, but indirectly influences it through environmental performance. Similarly, Journeault (2016) showed that eco-control indirectly affects financial performance through environmental performance. The results of these empirical studies suggest that EMCS improve environmental performance.

Although few studies analyze how SMCS affect social performance (Lisi, 2018; Wijethilake, Munir & Appuhami, 2018), these asserted that when a company implements CSR management to respond to social expectations, it can utilize SMCS to improve its financial, environmental, and social performance. Lisi (2018) showed that the use of social performance indicators has a positive influence on social performance. The use of social performance indicators in decision-making enables the integration of social activities into other key activities; therefore, the use of SMCS, including social performance indicators, can contribute to the improvement of social performance. In addition, Wijethilake, Munir and Appuhami (2018) showed that the enabling use of SMCS in the beliefs system and the interactive control system, to encourage voluntary participation of employees in CSR management, directly improves the financial performance of companies. Therefore, in this chapter, as "CSR" is defined as voluntarily incorporating environmental and social aspects into corporate business activities (European Commission, 2001), we examine how the use of SMCS affect CSR performance, formulate hypothesis 2 as follows:

**Hypothesis 2:** The use of SMCS improves the CSR performance.

## 2.4 *Impact of corporate governance on CSR performance*

Corporate governance makes it possible to construct reasonable management systems and decision-making systems, and to promote the commitment of employees to CSR activities, which can ultimately contribute to the improvement of organizational performance. Previous research that analyzed the relationship between corporate governance and CSR performance examined the impact of corporate governance on CSR performance using the board of directors, outside directors, institutional investors, and foreign investors among others, as elements of corporate governance.

For example, Johnson and Greening (1999) categorize CSR performance into the people dimension and the product quality dimension, and show that there is a positive partial relationship between CSR performance and the ownership ratio of the board of directors, institutional investors, and the Chief Executive Officer. Similarly, Neubaum and Zahra (2006) revealed that using the ownership ratio of institutional investors as a proxy variable of corporate governance indicates a positive influence on CSR performance. Coffey and Wang (1998) empirically showed that greater diversity of the board of directors, with more outside directors and female directors, has a positive influence on CSR performance. Hence, previous studies indicate that corporate governance improves CSR performance. Therefore, hypothesis 3.1 is as follows:

**Hypothesis 3.1:** Corporate governance improves the CSR performance.

Meanwhile, numerous studies have analyzed the direct impact of corporate governance on CSR performance, but have not discussed how corporate governance improves the CSR performance. Designing and utilizing SMCS effectively and efficiently in order to achieve the CSR strategy under the influence of corporate governance would not only promote the active participation of employees in CSR activities, but would also contribute to improving the CSR performance. In this chapter, in order to overcome the limitation of previous research by focusing on the use of SMCS, the direct and indirect influences of corporate governance on CSR performance are analyzed. In other words, this chapter examines the mediating effect of SMCS on the relationship between corporate governance and CSR performance. Therefore, hypothesis 3.2 is as follows:

**Hypothesis 3.2:** Corporate governance improves the CSR performance through the use of SMCS.

## 3. Research Design

### 3.1 *Analysis model*

This chapter analyzes the mediating effect of SMCS considering the mechanism through which corporate governance improves the CSR performance. Focusing on SMCS, the analytical model shown in Fig. 1 is built; this model helps verify the relationships between corporate governance, SMCS, and CSR performance.

### 3.2 *Data collection*

In order to analyze the relationships between corporate governance, SMCS, and CSR performance, data on corporate governance were obtained from NEEDS-Corporate Governance Evaluation System (Cges) and data on CSR performance were obtained from the 2017 CSR Company Directory. Data on the use of SMCS were obtained by conducting a questionnaire survey.

In particular, survey questionnaires were distributed to 1,325 Japanese companies across various industries listed in the "2016 CSR Companies" of Toyo Keizai Inc. The target respondents were CSR managers of the companies. The questionnaire was first validated using a pretest administered to three academics and five practitioners. This pretest confirmed their understanding of each measurement instrument.

As 175 questionnaires were returned, the response rate was 13.2%, of which 138 (10.4%) questionnaires were from the first mail-out and 37 (2.8%) were from the second mail-out. Additionally, 28 (2.1%) were omitted due to substantial missing data, resulting in 147 usable questionnaires (11.1%).

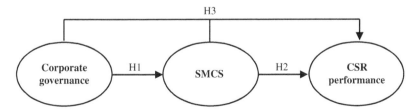

**Fig. 1.** Analysis model.

Different analyses for non-response bias were performed to confirm the validity of the data. First, a comparison between the respondents and non-respondents with respect to size (based on the number of employees and sales) and industry did not reveal any significant differences. Moreover, a comparison between the early respondents and late respondents did not reveal any significant differences. The results indicate that non-response bias was not likely to be a problem.

### 3.3 *Variable measurement*

Among the data provided by NEEDS-Cges, four indicators that are most used in previous research — size of the board of directors, ratio of outside directors, ownership ratio of institutional investors, and ownership ratio of foreign investors — were used for the measurement of corporate governance. These variables related to corporate governance are measured as a single item.

Next, SMCS are measured separately in four parts — beliefs system, boundary system, diagnostic control system, and interactive control system — based on Simons' (1995) LOC framework. Each question item was prepared with reference to Henri (2006), Widener (2007), and Arjaliès and Mundy (2013). There were 21 questions regarding SMCS: five on the beliefs system, four on the boundary system, six on the diagnostic control system, and six on the interactive control system. Each question item was set using a 7-point Likert scale. Furthermore, in order to capture SMCS as a package composed of four control systems, similar to Journeault (2016), second-order factor analysis was applied to each measured SMCS variable.

Finally, measurements of CSR performance were carried out, with a full score of 300 points using CSR evaluation items comprising human resources, and environment and social performances were measured with a full score of 100 points, excluding the evaluation items of corporate governance in the CSR evaluation item data provided by the "2017 CSR Company Directory" of Toyo Keizai Inc.

## 4. Results

### 4.1 *Evaluation of the measurement model*

Before verifying the hypotheses, it is necessary to consider the reliability and validity of each variable used for analysis. First, since the ceiling effect was observed for some of the questionnaire items, SMCS variables measured by the questionnaire survey were deleted and the reliability of each variable constituting the SMCS was checked using Cronbach's $\alpha$. As Cronbach's $\alpha$ was 0.8 or more, the reliability of each variable constituting SMCS was established. Subsequently, we investigated the validity of the SMCS variables by conducting an exploratory factor analysis in order to confirm whether each question item described the variable well.

Next, confirmatory factor analysis was carried out to examine convergence validity for the measurement variables constituting the analysis model. As a method to verify convergent validity, analysis was performed using standardized factor loading and average variance extracted (AVE). Generally, if the factor loading amount is 0.5 or more and the AVE is 0.5 or more, it is judged that there is convergence validity (Fornell & Larcker, 1981; Hair *et al.*, 2014); thus, convergent validity of all the variables was established. The results are shown in Table 1. Hypotheses verification is performed in Table 1 using each variable with high reliability and validity.

**Table 1.**   Descriptive statistics and result of confirmatory factor analysis.

| Variables | Min. | Max. | Ave. | SD | Factor loading | Cronbach $\alpha$ | AVE |
|---|---|---|---|---|---|---|---|
| **Corporate governance** | | | | | | | |
| Board of directors | 1.10 | 2.77 | 2.19 | 0.33 | | | |
| Outside directors | 0.00 | 0.67 | 0.22 | 0.12 | | | |
| Institutional investors | 0.00 | 0.76 | 0.29 | 0.19 | | — | |
| Foreign investors | 0.00 | 0.54 | 0.19 | 0.14 | | | |
| **SMCS** | | | | | | | |
| Beliefs | 1.5 | 7.0 | 5.33 | 1.22 | 0.793 | 0.952 | 0.866 |
| Boundary | 1.0 | 7.0 | 5.10 | 1.49 | 0.786 | | |
| Diagnostic | 1.0 | 7.0 | 4.44 | 1.64 | 0.863 | | |
| Interactive | 1.0 | 7.0 | 4.38 | 1.48 | 0.842 | | |
| **CSR performance** | | | | | | | |
| Human resources | 24.0 | 95.3 | 67.62 | 18.54 | 0.825 | 0.892 | 0.990 |
| Environmental | 20.0 | 98.6 | 72.59 | 19.66 | 0.855 | | |
| Social | 20.1 | 97.4 | 70.70 | 15.00 | 0.928 | | |

## 4.2 *Evaluation of the structural model*

As structural equation modeling (SEM) can be used to simultaneously analyze the causal relation and the correlation between variables, it was considered suitable for this study, which simultaneously analyzes the relationships between corporate governance, the use of SMCS, and CSR performance. In this chapter, hypotheses verification was performed using the standard coefficients and *t*-value that was calculated by the bootstrap method (Hall, 2008). The bootstrap method is mainly used to evaluate the significance of the standard coefficients in SEM (Tenenhaus *et al.*, 2005). The results of hypotheses verification are shown in Tables 2 and 3.

First, when confirming the standard coefficient related to hypothesis 1, there is a positive relationship between the board of directors and the use of SMCS (standard coefficient 0.195, *t*-value 2.489, $p < 0.05$); thus, it was suggested that managers who are influenced by the board of directors will utilize SMCS to encourage employees' participation in CSR activities. Next, a positive relationship was also confirmed in relation to the use of SMCS with outside directors (standard coefficient 0.194, *t*-value 2.558, $p < 0.05$). As outside directors play a role of monitoring to ensure fair

**Table 2.** Analysis results and hypotheses verification.

| Hypotheses | Causal relationship | Standard coefficient | Standard error | *t*-Value |
|---|---|---|---|---|
| H1 | Board of directors ⇒ SMCS | 0.195 | 0.226 | 2.489** |
| H1 | Outside directors ⇒ SMCS | 0.194 | 0.607 | 2.558** |
| H1 | Institutional investors ⇒ SMCS | 0.353 | 1.212 | 1.465 |
| H1 | Foreign investors ⇒ SMCS | 0.093 | 1.679 | 0.385 |
| H2 | SMCS ⇒ CSR performance | 0.329 | 1.169 | 4.046*** |
| H3-1 | Board of directors ⇒ CSR performance | 0.103 | 2.648 | 1.610 |
| H3-1 | Outside directors ⇒ CSR performance | 0.079 | 7.125 | 1.284 |
| H3-1 | Institutional investors ⇒ CSR performance | 0.278 | 14.067 | 1.428 |
| H3-1 | Foreign investors ⇒ CSR performance | 0.215 | 19.367 | 1.109 |

*Notes*: * $p < 0.1$; **$p < 0.05$; ***$p < 0.01$.

management activities, this role enables managers to carry out CSR activities effectively and efficiently; as such, they actively utilize SMCS. However, hypothesis 1 was partially adopted because the results with regard to the influence of institutional investors and foreign investors on the use of SMCS were not significant. Based on the results of the analysis of this chapter, SMCS that support the implementation of CSR activities are more strongly influenced by internal stakeholders, such as the board of directors and outside directors.

Second, hypothesis 2 was adopted (standard coefficient 0.329, $t$-value 4.046, $p < 0.01$) because the use of SMCS resulted in improved CSR performance. Based on the causal relationship between the use of SMCS and CSR performance, it can be presumed that the simultaneous use of multiple control systems enables the participation of employees in CSR activities, which contributes to the improvement of CSR performance. Although the relationship between EMCS and environmental performance has been analyzed in previous research (Henri & Journeault, 2010; Journeault, 2016), this chapter extends the scope of analysis of prior research and shows that SMCS can be used not only for environmental performance, but also for social performance.

Third, as shown in Table 2, not all the four variables relating to corporate governance directly improve the CSR performance. As shown in Table 3, however, verifying the meditating effect of SMCS in the relationship between corporate governance and CSR performance using Sobel test (1982) showed that SMCS are affected by corporate governance, which indirectly improves the CSR performance; thus, hypothesis 3 was

**Table 3.** The mediating effect of SMCS in the relationship between corporate governance and CSR performance.

| Hypotheses | Causal relationship | Indirect effect | Sobel test (Z) |
|---|---|---|---|
| H3-2 | Board of directors ⇒ SMCS ⇒ CSR performance | 0.064 | 2.119** |
| H3-2 | Outside directors ⇒ SMCS ⇒ CSR performance | 0.064 | 2.162** |
| H3-2 | Institutional investors ⇒ SMCS ⇒ CSR performance | — | — |
| H3-2 | Foreign investors ⇒ SMCS ⇒ CSR performance | — | — |

*Notes*: $*p < 0.1$; $**p < 0.05$; $***p < 0.01$.

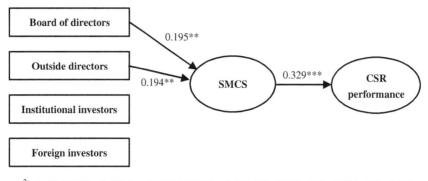

$X^2/df = 58.151/33 = 1.762$ ($p = 0.004$); RMSEA = 0.072; IFI = 0.979; TLI = 0.964; CFI = 0.978

$* p < 0.1$, $** p < 0.05$, $*** p < 0.01$

**Fig. 2.** Analysis results using the structural equation model.

partially adopted. Figure 2 shows the results of the verification of the hypotheses presented in this chapter.

## 5. Conclusions

Drawing from the LOC framework of Simons (1995), this chapter examined the mediating effect of SMCS on the relationship between corporate governance and CSR performance.

The results of the analysis showed that corporate governance, such as those involving board of directors and outside directors, has an impact on the use of SMCS to carry out the CSR strategy. Next, it was shown that the use of SMCS improves the CSR performance when managers use SMCS in encouraging the participation of organizational members in CSR activities. Finally, the result shows that corporate governance indirectly improves the CSR performance only when SMCS are mediated in the causal relation between corporate governance and CSR performance. Based on the above results, it is suggested that utilizing SMCS when carrying out the CSR strategy is essential, and it is particularly important to understand SMCS as a package rather than as an individual control means necessary for CSR management.

Understanding the factors that influence SMCS will enable companies to efficiently design and use SMCS. As corporate governance affects the management systems of the company and managers' decision-making, this chapter focused on the effect of SMCS in relation to corporate governance and CSR performance by using corporate governance variables as the antecedents of using SMCS. This chapter contributes to extant research on MCS by showing the mediating effect of SMCS, considering the mechanism through which corporate governance improves organizational performance. In previous research on MCS, organizational performance, including financial performance and environmental performance, was measured by questionnaire surveys; however, in this chapter, in addition to the data from the response of the questionnaire survey, the data provided by NEEDS-Cges and Toyo Keizai Inc. were used simultaneously. Thus, more objective results were obtained.

Finally, we present the direction of future research. This chapter confirmed the effect of using multiple control systems simultaneously, focusing on the use of SMCS for CSR management. However, the study did not analyze how the relation (configuration) between the control systems constituting SMCS affect the improvement of organizational performance, as claimed by Widener (2007). Therefore, in future research, it is necessary to empirically analyze the influence of the relationship between control systems that constitute SMCS on organizational performance, in order to devise ways to enhance the effect of SMCS. In addition, as the survey for the study was conducted in 2016, it may not be possible to generalize the results across other years. However, if we analyze the relationships between corporate governance, the use of SMCS, and organizational performance over the long term, it would be possible to elucidate the relationship more accurately. Moreover, as there are many unknown facets about SMCS, further long-term research in this field is necessary.

## References

Arjaliès, D. L. and Mundy, J. (2013). The use of management control systems to manage CSR strategy: A levers of control perspective. *Management Accounting Research* 24(4), 284–300.

Black, B. S., Jang, H. and Kim, W. (2006). Does corporate governance predict firm's market value? Evidence from Korea. *Journal of Law, Economics, and Organization* 22(2), 366–413.

Bushman, R. and Smith, A. (2001). Financial accounting information and corporate governance. *Journal of Accounting and Economics 32*(1–3), 237–334.

Coffey, B. S. and Wang, J. (1998). Board diversity and managerial as predictors of corporate social performance. *Journal of Business Ethics 17*(14), 1595–1603.

European Commission (2001). *Green Paper: Promoting a European Framework for Corporate Social Responsibility*. Commission of the European Communities.

Fornell, C. and Larcker, D. F. (1981). Evaluating structural equation models with unobservable variables and measurement error. *Journal of Marketing Research 18*, 39–50.

Hair, J. F., Black, W. C., Babin, B. J. and Anderson, R. E. (2014). *Multivariate Data Analysis*, 7th edn. Pearson.

Hall, M. (2008). The effect of comprehensive performance measurement systems on role clarity, psychological empowerment and managerial performance. *Accounting, Organizations and Society 33*(2–3), 141–163.

Henri, J. F. (2006). Management control systems and strategy: A resource-based perspective. *Accounting, Organizations and Society 31*(6), 529–558.

Henri, J. F. and Journeault, M. (2010). Eco-control: The influence of management control systems on environmental and economic performance. *Accounting, Organizations and Society 35*(1), 63–80.

Hoitash, U., Hoitash, R. and Bedard, J. C. (2009). Corporate governance and internal control over financial reporting: A comparison of regulatory regimes. *The Accounting Review 84*(3), 839–867.

Johnson, R. A. and Greening, D. W. (1999). The effects of corporate governance and institutional ownership types on corporate social performance. *Academy Management Journal 42*(5), 564–576.

Journeault, M. (2016). The influence of the eco-control package on environmental and economic performance: A natural resource-based approach. *Journal of Management Accounting Research 28*(2), 149–178.

Larcker, D. F., Richardson, S. A. and Tuna, I. (2007). Corporate governance, accounting outcomes, and organizational performance. *The Accounting Review 82*(4), 963–1008.

Lisi, I. E. (2018). Determinants and performance effects of social performance measurement systems. *Journal of Business Ethics, 152*(1), 225–251.

Merchant, K. A. and Van der Stede, W. A. (2007). *Management Control Systems: Performance Measurement Evaluation, and Incentives*, Harlow: Financial Times/Prentice Hall.

Neubaum, D. O. and Zahra, S. A. (2006). Institutional ownership and corporate social performance: The moderating effects of investment horizon, activism and coordination. *Journal of Management 32*(1), 108–131.

Pondeville, S., Swaen, V., and Rongé, Y. D. (2013). Environmental management control systems: The role of contextual and strategic factors. *Management Accounting Research 24*(4), 317–332.

Simons, R. (1995). *Levers of Control: How Managers Use Innovative Control Systems to Drive Strategic Renewal*. Harvard Business School Press.

Sobel, M. E. (1982). Asymptotic intervals for indirect effects in structural equation models. In Leinhart, S. (ed.) *Sociological Methodology*. San Francisco, CA: Jossey-Bass, pp. 290–312.

Tenenhaus, M., Vinzi, V. E., Chatelin, Y. M. and Lauro, C. (2005). PLS path modeling. *Computational Statistics and Data Analysis 18*(1), 159–205.

Widener, S. K. (2007). An empirical analysis of the levers of control framework. *Accounting, Organizations and Society 32*(7–8), 757–788.

Wijethilake, C., Munir, R. and Appuhami, R. (2018). Environmental innovation strategy and organizational performance: Enabling and controlling uses of management control systems. *Journal of Business Ethics*, *151*(4), 1139–1160.

Williamson, O. E. (1996). *The Mechanisms of Governance*. New York, NY: Oxford University Press.

## Chapter 4

# Legitimacy through Corporate Social Responsibility Rhetoric: An Analysis of Institutional Context and Language

Yuriko Nakao* and Katsuhiko Kokubu[†]

*Faculty of Business Administration, Tottori University of
Environmental Studies, Tottori, Tottori Prefecture, Japan
[†]Graduate School of Business Administration, Kobe University
Kobe, Hyōgo Prefecture, Japan

## 1. Introduction

Owing to important global environmental and social issues, corporate sustainability reporting is becoming a critical management practice for multinational companies. Since environmental, social, and governance investments have recently increased and investors make use of sustainability information (Amel-Zadeh & Serafeim, 2017), such information has been increasingly gaining significance. Further, influential guidelines on sustainability reporting, including Global Reporting Initiatives (GRI) standards and the framework of integrated reporting by International Integrated Reporting Council (IIRC), have been accelerating this trend.

In addition to quantitative information, qualitative information plays a pivotal role in sustainability reporting because the interpretation of top management of their social and environmental performance is critically important. However, as opposed to financial performance, the evaluation of social and environmental performance is ambiguous and likely to depend on personal judgement. Therefore, the language used in sustainability reports can significantly influence the judgement of information users. It could be misleading if top management intentionally uses language reflecting the institutional context, which consists of various phenomena over a particular period.

There is a limited number of previous studies that treat this problem, and those studies have been conducted based on interpretive text analysis (Laine, 2009; Mäkelä & Laine, 2011). Interpretive text analysis is a qualitative method, and cannot handle a large number of samples (Merkl-Davies, Brennan & Petros, 2012). Therefore, it is difficult to generalize their conclusions. However, in this chapter, we adopt a text-mining approach for the analysis of longitudinal text in sustainability reports. Text mining based on computer software can quantify natural languages and cover many observations.

Sustainability reporting could be employed as an information strategy to acquire legitimacy by top management (Hahn & Kühnen, 2013). However, under social and institutional pressure, top management is intended to gain legitimacy using a rhetorical strategy (Castelló & Lazano, 2011; Marais, 2012). This study aims to analyze such top-management legitimatizing activities through sustainability reporting in the long term.

As the institutional context influences the language of sustainability reporting over the long term, a continuing analysis is necessary. Therefore, we selected Japanese companies that have issued sustainability reports continuously since the late 1990s. In the analysis, this study focuses on the corporate social responsibility (CSR) rhetoric developed by Castelló and Lozano (2011), who classify legitimacy differences into three types of CSR rhetoric: strategic, institutional, and dialectic.

To finish this section, we would like to explain some technical words used in this study. "Language" is defined as a comprehensive concept including various linguistic elements including "text" and "terms." "Text" is the part of a sustainability report excluding the quantitative information, and "term" is a specific word or words selected through text-mining analysis.

## 2. Language and Sustainability Reporting for Legitimacy: Previous Literature

In this section, we review some previous studies on legitimacy using sustainability reporting. The main issues are the relationship between texts and institutions (Laine, 2009), a change in interpretation of the text (Tengblad & Ohlsson, 2010; Laine, 2010), and the language of CEO statements (Cong, Freedman & Park, 2014).

Laine (2009) focused on social change and information disclosure by text with an interpretive approach, based on the perspectives of social expectations and organizational legitimacy as well as new institutional sociology. This study analyzed Kemia Corporation, a leading Finnish chemical company, and she showed that environmental disclosure could be classified into five periods based on the time when Finnish media devoted more attention to the environment as an international business trend. In addition, she showed that the company used various rhetorical terms as responses to environmental problems in each period. Thus, Laine (2009) revealed changes in the language used across Kemia's 34 years of information disclosure and suggested there were changes in its rhetoric according to social institutional changes.

Laine (2010) examined whether the concept of sustainability is influenced by the society. The study adopted an interpretive approach, covering the annual and environmental reports of three major Finnish companies from 1987 to 2005. The analysis showed that each company described the concept of "sustainability" from different perspectives in the early 1990s. However, over time, their concepts converged to similar rhetoric rather than diverse ones. Although in the early 1990s, business was described as incompatible with sustainability, this study suggested that the interpretation of sustainability has changed over time and has become critical in business.

Tengblad and Ohlsson (2010) examined changes over time in the interpretation of the term "CSR" due to environmental changes surrounding enterprises. Their study used content analysis and analyzed CSR-related keywords in about 20 years of CEO statements in the annual reports of 15 Swedish companies. Consequently, they found the following terms related to CSR in 1981: "government", "import/export", and "inflation". In 2001, 20 years later, the terms were "sustainability", "ethics", and "morals." The authors noted that the trend of globalization has affected the language of CSR over time and that the interpretation of CSR is changing.

Cong, Freedman and Park (2014) focused on whether legitimacy is acquired using the CEO statement. They examined the relationship between the CEO statements and environmental performance. They evaluated scores for the environmental texts in the CEO statement, and used those scores as explaining variables; they then analyzed the relationship with environmental performance and used that as the explanatory variable. Their results showed a negative effect between environmental performance and environmental texts. This means that a CEO is likely to disclose more regarding poor environmental performance. This tendency was shown to be remarkable, particularly with poor environmental performance. They argued that these results support the acquisition of legitimacy through top-management texts.

As described above, these previous studies showed that institutional contexts influence language and CEOs are likely to legitimatize themselves using language. However, since the previous literature adopted interpretive text, the number of observations was small. Therefore, we used the text-mining approach in this study to uncover many observations.

## 3. Research Design

### 3.1 *Characteristics of CSR rhetoric*

We adopted the concept of CSR rhetoric developed by Castelló and Lozano (2011) for analyzing CEO-legitimatizing activities through sustainability reporting. They classified languages regarding CSR into 17 themes used in the sustainability reports and provided criteria to use language regarding each theme.

Castelló and Lozano (2011) revealed corporate rhetoric strategies when a company is trying to differentiate itself from others. They suggested that the purpose of those rhetoric strategies is legitimacy acquisition. Based on Suchman's (1995) theory identifying three legitimacies (pragmatic, cognitive, and moral), Castelló and Lozano (2011)

**Table 1.**  Characteristics of the three CSR rhetoric types (Castelló & Lozano, 2011, p. 22, Table 2).

| Characteristics | Strategic CSR rhetoric | Institutional CSR rhetoric | Dialectic CSR rhetoric |
|---|---|---|---|
| Discursive elements | Legitimated by the economic logic of the firm | Legitimated through the value of the enthymeme | Legitimated by appealing to an engaged dialog |
| Time scale orientation | Short- to mid-term | Long-term (sometimes used as temporal) | Long-term |
| Position in text | Supports the most important enthymemes | Used in introduction and linkages | Marginal, additional |
| Rhetoric strategy | Provides the logos | Provides the ethos | Supports the pathos |
| CSR Foundation | Positivistic | Positivistic | Post-positivistic |
| Main concepts | Performance | Social contract/duty | Inclusion; dialog |
| Management theories | CSP; strategic management; project management | Business ethics; stakeholder theory | Corporate citizenship/ political view of firm |
| Role of legitimacy | Pragmatic legitimacy | Cognitive legitimacy | Moral legitimacy |
| Message to stakeholders | We are accountable; we manage well | We are "good" and responsible; belong to the CSR community | We want to engage you in a dialog |

classified three rhetoric categories (strategic, institutional, and dialectic). The characteristics of these three CSR rhetoric types are summarized in Table 1.

Strategic CSR rhetoric is defined as "legitimated by the economic logic of the firm" (Castelló & Lozano, 2011, p. 22). This legitimization is related to strategic management based on liberalism and profit maximization. Castelló and Lozano (2011) suggested that "pragmatic legitimacy represents a fundamental challenge for corporations to persuade their stakeholders about the benefits of their products, procedures, and outputs" (Castelló & Lozano, 2011, p. 12).

Institutional CSR rhetoric is defined as "legitimated through the value of the enthymeme" (Castelló & Lozano, 2011, p. 22). Institutional rhetoric is starting to be embedded in the cognitive societal spectrum of good business practice. However, it is used ambiguously, and its language lacks in-depth meaning (Castelló & Lozano, 2011, p. 20). Castello and Lozano (2011) based on Scott (1991) explained that "cognitive legitimacy results from the acceptance of some broadly taken-for-granted assumptions available through cultural models which provide plausible explanation for the organization and its endeavours" (Castelló & Lozano, 2011, p. 12).

Dialectic CSR rhetoric is defined as "legitimated by appealing to an engaged dialogue" (Castelló & Lozano, 2011, p. 22). They indicated that dialectic CSR rhetoric has an aspirational character, and they interpret its enthymemes as an effort by firms to relate to their stakeholders based on dialogue and the public justification of the firms' societal contributions. Castelló and Lozano (2011) found moral legitimacy in this rhetoric. Castelló and Lozano (2011) based on Aldrich and Fiol (1994), Parsons (1960) and Suchman (1995) explained that "moral legitimacy, finally, reflects a positive normative evaluation of the organization and its activities" (Castelló & Lozano, 2011, p. 12).

Their study also showed the change in the trend from the use of institutional to dialectic CSR rhetoric over time. They suggested that dialectic rhetoric seems to signal a new understanding of the firm's role in society (Castelló & Lozano, 2011, p. 11). Including this perspective, we examine the trend of the three types of CSR rhetoric that changed over time in Japanese companies.

## 3.2 *Data*

This study analyzes the relationship between "institutional context" and "language", covering CEO statements in the sustainability reports of Japanese companies. Companies were selected based on the continuity of their sustainability reports. A survey conducted by the Ministry of Environment, Japan in 2001 documented that about 20% of the companies issued environmental reports. Thus, this study covers sustainability reports from 2001 to 2015. Furthermore, the sample companies comprise 54 companies that have issued sustainability reports for 15 consecutive years and that were among the top 100 by sales in 2015.

### 3.3 *Text mining and selected terms*

This study used text mining, which is an analytical tool for quantifying natural language text. Text mining is a method to automatically extract certain regularities from unstructured data (Kim, 2009). A feature of text mining is its division of text into "morphemes", which are the minimum semantic units of language data. The role of a text-mining software is to help place natural language into structured data, which becomes binary data with 0s and 1s. Incidentally, this study used IBM SPSS Text Analytics for Surveys 4.0.

In this study, many terms were outputted using text mining, and we selected terms with a frequency of 30 or more. The concept of CSR rhetoric developed was translated into Japanese. As we used three CSR rhetoric types developed by Castelló and Lozano (2011), we selected 11 terms for "strategic CSR rhetoric", 13 terms for "institutional CSR rhetoric", and 14 terms for "dialectic CSR rhetoric." Table 2 shows the CSR rhetoric terms selected in this study.

### 3.4 *Method of analysis*

We conducted the following two analyses to examine how the change in terms over time influences institutional contexts.

First, we examined the trends of increase and decrease in terms by year. These trend analyses enable an understanding of the relationship between the years and terms that could be influenced by specific events. These specific events make up the particular institutional context.

Second, we examined the changes over time of the CSR rhetoric. We examined whether the institutional contexts influence the legitimacy characterized by the CSR rhetoric terms. In this analysis, in addition to the mean of the frequency of terms, the coefficient of variation was also shown to illustrate the relative relation of fluctuations (increases and decreases) for each period.

In the second analysis, we divided the period into five sections based on the degree of sustainability in management: (1) 2001–2003: the early

**Table 2.**   CSR rhetoric terms selected in this study.

| Strategic CSR rhetoric | Frequency of terms | Institutional CSR rhetoric | Frequency of terms | Dialectic CSR rhetoric | Frequency of terms |
|---|---|---|---|---|---|
| Compliance | 190 | Global environmental Issues | 516 | 3R | 166 |
| Revenue | 150 | Global warming | 487 | Labor | 140 |
| Innovation | 155 | Reliability | 450 | Energy creation | 131 |
| Corporate Value | 155 | Stakeholder | 448 | Human Rights | 123 |
| Environmental Policy/target | 107 | Contribute | 374 | Life Cycle | 93 |
| Governance | 96 | CSR | 356 | Climate change | 91 |
| R & D | 92 | Communication | 226 | Biodiversity | 89 |
| CSR policy/ target | 77 | Social contribution | 204 | Member of society | 86 |
| Risk system | 70 | Ethics | 186 | Focus on the issue | 81 |
| Environmental vision | 52 | Sustainability | 162 | Forest | 80 |
| CSR system | 44 | Transparency | 160 | Global standards | 70 |
| | | Corporate citizenship | 134 | Anti-corruption | 62 |
| | | Dialogue | 102 | Diversity | 56 |
| | | | | CSR procurement | 31 |

period, (2) 2004–2006: the first diffusion period, (3) 2007–2009: the second diffusion period, (4) 2010–2012: the first maturity period, and (5) 2013–2015: the second maturity period.

*Environmental Reporting Guidelines* was published by the Ministry of Environment in Japan in 2000. Since then, corporate environmental disclosure in Japan has been increasing. For this reason, we named 2001–2003 the early period. In 2003, the concept of CSR was imported to Japan, mainly from Europe, and this was considered to be the first year of CSR in Japan. Hence, from 2004 to 2009 is called the diffusion period. In 2010, ISO 26000, an international standard of organizational social responsibility, was issued. This guidance explicitly delineates environmental and social issues that corporations manage and fairly influenced Japanese corporate activities. Thus, we named the time from 2010 to 2015 the maturity period.

## 4. Results

### 4.1 *Trends in the frequency of terms*

To capture the trend of the degree of influence of institutional context to terms, we concentrated on the terms that increase more than threefold from the previous year. These terms are "CSR", "compliance", "dialogue", "governance", "climate change", "biodiversity", and "diversity." Table 2 shows institutions related to these terms.

The term "CSR" increased from one in 2003 to 21 in 2004. In 2003, *The Evolution of the Market and CSR Management* was published by Japanese Association of Corporate Executives. This report influenced Japanese companies to promote the concept of CSR. Tanimoto (2004) called the year 2003 as "the first year of CSR" in Japan.

It is likely that the influence of these guidelines is related to the increase in the frequency of the term "CSR."

The term "compliance" also increased from 2004 to 2006. The trend influenced the enactment of the "Company Law" in 2006. This law contains strengthening of compliance structures as a form of risk management.

The terms "governance" increased from five in 2013 to 15 in 2014 and 21 in 2015, and "dialogue" increased from three in 2014 to 14 in 2015. In Japan, the Stewardship Code was published in 2014 (FSA, 2014), and the Corporate Governance Code was published in 2015 (TSE, 2015). These codes emphasized the dialogue between the management and investors. The trend of these terms is considered to be influenced by these codes.

The term "climate change" increased from two in 2006 to eight in 2007 and 13 in 2008. This is considered to be influenced by the former US Vice President Al Gore and Intergovernmental Panel on Climate Change (IPCC) being awarded the Nobel Peace Prize in 2007, and the adoption of the "Declaration of Leaders Meeting of Major Economies on Energy Security and Climate Change" at the G8 summit in Toyako, Hokkaido in 2008. These events are considered to have strongly influenced the use of the term climate change in CEOs' statements in sustainability reports.

The term "biodiversity" increased from two in 2007 to seven in 2008, six in 2009, and 17 in 2010. *The Guidelines for Private Sector Engagement in Biodiversity* was published in 2009 by the Ministry of Environment.

Furthermore, the 10th COP to the Convention on Biological Diversity was held in Aichi in 2010. This is considered to be the reason for the increase in the frequency of the terms related to "biodiversity."

The term "diversity" increased from four in 2013 to 16 in 2014 and 14 in 2015. This trend is considered to be the result of the Ministry of Economy, Trade, and Industry's implementation of the "Diversity Management Selection 100" award in 2012, in collaboration with the Tokyo Stock Exchange, which is presented to companies for improving their corporate value through the promotion of diversity. These factors are considered to have led to the recognition and spread of diversity.

The frequency of the term "CSR" decreased from 2011 onward. The frequency of "CSR" was 34 in 2010, and it decreased to 29 in 2011 and 24 in 2015. The trend may be explained by the fact that the effect of differentiating CSR terms is penetrating the business sector and its usage is decreasing.

## 4.2 *CSR rhetoric changes terms*

In this section, we analyzed the trends over five periods of institutional context based on the three CSR rhetoric types. Table 3 shows how the terms of strategic, institutional, and dialectic CSR rhetoric have changed in the five previously defined periods. The size of the circle indicates the frequency of the CSR rhetoric term; the darker the colour of the circle, the higher the rate of frequency. The mean and coefficient of variation for each term are shown in the right column, and the mean of the frequency and coefficient of variation in the five periods are shown at the bottom of Table 3.

The mean of the frequency of terms from 2001 to 2003 was 19.03, which is the lowest, and the coefficient was 0.71, which is also the lowest. On the other hand, during the second maturity period, the mean of the frequency of terms was the highest at 39.45, and the coefficient of variation was 1.46; this means that CSR rhetoric terms were considerably diffused during these periods.

Regarding the strategic CSR rhetoric, circles with 40 or more reference terms are shown from the first diffusion period. Strategic CSR rhetoric tended to be consistently used from the diffusion period to the maturity

**Table 3.** Changes in the three CSR rhetoric types.

| | Terms | Early period 2001–2003 | First half of the diffusion period 2004–2006 | Second half of the diffusion period 2007–2009 | First half of the maturity period 2010–2012 | Second half of the maturity period 2013–2015 | Mean | Coefficient of Variation |
|---|---|---|---|---|---|---|---|---|
| Strategic CSR rhetoric | Compliance | | | | | | 38.00 | 2.32 |
| | Revenue | | | | | | 30.00 | 2.43 |
| | Innovation | | | | | | 31.00 | 1.83 |
| | Corporate Value | | | | | | 31.00 | 2.17 |
| | Environmental Policy / target | | | | | | 21.40 | 3.39 |
| | Governance | | | | | | 19.20 | 1.44 |
| | R & D | | | | | | 18.40 | 2.93 |
| | CSR policy / target | | | | | | 15.40 | 1.80 |
| | Risk system | | | | | | 14.00 | 4.52 |
| | Environmental vision | | | | | | 10.40 | 2.72 |
| | CSR system | | | | | | 8.80 | 1.32 |
| Institutional CSR rhetoric | Global environmental Issues | | | | | | 103.20 | 6.69 |
| | Global warming | | | | | | 97.40 | 6.00 |
| | Reliability | | | | | | 90.00 | 3.05 |
| | Stakeholder | | | | | | 89.60 | 2.38 |
| | Contribute | | | | | | 74.80 | 3.82 |
| | CSR | | | | | | 71.20 | 1.96 |
| | Communication | | | | | | 45.20 | 5.95 |
| | Social contribution | | | | | | 40.80 | 3.16 |
| | Ethics | | | | | | 37.20 | 2.24 |
| | Sustainability | | | | | | 32.40 | 5.27 |
| | Transparency | | | | | | 32.00 | 3.73 |
| | Corporate citizenship | | | | | | 26.80 | 2.89 |
| | Dialogue | | | | | | 20.40 | 2.13 |
| Dialectic CSR rhetoric | 3R | | | | | | 33.20 | 1.59 |
| | Labor | | | | | | 28.00 | 2.17 |
| | Renewable energy creation | | | | | | 26.20 | 2.96 |
| | Human Rights | | | | | | 24.60 | 1.63 |
| | Life Cycle | | | | | | 18.60 | 8.63 |
| | Climate change | | | | | | 18.20 | 1.62 |
| | Biodiversity | | | | | | 17.80 | 1.29 |
| | Member of society | | | | | | 17.20 | 2.24 |
| | Focus on the issue | | | | | | 16.20 | 0.91 |
| | Forest | | | | | | 16.00 | 7.63 |
| | Global standards | | | | | | 14.00 | 1.68 |
| | Anti-corruption | | | | | | 12.40 | 1.11 |
| | Diversity | | | | | | 11.20 | 0.91 |
| | CSR procurement | | | | | | 6.20 | 1.41 |
| **Mean** | | 19.03 | 34.42 | 37.39 | 35.29 | 39.45 | | |
| **Coefficient of Variation** | | 0.71 | 1.15 | 1.12 | 1.23 | 1.46 | | |

Frequency of Terms: 0~39, 40~59, 60~79, 80~99, 100~

period. As the coefficient of variation was relatively low, it can be said that strategic CSR rhetoric was used regardless of the influence of institutional context. Strategic CSR rhetoric represents pragmatic legitimacy. Therefore, this legitimization trend can be seen for a long period regardless of the institutional contexts.

Institutional CSR rhetoric has a high overall circle in the early period (2001–2003) compared to the other two rhetoric types. Institutional CSR rhetoric was used in the early period in order to gain cognitive legitimacy. In particular, institutional CSR rhetoric was most used during the second diffusion period (2007–2009). In addition, institutional CSR rhetoric tended to have a high coefficient of variation compared to strategic and dialectic CSR rhetoric. A high coefficient of variation means that the frequency of terms varies from each period. Therefore, this tendency shows that institutional CSR rhetoric tends to be more likely influenced by the institutional context. Institutional CSR rhetoric represents cognitive legitimacy. This legitimization trend can be seen in the diffusion period.

Finally, for dialectic CSR rhetoric, the frequency of terms was below 39 in the early and diffusion periods. However, after 2010, during the maturity period, the term frequencies exceeded 40. In addition, the coefficient of variation of the dialectic CSR rhetoric is relatively low. Therefore, it can be considered that this rhetoric is not much influenced by institutional contexts. In addition, sustainability management has penetrated the corporations in the mature period. In this period, the trend of using the dialectic CSR rhetoric is likely because the corporation represents moral legitimacy. The trend from the use of institutional CSR rhetoric to dialectic CSR rhetoric over time revealed in this study is consistent with the results of Castelló and Lozano (2011).

## 5. Discussion and Conclusion

We analyzed the relationship between institutional context and language based on the CEO statements of Japanese companies' sustainability reports using text mining. The results clarified the following two points. First, the changes regarding specific events in the years before and after are related to the institutional context, which can be found in the CEO statements. The phenomenon indicates that the CEOs' selected language is affected by social pressure. Second, CSR rhetoric has been shown to emphasize the changes from institutional to dialectic CSR rhetoric from the diffusion stage to the maturity period in sustainability management. In other words, the CEO rhetoric strategy changed from cognitive legitimacy (institutional CSR) to moral legitimacy (dialectic CSR).

Therefore, the CEOs' choice of language is influenced by the institutional environment, reflecting social pressure, and the contemporary context influences the rhetorical strategy. Thus, the users of sustainability report information should appropriately understand the tendency of the language used by CEOs to avoid misunderstanding. Unlike the interpretive text analyses of a small number of reports, this study examined the language of many reports using the text-mining software, so the results are more robust than those of previous studies.

However, although we quantitatively analyzed the language of CEOs' statements and clarified their trends, we did not deeply discuss the causal relationship between language and institutional context. Further analyses will be necessary to investigate this point.

# References

Amel-Zadeh, A. and Serafeim, G. (2017). Why and how investors use ESG information: Evidence from a global survey. *Harvard Business School Accounting & Management Unit Working Paper.* https://ssrn.com/abstract=2925310 or http://dx.doi.org/10.2139/ssrn.2925310.

Aldrich, H. E. and Fiol, C. M. (1994). Fools rush in? The institutional context of industry creation. *Academy of Management Review 19*(4), 645–670.

Castelló, I. and Lozano, J. M. (2011). Searching for new forms of legitimacy through corporate responsibility rhetoric. *Journal of Business Ethics 100*(1), 11–29.

Cong, Y., Freedman, M. and Park, J. D. (2014). Tone at the top: CEO environmental rhetoric and environmental performance. *Advance Accounting 30*(2), 322–327.

FSA (2014), Principles for Responsible Institutional Investors — Japan's Stewardship Code. The Financial Services Agency in Japan.

Hahn, R. and Kühnen, M. (2013). Determinants of sustainability reporting: A review of results, trends, theory, and opportunities in an expanding field of research. *Journal of Cleaner Production 59*, 5–21.

Kim, M. (2009). *Introduction to Statistical Science of Text Data.* Iwanami Shoten, Analysis Laboratory (in Japanese).

Laine, M. (2009). Ensuring legitimacy through rhetorical changes? *Accounting, Auditing & Accountability Journal 22*(7), 1029–1054.

Laine, M. (2010). Towards sustaining the status quo: Business talk of sustainability in Finnish corporate disclosures 1987–2005. *European Accounting Review 19*(2), 247–274.

Mäkelä, H. and Laine, M. (2011). A CEO with many messages: Comparing the ideological representations provided by different corporate reports. *Accounting Forum 35*(4), 217–231.

Marais, M. (2012). CEO rhetorical strategies for corporate social responsibility (CSR). *Society and Business Review 7*(3), 223–243.

Merkl-Davies, D. M., Brennan, N. M. and Petros, V. (2012). Text analysis methodologies in corporate narrative reporting research. *Conceptual Paper.* https://www.academia.edu/2173695/Text_Analysis_Methodologies_in_Corporate_Narrative_Reporting_Research, Accessed 8 September 2014.

Parsons, T. (1960). *Structure and Process in Modern Societies.* New York Free Press.

Scott, W. R. (1991). Unpacking Institutional Arguments. In Powel, W. W. and DiMaggio, P. J. (eds.) *The New Institutionalism in Organizational Analysis.* University of Chicago Press, pp. 164–182.

Suchman, M. (1995). Managing legitimacy: Strategic and institutional approaches. *Academy of Management Review 120*, 21–571.

Tanimoto, K. (2004). Changes in the market society and corporate social responsibility. *Asian Business & Management 3*(2), 151–172.

Tengblad, S. and Ohlsson, C. (2010). The framing of corporate social responsibility and the globalization of national business systems: A longitudinal case study. *Journal of Business Ethics 93*(4), 653–669.

TSE (2015). Japan's corporate governance code. Tokyo Stock Exchange.

# Part 2

# MFCA Development

## Chapter 5

# Development and Possibilities of MFCA as a Tool of Sustainability Management: In View of Japanese, German, and Some Asian Experiences

Michiyasu Nakajima

*Faculty of Business and Commerce, Kansai University*
*Osaka Prefecture, Japan*

## 1. Introduction

Material Flow Cost Accounting (MFCA) was developed as a tool of Environmental Management Accounting (EMA) in Japan since 2000. The basic idea of MFCA originated from corporate projects coordinated by Institut für Management und Umwelt (IMU), Augsburg[1] in Germany since the 1990s (Nakajima & Kokubu, 2001, 2008; IMU & ZWW, 2003; Wagner, 2015). In this chapter, we call MFCA that was developed in its first phase by IMU as "German MFCA" (Strobel & Redmann, 2000, 2001), and in the second phase of MFCA experiences in Japan as "Japanese MFCA" (METI Japan, 2001, 2010; Nakajima & Kokubu, 2001, 2008).

Since 2007, after the international standardization of MFCA as ISO 14051 (ISO, 2011), MFCA started to expand rapidly to other Asian

---

[1] https://imu-augsburg.de (5 September 2018).

industries.[2] Stimulated by the international standardization process of MFCA, the fundamental idea and procedures of MFCA were shared with other Asian countries, strongly facilitated by the available Japanese case examples in English. The Japanese industrial experiences were generalized by other Asian industries as strong models of simultaneously achieving cost reduction and environmental protection. As a result, many Asian industries tried to introduce MFCA into their own production processes as a process improvement tool, a new kind of Kaizen tool. And, referring to the international ISO standard, the Asian industries have used MFCA as a globally accepted and authorized tool for EMA.

In this chapter, when MFCA is used in a company, we point out the important factor to develop MFCA as a tool of sustainability management. First, in Section 2, the characteristics of German and Japanese MFCA will be outlined to clarify the basic idea of MFCA. And we can understand how the framework of MFCA was established in Japan as ISO (ISO, 2011). In Section 3, one of the latest MFCA case examples in Japan will be illustrated, and some critical issues to develop MFCA as a sustainability management tool. In Section 4, we will show that many Asian MFCA users face difficulties to contribute to sustainability by using MFCA (ISO14051). Finally, we will conclude that we need to keep both usability of German MFCA and Japanese MFCA.

## 2. MFCA Development from Germany to Japan to International Standardization

### 2.1 *Original German MFCA*

Originally the method of MFCA had been developed at IMU, Augsburg, Germany. IMU published first discussion papers to the MFCA approach in 2000 (e.g., Strobel & Redmann, 2000, 2001). The IMU approach started by mapping material flows throughout a company from input to output. The complex flow of material first was recorded in physical terms, preferably in kilogram for mass balancing purposes. Other physical units (cubic meter, pieces, etc.) were used as first substitutes in case the weight

---

[2]This dissemination of MFCA has been strongly supported by APO (Asian Productivity Organization) as a tool of Green Productivity since 2010.

units were not available. This exercise showed that companies regularly only knew the amount of material that was supposed to go into the product (via bill of material) but did not know the amounts of material that did not end up in the product (e.g., emissions as kilogram in waste or tons of gases). And there was no clear record to the exact sources of waste or emissions as well as to the costs involved with these unrecorded material flows. The IMU approach then started to track and document these flows in physical as well as in monetary terms. This for production management was the prerequisite on the one hand to avoid waste and emissions up front and on the other hand with the higher transparency of the "real waste cost" focus on cost-saving potentials.

First German MFCA projects were introduced by IMU in several German companies supported by the German governmental Eco-Efficiency Project in the 1990s (IMU & ZWW, 2003; Wagner, 2015). The companies started by tracing all material flows from corporate input to output. The analyzed input–output system was the scope of a company.

Which materials did enter the company, and were they recorded in kilograms and dollars?

Where did they go, where were they transformed or stored?

And where did they leave the company during production — as waste, as emission, or as recycling material?

These material flows throughout the company were followed by mass balances at each transformation center, again in kilograms and dollars. As a major result, the material flow analyses showed that the material flow costs of waste (including input material cost, conversion cost and disposal cost) were surprisingly high. As a rough estimate, companies saw, reported and controlled only about 10% of the total "real" material costs that were linked to material flows ending up as waste. This discovery gave strong impulses to reduce waste and by this to save material (resources), reduce environmental impacts, and save costs.

Typically, the German companies, after a first round of manual data collection, headed for processing the material flow data within the already existing Enterprise Resource Planning (ERP) systems like SAP or Oracle, as many of the required material control data already existed in the ERP systems, e.g., input material (purchasing) data, stocks, material in product (bill of material), etc. (Nakajima & Kokubu, 2001, 2008; IMU & ZWW, 2003; Wagner & Enzler, 2005).

## 2.2  Japanese MFCA

The Japanese MFCA approach started from the basic ideas and procedures of the German MFCA after the visit of a Japanese delegate to IMU in 2000 (Nakajima & Kokubu, 2001). The shared MFCA methodology facilitated a transparency and a quantification of material movements, stocks, and inventory changes. The mapping of costs along the material flows distinguished between input material cost, conversion cost or "system cost" (including, e.g., labor cost, depreciation, and energy cost), and output cost. The Japanese MFCA endeavors started by first explaining and defining the MFCA concept and by designing a working plan and procedures to conduct MFCA analysis in a Japanese industrial site (METI Japan, 2001).

In 2000, the Japanese government took up the German experiences and started a project offering the MFCA management tool to companies with the purpose to reach two targets simultaneously: promoting environmental protection on the one hand and creating new business chances on the other hand (METI Japan, 2001). In the past, these two targets have been widely seen as contradictory. In this project, MFCA was introduced as a management accounting tool, which could be relevant for business practice by tracing cost-saving potentials through resource and material efficiency measures, and by reducing environmental impacts. The Japanese project established a working group on MFCA in 2000.

The Japanese approach, less complex and more pragmatic, compared to the first German approach, focused typically on the manual data collection with regard to selected production processes or wasted material flows. The detailed and comprehensive assessment of material flows from input to output in a process regularly showed considerable saving potentials in terms of wasted material and corresponding cost (METI Japan, 2001; Nakajima & Kokubu, 2001, 2008). The successful case studies, supported by METI, resulted in a rapid dissemination of the approach in Japanese industries. Around 2000 Japanese companies still considered environmental management as an add-on and costly exercise, in addition to core production management. But the MFCA case examples showed new opportunities for cost reduction in manufacturing processes. From a conventional viewpoint (applying, e.g., Total Productive Maintenance (TPM) and Quality Circle (QC)), companies could not become aware of the significance of the considerable wasted material produced by their own manufacturing processes. In Japan, MFCA was accepted as a new Kaizen tool. Many Japanese companies introduced MFCA into their manufacturing processes, in METI and other projects, and successful case examples were published by Kaizen experts (Anjo & Shimogaki, 2011).

The METI working group developed MFCA as an EMA tool encouraging companies to improve their environmental management systems and by this gain economic benefits based on a more accurate and rigorous material flow control. As a result, more than 200 corporate MFCA case examples could be made publicly available since 2000 (Kokubu & Nakajima, 2018). Also, these Japanese companies continued to further develop the MFCA methodology as a relevant EMA approach. Primarily, Japanese MFCA along material flow assesses each process and workplace (e.g., a machine or an equipment). At every point of material transformation (so-called "quantity centers"), MFCA shows volumes of each wasted material and evaluates costs of each wasted material. These costs of wasted materials, in general unexpectedly high, again stimulate impressive incentives to start Kaizen activities. Japanese MFCA in most cases starts with a pin point analysis of a selected manufacturing process and then expands the scope of MFCA analysis to other manufacturing areas. Japanese case examples from various industry sectors have been published and also translated into English (METI Japan, 2010; ISO-EMA Japan, 2007a, 2007b).

## 2.3 *Common Principles of German MFCA and Japanese MFCA*

Basically, the scope of MFCA can vary in range. Also, focus and procedures might be changed according to company's demand. But both, the Japanese and the German MFCA rely on common methodological principles (ISO, 2011).

1. The subjects of tracking material flows and stocks are particular input materials.

Along manufacturing processes, materials generally are mixed, transformed, separated, or assembled. After production processing, however,

**Fig 1.** Traditional recognition of production processes.

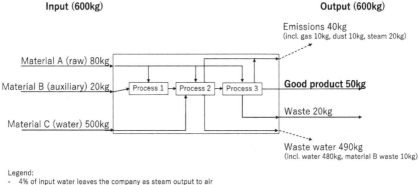

**Fig 2.** Simplified material flow chart (MFCA mass balance).

the data of traditional production management and cost accounting is aggregated. For example, materials A and B are input to a process which manufactures 500 pieces of good product, shown in Fig. 1. The information of traditional production management provides data on input of material A and B, and on number of good products as output. The input data of materials are aggregated to number of good products.

As shown in Fig. 2, MFCA traces the exact amount of material A, B, and C going into the products as the output, but also the amounts of wasted materials going to air, water, and soil, as waste or for recycling or even as by-products.

In MFCA, the wasted material is primarily called as "material loss." And then in Japanese terminology, materials going into the primary products are considered as "positive product", while the rest are defined as "negative product" (Nakajima & Kokubu, 2001).

2.  The method to physically trace materials along the entire flow of materials at quantity centers is the mass balance. Masses from input to output at each quantity center according to thermodynamic laws have to balance. Increasing or decreasing stocks have to be considered. Only by mass balancing, material losses can be traced and accounted for in physical terms, as shown in Fig. 2.

## 2.4 *MFCA as international standard*

The international ISO-standardization process (ISO: International Organization for Standardization) of MFCA starting in 2007 has launched the dissemination of MFCA as a tool of management in many countries around the world. The international standardization of MFCA has been proposed and mainly led by Japanese government and other Japanese industry associations, based on the Japanese MFCA project experiences since 2000.

Before the formal proposal of MFCA to ISO in 2007, Japan Industrial Standards Committee (JISC) published and circulated two documents (ISC-EMA, 2007a, 2007b) at the plenary meeting of ISO/TC207 in Beijing, China. These documents presented the theoretical, methodological, and practical baseline of Japanese MFCA. They emphasized that MFCA was one of the most relevant corporate tools in EMA to achieve "both a reduction in the environmental impact and a real economic benefit" (ISC-EMA, 2007a, p. 13). ISC-EMA (2007b) disclosed a number of MFCA case examples from Japanese companies such as Nitto Denko, Canon, Tanabe-Seiyaku, Sony EMCS, Matsushita Electric Industrial (Panasonic), Nippon Paint, etc. These MFCA case examples in general started by depicting a material flow chart (a type of process mapping); they numbered the amounts of material inputs and outputs before and after MFCA improvements, based on actual practical information. By this they were able to exemplify the economic benefits derived from MFCA applications. Companies became aware that up to now they had not comprehensively monitored the material efficiency of their manufacturing process. Consequently, famous Japanese cost-leader companies on the basis of the new MFCA approach were able to show considerable cost reductions, especially in mass production.

Also in Germany, the publication of the ISO 14051 MFCA standard stimulated new German MFCA projects targeting material efficiency and focusing on cost reductions in reference to the Japanese experiences (Schmidt & Nakajima, 2013).

The state of Baden-Wurttemberg in Germany, for example, introduced a governmental project on Resource Efficiency Management in 2013 (Schmidt *et al.*, 2017). This project documented 100 case examples of corporate resource efficiency management, including MFCA case examples (Schmidt *et al.*, 2017). However, the MFCA case examples were not declared as MFCA case examples in this book (Schmidt *et al.*, 2017). Out of competitive reasons, the companies hesitated to publicly disclose MFCA cost-saving data from improved material efficiency.

The author had a chance to visit some of these German MFCA companies. The companies' approach, based on ISO 14051, was to follow the (Japanese) MFCA experience applying a governmentally proposed MFCA software (bw!MFCA-Software, Schmidt *et al.*, 2017). The software was implemented in order to digitalize, calculate, and analyze MFCA data, including environmental aspects, such as $CO_2$ emission data and life cycle assessment (LCA) information. Their projects also referred to other Japanese on-site management tools, such as Kaizen, Lean Management, etc. But these German MFCA companies did not achieve comparable results or improve process efficiency as in the Japanese case examples.

## 3. A Japanese MFCA Case Study

The author has conducted MFCA projects since 2000 until now. Table 1 shows the result of a typical, recent MFCA project in a Japanese manufacturing company. The company produces engine parts for the automotive industry. The data refers to one particular year, estimated by MFCA analyses. In this case, the MFCA project mainly focused on the flow of materials and energy, and on waste management. It did not consider system costs (e.g., labor cost and depreciation).

This manufacturing process consumes much water. Table 1 shows the disproportionally high amount of water compared to other inputs to the manufacturing process (when measured in mass units — kilogram). At

**Table 1.** MFCA case study in Japanese automotive industry.

| Mass data | |
| --- | --- |
| All Inputs | 13,781,626 kg |
|   Positive product | 372,727 kg |
|   Negative product | 13,408,899 kg |
| All inputs without water | |
|   All inputs | 476,526 kg |
|   Positive product | 372,727 kg |
|   Negative product | 103,799 kg |
|   Water consumption | 13,305,100 kg |
|   Electlicity consumption | 1,085,015 Kwh |
| Cost data | |
|   Costs of all input materials, waste management and energy | 545,501,039 J¥ |
|   Cost of positive product | 379,809,732 J¥ |
|   Cost of negative product | 165,691,307 J¥ |
|   Breakdown: Cost of electricity | 17,794,249 J¥ |

the beginning of this MFCA project, even though some staff members had rough information on high-water consumption, could the topic be not recognized as a management issue. This recognition was changed after MFCA data presentation. On the other hand, looking at the manufacturing process in terms of cost, the water input cost (= purchasing cost) is 0, as water procurement is accomplished by a company-owned well.

Also, Table 1 shows the small cost fraction of energy cost compared to other cost fractions. This result is typical for industries.

Figure 3 shows examples to summarize this MFCA project.

In Fig. 3, the top two diagrams illustrate the proportion of positive and negative products in mass units. The upper left diagram shows the proportion of the positive and the negative products, including water consumption in mass units (e.g., water as input material C in Fig. 2). Considered from a physical point of view in mass units, 97% of all input materials end up as negative products. Only 3% of the input materials go into the product (positive product in MFCA terms). On the other hand, if water

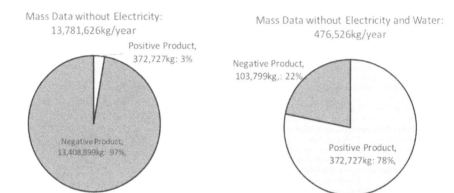

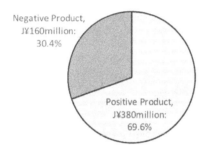

**Fig 3.**   A summary of MFCA project.

consumption is not included in the materials data, the top right-hand diagram in Fig. 3 shows a different proportion of positive and negative products again in mass units. The negative product ratio changes to 22% of
input materials. This dimension is common for Japanese industries.

This MFCA project also revealed a substantial number of defective
products. The results in Fig. 3 seem even more remarkable, considering
that defective products so far had not been recognized as material losses.
This production line (in mass units) permanently generates 22% material
losses (not including waste water).

The bottom diagram in Fig. 3 shows the proportion of positive and
negative products, including water consumption, now in monetary terms.
The negative product cost ratio is 30.4% of all input material costs,

including waste treatment cost and energy cost. This MFCA information identifies the monetary dimension of material losses. It also suggests thinking about improvement measures. Typically for this type of MFCA projects, the company then starts to examine the causes of material losses and to develop targeted action plans in order to improve material efficiency. Typically also, at this point, the interest of most companies notably moves to the cost information.

On the other hand, the project experiences show that the demonstration and availability of MFCA mass data can help support the increasing recognition of information on resource consumption, such as water consumption, waste water, emissions, metal or plastic waste, and other material losses. In corporate practice of MFCA projects, management first of all, especially the MFCA beginner, focuses on cost reduction. But MFCA can support a wider range of performance targets than "just" cost reduction. The MFCA offers a new transparency of production processes and new opportunities to improve material efficiency. As a result, it serves as an accounting tool to support environmental and sustainability targets as well. And by this it serves to support a long-term corporate survival strategy, a strategy to ensure the mid- and long-term existence of a company.

Not to forget that MFCA from its origins had been created as a contribution to reach a more sustainable economy (Wagner, 2015).

Section 4 reports on the transfer of Japanese MFCA to other Asian industries.

## 4. MFCA Experiences in Asian Industries

METI Japan (2010) published 23 successful case examples in companies and the supply chain.[3] This booklet was to support the international standardization of MFCA. Through this companies in other Asian countries became interested in MFCA and started to apply MFCA in their own company (Kokubu & Nakajima, 2018; Ki-Hoon & Schaltegger, 2018). And then, in 2014, Asian Productivity Organization (APO) offered a number of seminars to introduce MFCA within the Green Productivity

---

[3]For MFCA in supply chain see Nakajima, Kimura and Wagner (2015) and Kokubu *et al.* (2015).

program (APO, 2014). APO invited company staffs, consultants and governmental representatives from several Asian countries to its site in Japan and for internet meetings. As a major impression from the corporate MFCA case studies as well as from dozens of MFCA seminars, the author experienced a dominant trend: even though the users of MFCA did understand that MFCA was designed to serve environmental protection purposes, in corporate reality, the focus to use MFCA always shifted toward cost reduction purposes. Nevertheless, the company uses MFCA only for cost reduction; MFCA was changed as an authorized tool for a company to obtain an evidence to create a sustainable management.

Malaysia Productivity Corporation (MPC) is a counterpart of APO in Malaysia. MPC has conducted MFCA projects in Malaysian companies since 2010, also publishing case examples as Green Productivity, e.g., in *The Application of Material Flow Cost Accounting in Malaysia* (MPC, 2012). Figure 4 shows the aggregated costs of material loss for five case studies. The MFCA cost evaluation included material cost, energy cost, labor cost, and others cost. In Fig. 4, e.g., "$ 138/M" shows the monthly cost of material loss of a brake lining manufacturing company (40 workers, $23 million of annual sales). The MFCA project helped this company achieve a yearly reduction of material loss cost of approximately $130,000. All case examples include information on environmental aspects (e.g., $CO_2$ emission). But at the end, cost reduction always proved as a strongest management incentive.

**Fig 4.**   Cost of monthly material losses in five Malaysian case examples (Yap, 2017).

The same observations could be affirmed at the APO seminar of MFCA, Tehran, Iran.[4] Delegates from Japan, Germany, Thailand, Malaysia, India, Iran, Cambodia, Vietnam, China, and Taipei discussed MFCA experiences. Most MFCA projects in Asian industries focused on cost reduction as a major result. In theory, all the participants agreed that MFCA was an EMA tool to achieve environmental protection results, e.g., by discussing the integration of MFCA analysis and LCA. Still the main interest shifted back on how to improve manufacturing processes and on possible cost reductions.

The author's analysis of practical MFCA experiences and supported manufacturing processes in Indonesia, Malaysia, Philippines, and Taiwan by MFCA again confirmed the same tendency. MFCA is used as an internal process inside a company. Even after explicitly discussing environmental aspects, material losses and mass aspects (kilogram), the company's interest rapidly turns back to aspects of costs (material loss costs) and internal company issues.

At the same time, the author, visiting the MFCA projects, has experienced massive industrial environmental pollutions such as dust on roads, in town, in rivers, forests, nature, and life (Fig. 5).

Industrial nations like Japan or Germany have experienced critical pollutions from factory emissions. Asian countries do not have to go through same experiences.

MFCA is not only a tool to improve internal material efficiency and secure cost reductions, but also can help reduce internal environmental impacts by reducing resource consumption (material in waste, to air, to soil, to water, energy losses, etc.). MFCA can also help recognize emissions to the outside world (to ecosystem and society) in mass unit. However, we need to develop MFCA as a tool for decision-making, including, e.g., social costs and benefits,[5] in corporate management.

---

[4] International Conference on Material Flow Cost Accounting, 19–21 September 2017, Teheran Iran, sponsored by APO.

[5] For example, recently ISO14007 (Environmental management: Determining environmental costs and benefits — Guidance) and ISO14008 (Monetary valuation of environmental impacts and related environmental aspects) have been discussed to be published. We will have a possibility to integrate MFCA with these ISOs.

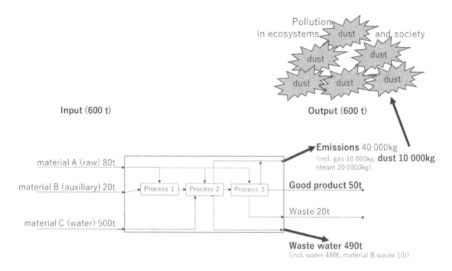

**Fig 5.**   Material flows ending in product, in air, water, and soil.

## 5. Conclusion

MFCA is an accounting tool providing information to production management and top management for productivity, strategy, environmental, and sustainability purposes. MFCA can be applied by traditional production management, and by looking at manufacturing processes from a different perspective. Also with a traditional management mind-set, unexpected possibilities for cost reduction can be located. This is the important result for MFCA users introducing MFCA into their business processes, in order to achieve economic benefits accompanied by the elimination of material inefficiencies. But this is not the only usefulness and relevance of MFCA as a management tool. MFCA is originally a tool to increase transparency of material and resource flows[6] from resource extraction to transformation, dissipation, and disposal. MFCA is a tool to increase transparency on quantities and cost of resources efficiently used or inefficiently wasted in industry, and by this becomes a basic tool for sustainability management.

In addition, today's companies are not only confronted with cost-saving pressures, but with a complex challenge of legal, societal, and competitive

---

[6]Materials here are defined as processed resources.

pressures. Political and client pressures are strong on environmental impact reduction, climate issues, and social responsibility. The Volkswagen AG example of the last two years showed the global corporate consequences of underestimating emission issues, as environmental topics for long have not been considered as relevant for business.

MFCA is able to bridge the gap between efforts of traditional management and its imperative orientation toward cost saving on the one hand and modern management on the other facing new political and societal challenges toward pollution reduction and environmental protection.

## Acknowledgment

The author is very grateful to Prof. Dr. Bernd Wagner, University of Augsburg Germany, for the strong support and the many helpful contributions and discussions during the process of finishing this chapter.

## References

Anjo, Y. and Shimogaki, A. (2011). *Zusetsu MFCA (Material Flow Cost Accounting) — ISO14051 to make a transparency of losses on materials and energy*. JIPM Solution (in Japanese).

APO (Asian Productivity Organization) (2014). *Manual on Material Flow Cost Accounting: ISO14051*. APO.

IMU (Institute für Management und Umwelt) and ZWW (Zentrum für Weiterbildung und Wissenstransfer, University of Augsburg) (2003). *Flussmanagement für Produktionsunternehmen. Material- und Informationsflüsse nachhalting gestalten*. Redline Wirtshaft (in German).

ISC-EMA Japan (International Standardization Committee for Environmental Management Accounting, Japan) (2007a). *Preliminary Proposal for International Standardization of Material Flow-Based Environmental Management Accounting*. JISC (Japan Industrial Standards Committee).

ISC-EMA Japan (2007b). *Preliminary Proposal for International Standardization of Material Flow-Based Environmental Management Accounting: Annex*. JISC.

ISO (International Organization for Standardization) (2011). *ISO14051 Environmental Management — Material Flow Cost Accounting General Framework*. ISO.

Ki-Hoon, L. and Schaltegger, S. (2018). *Asia Pacific Perspectives.* Eco-Efficiency in Industry and Science. Springer.

Kokubu, K., Itsubo, N., Nakajima, M. and Yamada, T. (2015). *Low-carbon Supply Chain Management.* Chuokeizai-sha Inc. (in Japanese).

Kokubu, K. and Nakajima, M. (2018). *Material Flow Cost Accounting Theory and Practice.* Doubunkan Shuppan (in Japanese).

METI Japan (2001). *Workbook of Environmental Management Accounting Methods.* METI Japan.

METI Japan (2010). *Material Flow Cost Accounting: MFCA Case Examples.* METI Japan.

MPC (Malaysia Productivity Corporation) (2012). *The Application of Material Flow Cost Accounting in Malaysia.* MPC.

Nakajima, M. and Kokubu, K. (2001). *Material Flow Cost Accounting.* Nikkei Inc. (in Japanese).

Nakajima, M. and Kokubu, K. (2008). *Material Flow Cost Accounting*, 2nd edn. Nikkei Publishing Inc. (in Japanese).

Nakajima, M., Kimura, A. and Wagner, B. (2015). Introduction of MFCA to the supply chain: A questionnaire research on challenges of constructing a low-carbon supply chain to promote resource efficiency. *Journal of Cleaner Production 108*, Part B, 1302–1309.

Schmidt, M. and Nakajima, M. (2013). Material flow cost accounting as an approach to improve resource efficiency in manufacturing companies. *Resources 2*(3), 358–369.

Schmidt, M., Spieth, H., Bauer, J. and Haubach, C. (2017). *100 Betriebe für Ressourceffizienz — Band 1 Praxisbeispiele aus der produzierenden Wirtshaft.* Springer Spektrum.

Strobel, M. and Redmann, C. (2000, 2001). *Flow Cost Accounting.* IMU.

Yap, A. (2017). Application of MFCA as Green Productivity Tool16-IN-22-GE-CON-A. *International Conference on MFCA*, 19–21 September, Tehran. APO.

Wagner, B. (2015). A report on the origins of MFCA research activities. *Journal of Cleaner Production 108*, Part B, 1255–1261.

Wagner, B. and Enzler, A. (2005). *Material Flow Management. Sustainability and Innovation.* Springer.

Chapter 6

# How Does Material Flow Cost Accounting Continue in Practice?: The Effective Policy from a Questionnaire Survey

Tatsumasa Tennojiya*, Akira Higashida[†],
Hirotsugu Kitada[‡] and Jaehong Kim[§]

*Graduate School of Humanities and Social Sciences,
Okayama University, Japan
[†]Faculty of Business Management, Meijo University, Japan
[‡]Faculty of Business Administration, Hosei University, Japan
[§]Faculty of Economics, Kanto Gakuen University, Japan

## 1. Introduction

Material flow cost accounting (MFCA) is an environmental management accounting tool that was integrated into the ISO 14000 family in 2011 as ISO 14051. It is a noteworthy means of seeking a sustainable society (ISO, 2011). The ISO (2011, p. v) describes MFCA as "a management tool that can assist organizations to better understand the potential environmental and financial consequences of their material and energy use practices, and seek opportunities to achieve both environmental and financial improvements via changes in those practices." The MFCA is so useful for sustainability management that ISO 14052, which offers guidance for practical implementation of MFCA in a supply chain, was also published in 2017 (ISO, 2017). Further, discussions about ISO 14053, which relates to MFCA's international standardization for small- and medium-sized enterprises (SMEs), is also underway.

It is helpful to recognize the difference between MFCA and traditional cost accounting to fully grasp the characteristics of MFCA. As MFCA is defined as a "tool for quantifying the flows and stocks of materials in processes or production lines in both physical and monetary units" (ISO, 2011, p. 3), its calculation focuses on the materials itself. "Materials" can be divided into two categories here: those intended as parts of products (e.g., raw materials, auxiliary materials, and intermediate products) and those that are not (e.g., cleaning solvents and chemical catalysts). Further, MFCA includes means to calculate the cost of waste products by focusing on each type of the materials. This cost is not generally calculated under traditional cost accounting, which primarily aims to determine the profits gained through product sales. Therefore, waste product costs are naturally regarded as a part of sales costs. Meanwhile, the waste product costs in MFCA can be distinguished from other product costs. By using indexes of actual resource efficiencies, costs can be assigned or allocated to products as well as their wastes. Accordingly, MFCA can provide information about the cost of waste products and inefficiencies of materials in the process, which can then compel organizations' managers to make better decisions regarding material consumption.

Recently, MFCA has received more attention in academia. For example, MFCA was selected as a key topic in the *2013 Environmental and Sustainability Management Accounting Network* conference (Nakazawa, Tennojiya & Kokubu, 2013) and in the *Journal of Cleaner Production* (Guenther *et al.*, 2015). Academic research has been conducted from various perspectives to contribute to the knowledge regarding MFCA. By considering this tendency, Christ and Burritt's (2015) review of MFCA studies suggests a possible direction for future research by illustrating seven future research questions and 16 subresearch questions. From this research agenda's diverse directions, this chapter addresses MFCA's continuation. Challenging this issue is significant, as MFCA can play an important role in building a sustainable society if more companies use it continuously.

Research — conducted primarily in Japan — has discussed the issue of MFCA's continuous use (Kokubu, 2007; Seki & Anjo, 2016; Okada, 2018). Kokubu (2007) theoretically recognized two problems in the continuous implementation of MFCA: (1) its controllability, as it is difficult to decrease the losses calculated by MFCA in an existing range of controllability, and (2) its priority, as top management generally prioritizes opportunities to improve revenues over decreasing costs. The author also considers solutions to these problems: adjusting the range of controllability through top management's engagement and constructing environments that prioritize activities to reach MFCA targets, respectively. Further, he extracts a concrete means to achieve these solutions from three case studies of successful companies, in terms of their continuous use of MFCA. These include the implementation of a meeting involving the entire company to report results, using a product improvement tool, and establishing goals for the entire company. Seki and Anjo (2016) also address this problem by considering the factors of continuous use through a case study of an SME that continuously implemented MFCA. The authors recognize such success factors — (1) the long-term perspective on using MFCA, (2) company's capability which enables every member's participation, and (3) understanding by top management. Okada (2018) also uses a single case study of another company to reveal a shared thinking among members about costs as a success factor in the continuous use of MFCA.

As mentioned previously, some research has already addressed the issue of the continuation of MFCA. Meanwhile, little is known in practice due to the limited number of examples. Therefore, this study attempts to accumulate knowledge about the continuous use of MFCA in practice. We propose the following question to achieve this objective: What are the factors deterring the continuous use of MFCA? This question will be answered using data from a questionnaire survey designed to understand the actual conditions of continuous MFCA use. Further, we use this data to also consider an effective policy to enable the continuous use of MFCA, which leads to a better, more sustainable world.

The remainder of this chapter is structured as follows. Section 2 describes the research method employed for this chapter. Section 3 states and discusses the empirical findings. Section 4 summarizes the study and suggests some directions for future research.

## 2. Research Design

### 2.1 *Questionnaire survey*

While the prototype of MFCA was developed in Germany in the late 1980s and early 1990s (Wagner, 2015), scholars and practitioners in Japan have played an important role in developing and diffusing MFCA in practice. Japan's Ministry of Economy, Trade and Industry (METI) has strongly supported the promotion of MFCA after an academic researcher introduced the concept in 2000. Many of the companies that implemented MFCA from 2001 to 2010 were subsidized by METI, and over 300 companies have implemented MFCA following its support (Schmidt & Nakajima, 2013).

As a management accounting tool, MFCA's use is voluntary; therefore, a company's performance through MFCA is not generally made public. Meanwhile, many cases of MFCA adoption in Japan were disclosed in a report that carried details of subsidies from METI (e.g., METI, 2010), which leads to high accessibility to companies that have experience in implementing MFCA. This study exploits this feature.

In 2016, we first checked all reports of the projects supported by METI to compile a list of MFCA companies. Further, we complemented this data through Internet searches, as some companies independently adopt MFCA regardless of METI's support. Accordingly, our list consisted of 219 companies, and we then sent our questionnaire to these companies. Ultimately, 27 companies responded to our questionnaire, with a response rate of 12.3%. While the questionnaire's objectives cover a wide range, we use only a part of it in the study, or the eight questions about the problems in MFCA activities. We excluded deficient responses, and consequently, data from 22 companies were found to be useable.

### 2.2 *Variables*

This study focuses on the issue of MFCA design and other possible factors in the continuation of MFCA. Questions about the MFCA design were primarily constructed based on the "perceived attributes of innovation", which is a component of Rogers's (2003) diffusion theory. Rogers (2003, p. 12) defines innovation as "an idea, practice, or object that is perceived as new by an individual or other unit of adoption." The perceived attributes of innovation explain the speed of an innovation's adoption.

Rogers (2003) identifies five perceived attributes of innovation, namely relative advantage, compatibility, complexity, trialability, and observability. First, relative advantage is "the degree to which an innovation is perceived as being better than the idea it supersedes. The degree of relative advantage is often expressed as economic profitability, as conveying social prestige, or in other ways. The nature of the innovation determines what specific type of relative advantage (economic, social, and the like) is important to adopters, although the characteristics of potential adopters may also affect which specific sub-dimensions of relative advantage are most important" (Rogers, 2003, p. 229).

Second, compatibility is "the degree to which an innovation is perceived as consistent with the existing values, past experiences, and needs of potential adopters. An idea that is more compatible is less uncertain to the potential adopter and fits more closely with the individual's situation. Such compatibility helps the individual give meaning to the new idea so that it is regarded as more familiar. An innovation can be compatible or incompatible with (1) sociocultural values and beliefs, (2) previously introduced ideas, and/or (3) client needs for the innovation" (Rogers, 2003, p. 240).

Third, complexity is "the degree to which an innovation is perceived as relatively difficult to understand and use" (Rogers, 2003, p. 257). Fourth, trialability is "the degree to which an innovation may be experimented with on a limited basis" (Rogers, 2003, p. 258). Finally, observability is "the degree to which the results of innovation are visible to others" (ibid.).

Here, the greater the adopter's perceived relative advantage, compatibility, trialability, and the observability of innovation, the more rapid the adoption rate. Further, an innovation's complexity negatively relates to the adoption rate. These attributes can reflect an MFCA design, and become a variable determining its rate of adoption. Therefore, existing studies have also focused on the concepts that consider the factors of MFCA adoption (e.g., Sulong, Sulaiman & Northayati, 2015). Meanwhile, we attempt to employ the concepts in a more extended manner by assuming that they can be used not only during the initial decision — when companies decide whether to implement MFCA — but also in subsequent decisions, when companies decide whether to continue such MFCA activities. We consider the factors in the continuous use of MFCA by attempting to use these concepts without modification, except for trialability. The concept of trialability is unfit in this context, as all questionnaire respondents have already implemented MFCA. Therefore, this study changes "trialability" to "developability," which means "the degree to which the innovation results indicate its worth in use." The changed concept reveals that the better the company's perception of each MFCA attribute, the easier the decision to use MFCA continuously.

Other possible obstacles can also be considered. This study recognizes three factors aside from MFCA design. First, resistance from the production site must be considered, an issue that has received attention in the management accounting research context. For example, Malmi (1997) focuses on a factory's resistance against implementing the activity-based costing (ABC) system through one company, then identifies three origins of adopters' resistance: the economic rationale, politics, and culture. Results by Seki and Anjo (2016) and Okada (2018) imply that this issue is relevant even in an MFCA context because the MFCA calculation process requires data gathered from the production site. Further, improvements related to MFCA calculation are primarily conducted by people at the production site. Therefore, cooperating with them is important in continuing MFCA activity.

Another factor is insufficient budget for MFCA activities. In Japan, METI financially supported the promotion of MFCA, and MFCA consultants were sent to companies for free. Thus, a sufficient budget is not an important factor in the decision process regarding MFCA's initial implementation in many cases in Japan. However, one important issue may involve determining whether these companies will continue MFCA without support from METI. Further, the importance of top management's understanding, which Kokubu (2007) and Seki and Anjo (2016) recognize as enablers, may also influence the budget problem. If top management does not understand such activities and the budget is lacking, it will be difficult to continue them.

Another factor is the interruption of knowledge by changes in personnel, as MFCA activities only seem to continue when someone recognizes its importance and knows how to use it. Thus, MFCA activity will cease if no one knows how to activate it; consequently, our research design also addresses this issue, although extant studies of MFCA have yet to explore it.

Thus far, we have considered eight factors influencing the continuous use of MFCA: five factors that relate to MFCA design, and three others that involve issues in MFCA activity. Each factor is respectively assigned questions that we use in this research (see Appendix A).

## 3. Discussion

### 3.1 *Questionnaire survey results*

The data used in this research include questions regarding problems with MFCA. We asked respondents about the extent to which each question fits their company's MFCA activity. Table 1 illustrates all variables' descriptive statistics.

Table 1 notes that companies with experience in implementing MFCA acknowledge issues with developability (4.55), observability (4.55), and complexity (4.50) relative to the MFCA design; further, they acknowledge the interruption of knowledge through personnel changes (4.82) at relatively high levels. Meanwhile, resistance (3.45) is less recognized as a problem in MFCA.

This study's sample comprised two types of companies; one includes companies with experience in continuously using MFCA, while the other

**Table 1.** Descriptive statistics of all samples.

|  | Mean | Std. Dev. | Min | Max |
|---|---|---|---|---|
| complexity | 4.50 | 1.54 | 2 | 7 |
| r_advantage | 4.23 | 1.80 | 1 | 7 |
| compatibility | 3.86 | 1.42 | 1 | 7 |
| developability | 4.55 | 1.63 | 1 | 7 |
| observability | 4.55 | 1.53 | 2 | 7 |
| resistance | 3.45 | 1.30 | 1 | 7 |
| budget | 4.14 | 1.46 | 1 | 7 |
| knowledge | 4.82 | 1.50 | 2 | 7 |

includes those without such experience. We then create two subsamples to answer the research question and establish the criterion of continuation as two years' experience. A two-year criterion is selected due to Japan's particular context. As mentioned in Section 2, many companies have implemented MFCA based on METI's financial support, which became available as per the Japanese government's fiscal year (from the beginning of April of the reference year to March-end of the following year). This study assures continuation by only regarding companies implementing MFCA for over two years as those that continuously use MFCA. Table 2 displays the subsamples' descriptive statistics.

Table 2 indicates that companies with experience in continuously using MFCA are less likely to recognize its problems, a trend observed across all variables. Although the calculation of the t-test showed that the differences were not statistically significant, these variables seem to deserve consideration in the continuation of MFCA.

Further, different perceptions might exist between the different company types. Companies with experience in using MFCA continuously recognize the issues regarding complexity (4.22), relative advantage (4.11), and observability (4.11) relative to MFCA design — and the interruption of knowledge by changes in personnel (4.67) at relatively high levels. However, companies with no experience recognize issues with developability (5.00), observability (4.85), and complexity (4.69) relative to MFCA

**Table 2.** Subsamples' descriptive statistics.

| Continuous Use | Yes ($n = 9$) | | No ($n = 13$) | |
|---|---|---|---|---|
| | Mean | Std. Dev. | Mean | Std. Dev. |
| complexity | 4.22 | 1.64 | 4.69 | 1.49 |
| r_advantage | 4.11 | 1.83 | 4.31 | 1.84 |
| compatibility | 3.33 | 1.12 | 4.23 | 1.54 |
| developability | 3.89 | 1.90 | 5.00 | 1.29 |
| observability | 4.11 | 1.54 | 4.85 | 1.52 |
| resistance | 2.89 | 1.27 | 3.85 | 1.21 |
| budget | 3.67 | 1.66 | 4.46 | 1.27 |
| knowledge | 4.67 | 1.32 | 4.92 | 1.66 |

design, and the interruption of knowledge by changes in personnel (4.92) at relatively high levels. The results reveal that companies with no experience in continuously using MFCA tend to more often recognize problems with its developability compared to companies with such experience.

## 3.2 *Policy to resolve the problem*

The findings suggest we must discuss a policy not only to improve MFCA design, but also to resolve the problems presented in this research. We address this issue by focusing on two factors most recognized by companies with no experience in continuing MFCA, "developability" and the "interruption of knowledge by a change in personnel."

The results imply that MFCA design should involve a policy with the intent to improve the MFCA's relative advantage, compatibility, developability, and observability, or decrease its complexity; this is important in urging companies to continuously use MFCA. Simultaneously, it might be crucial to distinguish an approach for companies with experience in continuously using MFCA. Regarding these experienced companies, seven of nine had ceased MFCA activities at the time of the questionnaire survey. Therefore, it is also necessary to consider such an approach for companies with continuous experience. However, the results do not reflect any characteristics, although it can be said that the MFCA's complexity and relative advantage are recognized as more highly ranked problems in experienced companies than in unexperienced ones. Alternatively, the MFCA can also focus on the data from companies with no experience. The MFCA's developability is regarded as the highest priority problem in unexperienced companies, while experienced companies place a medium priority on this problem. This result implies a lack of information regarding the further development of MFCA in practice. To urge companies to continuously use MFCA, companies must know how to horizontally and/or vertically expand MFCA. Therefore, a policy is necessary that can help companies understand the MFCA's development. For example, the case study by Higashida, Kokubu and Shinohara (2017) of a company that successfully implemented MFCA company-wide emphasizes the importance of MFCA's integration into key personnel needs. Further, relative to MFCA's development in the company, the authors also described the factory in which MFCA was implemented as an initial trial. The company in this example used the term "material flow cost activity" instead of MFCA to avoid resistance from those on the production line, and MFCA was incorporated with indicators regarding production improvement. In this manner, one policy might involve disclosing and explaining cases of successful companies in terms of horizontally and/or vertically expanding MFCA. Further, we must learn how to develop MFCA from these companies.

The problem of knowledge interruptions due to changes in personnel is recognized at a high level. One company in our sample clearly notes in the free description section of the questionnaire that the "personnel change of the MFCA promoter discontinued the MFCA activity." This result implies that MFCA philosophy and knowledge has not become popular in factories. Seki and Anjo (2016) describe one company with a long-term view of using MFCA and a capability to enable all members' participation as well as top management's understanding of the concept. These points might mitigate the influence of personnel change. Günther and Gäbler's (2014) quantitative meta-analysis of the antecedents of the adoption and success of strategic cost management methods argues for the importance of employees' commitment to cost management in continuously using such methods. The authors further assert that "commonly derived targets, interdisciplinary, cross-functional teamwork, and a distinct support for the process by management are able to significantly strengthen the identification of the employees with cost management" (Günther & Gäbler, 2014, p. 182). This assertion is consistent with knowledge from Seki and Anjo (2016) and with such solutions as described by Kokubu (2007), including the implementation of a company-wide meeting to report results and establishing goals across the entire company. If employees are highly committed to MFCA, personnel changes seem to have a naturally low negative impact. Therefore, the method to drive employees' commitment to MFCA deserves further discussion in the context of continuing MFCA. Similarly, it might also be useful to consider knowledge creation through MFCA in terms of mannerisms to mitigate the problem. Kitada, Kokubu and Tennojiya (2013) used a case in which MFCA was implemented in an SME to determine that MFCA measurement and calculation practices created a field of local knowledge. If such a function works well, personnel change impacts might be mitigated. Therefore, how MFCA acts as a tool to promote knowledge creation must also be discussed.

Thus far, we have recognized the problems in MFCA activity. However, these problems seem to be connected by the complementary capabilities within companies. Further, the perceived attributes of innovation are determined by companies' perceptions, and therefore, these concepts strongly depend on each company's abilities. For example, if members share cost-related perceptions, as Okada (2018) describes, or members have already activated product improvement tools, as Kokubu (2007) notes, high compatibility is easily achieved. Other factors, such as knowledge interruption, also seem to be influenced by complementary capabilities. As previously mentioned, employees' commitment and knowledge might affect MFCA continuation. Further, Darnall's and Edwards's (2006) research on the adoption of environmental management systems clarified that companies with complementary capabilities — such as quality-based management systems, inventory control management systems, and pollution prevention — could adopt environmental management systems at a lower cost. Such discussions are applicable to the MFCA context. Thus, the following question must be addressed: What types of complementary capabilities influence the continuous use of MFCA?

## 4. Conclusion

This chapter has attempted to answer the following research question to accumulate knowledge regarding the continuous use of MFCA in practice: What are the factors that impede the continuous use of MFCA? Our questionnaire survey results indicate that companies significantly recognize problems such as MFCA's developability and the interruption of knowledge by personnel changes at a relatively high level. Further, an effective policy to promote companies' continuous use of MFCA should focus on these two primary obstacles. From the MFCA developability perspective, we highlight the importance of disclosing and explaining cases of companies with experience in horizontally and/or vertically expanding MFCA. Meanwhile, in terms of a problem with knowledge interruption, we emphasize the need for discussion about how to improve employees' commitment to MFCA and for MFCA to function as a knowledge creation tool. Further, we discuss the possibility of its complementary capacity, as factors can promote such an experience. To our knowledge, this study is the first to use a questionnaire survey to address the problem of the continuous use of MFCA. Our findings can act as a foundation for future research.

The study also contributes to diffusion theory, as we explore the concept of "developability" as a perceived innovation attribute in evaluating a tool's continuous ability. Moreover, our results recognize "developability" as a key issue in the continuation of MFCA. The success of this research analysis may justify the superiority of "developability" instead of "trialability" when employing the "perceived attributes of innovation" to address the issue of continuous use. Further, this research on MFCA can be applied to evaluate other tools in general, and their continuous use in particular.

This study's limitations primarily relate to the sample size and coverage of problems. Specifically, the limited sample size influences our research results, as we can grasp trends but with no statistically significant differences. Further, it remains an open question why seven of nine experienced companies ceased MFCA activities at the time of the questionnaire survey. However, the study contributes by accumulating knowledge about the continuous use of MFCA in practice, which was scarcely explored before this study. Future policymaking research should focus on the intent to urge companies to continuously use MFCA to pursue a sustainable world.

## A. Appendix — Questionnaire Items

*Issue: The problem with MFCA activity*

*To what extent do the following questions fit your company's MFCA activity? (1–7)*

1. The MFCA calculation process is complex. (*complexity*)
2. Effects to anticipate thorough MFCA implementation are already fulfilled through other existing management tools. (*relative advantage*)
3. Effects to expect through MFCA implementation are not strategic priority issues. (*compatibility*)

4. Experience with early implementation of MFCA does not allow the company to evaluate the possibility of its development. (*developability*)
5. The MFCA analysis results are difficult to understand for employees in other departments. (*observability*)
6. Resistance to and opposition against conducting MFCA activities exist at the production site. (*resistance*)
7. A budget is lacking to improve MFCA activity. (*budget*)
8. Knowledge and activity cannot continue because of changes in the personnel in charge of MFCA activities. (*knowledge*)

## Acknowledgments

This work was supported by The Melco Foundation 2015009 and JSPS KAKENHI JP 18K12911.

## References

Christ, K. L. and Burritt, R. L. (2015). Material flow cost accounting: A review and agenda for future research. *Journal of Cleaner Production 108*, 1378–1389.

Darnall, N. and Edwards Jr., D. (2006). Predicting the cost of environmental management system adoption: The role of capabilities, resources and ownership structure. *Strategic Management Journal 27*, 301–320.

Guenther, E., Jasch, C., Schmidt, M., Wagner, B. and Ilg, P. (2015). Material flow cost accounting: Looking back and ahead. *Journal of Cleaner Production 108*, 1249–1254.

Günther, T. W. and Gäbler, S. (2014). Antecedents of the adoption and success of strategic cost methods: A meta-analytic investigation. *Journal of Business Economics 84*, 145–190.

Higashida, A., Kokubu, K. and Shinohara, A. (2017). Creation and transformation of visibility: Time series analysis of material flow cost accounting practice. In Kokubu, K., Sawabe, N. and Matsushima, N. (eds.) *Calculation and Organizing Practices: Reconnecting Accounting Research and Organizational Theory*. Yuhikaku, pp. 117–136 (in Japanese).

ISO (2011). *ISO14051: Environmental Management — Material Flow Cost Accounting — General Framework*. ISO.

ISO (2017). *ISO14052: Environmental Management — Material Flow Cost Accounting — Guidance for Practical Implementation in a Supply Chain.* ISO.

Kitada, H., Kokubu, K. and Tennojiya, T. (2013). Technological empowerment: Creating local knowledge with calculating practice. *7th Asia Pacific Interdisciplinary Research in Accounting (APIRA) Conference Paper.*

Kokubu, K. (2007). Continuous implementation of material flow cost accounting. *The Kokumin-Keizai Zasshi (Journal of Economics & Business Administration) 196*(5), 47–61 (in Japanese).

Malmi, T. (1997). Towards explaining activity-based costing failure: Accounting and control in a decentralized organization. *Management Accounting Research 8*(4), 459–480.

METI (2010). *Material Flow Cost Accounting: MFCA Case Examples.* Ministry of Economy, Trade and Industry, Japan.

Nakazawa, Y., Tennojiya, T. and Kokubu, K. (2013). A trend of international studies on MFCA: An analysis of presented researches at EMAN 2013. *Environmental Management 49*(10), 70–74 (in Japanese).

Okada, K. (2018). Continuous adaptation of MFCA: The case analysis of the Owari company. In Kokubu, K. and Nakajima, M. (eds.) *Material Flow Cost Accounting Theory and Practice.* Dobunkan Publishing, pp. 158–175 (in Japanese).

Rogers, M. (2003). *Diffusion of Innovation: Fifth Edition.* New York, NY: Free Press.

Schmidt, M. and Nakajima, M. (2013). Material flow cost accounting as an approach to improve resource efficiency in manufacturing companies. *Resource 2*(3), 358–369.

Seki, R. and Anjo, Y. (2016). The possibility of MFCA as a management tool: The case of Komagane Denka Co. *Melco Journal of Management Accounting Research 8*(2), 35–47 (in Japanese).

Sulong, F., Sulaiman, M. and Northayati, M. A. (2015). Material flow cost accounting (MFCA) enablers and barriers: The case of a Malaysian small and medium-sized enterprise (SME). *Journal of Cleaner Production 108*, 1365–1374.

Wagner, B. (2015). A report on the origins of material flow cost accounting (MFCA) research activities. *Journal of Cleaner Production 108*, 1255–1261.

Chapter 7

# Toward Sustainable Production: The Role of Emotion in Material Flow Cost Accounting Practices

Kana Okada*, Naoko Komori[†] and Katsuhiko Kokubu[‡]

*Faculty of Business Administration,
Osaka University of Economics, Osaka, Osaka Prefecture, Japan
[†]Management School, Sheffield University, UK
[‡]Graduate School of Business Administration, Kobe University
Kobe, Hyōgo Prefecture, Japan

## 1. Introduction

The Sustainable Development Goals (SDGs) that was published by the United Nations in 2015 have been embraced by a range of actors, including public sector and private sector organizations, NGOs, and accounting professionals worldwide. The SDG framework includes 17 goals that relate to the social, ecological, and economic outcomes required for achieving environmental and human development, and are expected to be delivered by 2030. While being referred to by policymaking communities rapidly, these "global goals" are expected to provide a guide for development across nations.

However, the methods to achieve the SDGs are inevitably affected by the national "local" context, and their corresponding processes impact each society differently (Komori, 2015; Belal *et al.*, 2017). In translating universal, "global" SDGs into local organizational and social contexts, accounting plays a pivotal role, and has been argued to affect strategizing, thus guiding organizations to achieve the SDGs (Bebbington & Unerman, 2018). However, SDGs are criticized as being ideologically Eurocentric and neo-liberal in nature (Weber, 2017). Therefore, it becomes important to examine the ways in which sustainability and environmental agendas are coped with and resolved within a different (i.e., Asian) socio-cultural context. Such an exploration will shed light on the role of accounting in translating SDGs, which has not yet been established in Western-led discussions.

With this in mind, this chapter discusses a case study of Material Flow Cost Accounting (MFCA), a significant accounting practice of Japanese manufacturing companies, which has sustained the process of *Monozukuri* ("manufacturing craftsmanship", the Japanese term for "sustainable manufacturing") (Fujimoto, 1999). Hitherto, it has been used to evaluate opportunities, effectiveness, and the potential of technology improvement for cost reduction regarding the environment. Japan is now leading its international standardization.

MFCA could be a significant technical tool to realize Goal 12, "Ensure sustainable consumption and production patterns (Responsible consumption and production)". The International Federation of Accounting (IFAC) has identified eight SDGs (out of 17) which accounting and the accounting professional could contribute to (IFAC, 2016) and Goal 12 is one of them. To date, several scholars have argued the significance of creating a balance between the economy and the environment (Burritt & Schaltegger, 2010).

Initially developed in Germany (Wagner, 2015), MFCA has been widely implemented in Japanese manufacturing firms as an environmental management accounting practice that responds to the need of creating the above-mentioned balance in the production processes. It does so by helping harmonize the different and often conflicting values and priorities of the economy and the environment. MFCA enables reducing the waste of material resources and energy by identifying material loss costs separately from product costs. Working with the International Organization for Standardization (ISO) to develop and publish its international standards ISO 14051 and 14052, Japan is now taking the initiative to establish these standards.[1]

---

[1]Professor Kokubu served as a convener for ISO/TC207/WG8.

Although the significance of the role of accounting and accounting professionals for achieving the SDGs is well recognized, how to achieve and continue them remains largely unexplored. The examination of the continuous practices of MFCA would thus provide insight into the ways in which accounting serves to shape the process for delivering sustainable production.

This study thus explores the reasons why MFCA has been introduced and maintained as an accounting practice by Japanese manufacturing companies by using the concept of "practice theory." Practice theory is relevant in the accounting context to "elaborate the ways in which specific organizational members sought to use accounting to achieve, if not grand strategic missions, at least specific subsets of organizational objectives" (Ahrens & Chapman, 2007, p. 4). While MFCA as a practice has significant global impact, the differences in linguistic and socio-cultural contexts make it difficult for the academic knowledge on MFCA to be translated and "travel" beyond national boundaries. With emphasis on field observations and paying attention to the relevant translation processes, practice theory could potentially highlight the ways in which MFCA has been used in the manufacturing processes in Japan. Accounting research incorporating sustainability agendas has mainly developed in terms of reporting standards and practices (e.g., GRI). However, less attention has been paid to its relationship with everyday management accounting practices. By applying practice theory, this study helps translate how the processes of MFCA practice are constructed within the organizational and socio-cultural context of Japan. It specifically sheds light on the significant role of emotion to create balance between the economy and the environment.

This chapter first reviews the literature on MFCA and highlights the gaps in the existing studies in Section 2. Section 3 discusses the relevance of practice theory to address these gaps. This is followed by the case study of Naniwa Company (a fictitious name) in Section 4. Drawing on Shatzki's practice theory (1996), this chapter shows how MFCA has been introduced and practiced in the socio-cultural context of Japan. This chapter concludes by discussing the significance of emotion, which is found to play a significant role in achieving and continuing sustainability goals through accounting practice.

## 2. From Local to Global: Developing the Knowledge and Practice of MFCA

MFCA has been researched and developed through case studies by both the government and industry. Specifically, since its development by the Institut für Management und Umwelt (IMU) at the end of the 1990s, MFCA has proven its efficacy in projects conducted by the German Government or the Bayern state (Kokubu, 2007; Wagner, 2015). It was subsequently introduced in Japan in 2000. Several case studies commissioned by the Ministry of Economy, Trade and Industry (METI) were conducted on this topic. Then, the ISO standardization of MFCA was discussed at Japan's initiative, which materialized with the publication of ISO 14051 in 2011. As of 2009, more than 150 firms were the object of case studies in the form of projects conducted in Japan (Nakajima, 2009); the number of cases is increasing now. Many of the cases are conducted by METI in Japan as projects (Okada & Kokubu, 2018).

One major objective of MFCA is reducing the environmental burden, while at the same time, improving profitability (ISO 14051, 2011; Kokubu & Kitada, 2015). It can be defined as a method of calculating costs according to the actual flow (flow and stock) of materials. As per ISO 14051, under MFCA, "the flows and stocks of materials within an organization are traced and quantified in physical units (e.g., mass, volume) and the costs associated with those material flows are also evaluated" (ISO 14051, 2011, p. 1). Calculating the quantity for each input material and multiplying it by the unit price enhances the transparency of the use of materials and energy. In the manufacturing industry, raw materials constitute a large part of the product, and more precise quantitative techniques are necessary to calculate and classify cost and waste. As such, by applying MFCA, cost is calculated not only for final products, but also for waste. This largely departs from traditional cost accounting. In traditional cost calculation, waste is not calculated separately from the product. By evaluating the cost of waste in the same way as for a product, MFCA enables us "to grasp how much money has been thrown away" (Kokubu, 2010).

In parallel to the government and industry case studies, MFCA has also been pursued academically. Such studies could be categorized into three key areas.

In the early period of its introduction, MFCA's distinctive nature from traditional management accounting and the problems caused by such differences have been discussed (e.g., Nakajima & Kokubu, 2003). This is followed by a second stream of research that is related to an expansion in the use of MFCA and the associated challenges. Numerous studies discuss the potential and effectiveness of MFCA expansion into supply chains (Higashida, 2008; Kokubu, 2011; Nakajima, 2009; Okada & Kokubu, 2018). The expansion of MFCA beyond single companies enables determining losses for supplier or downstream companies as well, thus helping increase resource efficiency throughout the supply chain. Previous studies mostly discuss the role of MFCA in an interfirm context and how to make its expansion successful. Higashida (2008) and Nakajima (2009) point out that MFCA plays the role of an information system that connects the buyer to the supplier. It is thus important for managers to be responsible for the entire process, from product design to operations, since they play the key role of mediators in linking the focal company with other companies (Higashida, 2010). Historically, companies that strongly promoted the diffusion of MFCA throughout the entire supply chain were also successful in decreasing material loss (Nakajima & Kimura, 2012, 2014; Kimura & Nakajima, 2013).

This leads to the third body of studies, which discusses the limitations or challenges of MFCA (Kokubu, 2007; Higashida, 2008; Higashida & Kokubu, 2014). Theoretically, corporate business activities are likely to be governed by the economic behavior principle: there is a trade-off between decreasing input costs and increasing future revenue profitability, and the latter is generally prioritized over the reduction of environmental impacts (Kokubu, 2007). Such conflicts with the economic behavior principle cannot be easily resolved. Although any area for improvement is detected via the use of MFCA, economic interest typically takes over. Higashida and Kokubu (2014) highlight that this tendency becomes more prominent for long-term implementation and continuous application. This highlights that, for the effective operation of MFCA, the "institutional support from outside the company" (Higashida & Kokubu, 2014, p. 98) becomes indispensable to help the "society and markets positively evaluate companies introducing MFCA" (Kokubu, 2007, pp. 55–56). The conflict between economic principles and environmental protection is strongly linked to the main limitation of MFCA, which also represents the issues related to its expansion (Kokubu, 2007; Higashida & Kokubu, 2014). As such, the need to encourage environmental impact reduction from outside the firm becomes essential. In the SDGs context, it is important to support from outside the firm in the same way.

Although studied extensively, the existing research on MFCA was predominantly conducted by Japanese scholars, meaning its findings are less likely to be shared beyond the Japanese context. Such research gap resulted from the differences in research epistemology and methodology compared to international accounting research, and potentially limits the internationalization of accounting knowledge (Humphrey & Gendron, 2015). However, if carefully applied, Western-led theory could help offer innovative ways of translating indigenous phenomena and knowledge (Kamla & Komori, 2018). Practice theory, for example, could help highlight how MFCA has been used and developed in practice, reconfiguring organizational relationships by making losses more visible and transparent (Kitada, 2011). The continuous application of MFCA thus became possible because the organizational mechanism among practicing members and the interactions among them supported MFCA processes. The application of practice theory by Schatzki (1996) is relevant to understanding such intricate mechanisms and help develop knowledge to be shared beyond national boundaries.

## 3. Practice Theory

The practice theory developed by Schatzki (1996, 2002, 2005, 2011) provides an effective angle to understand the dimension of accounting practices that cannot be explained by rational reasoning. Practice is defined as "organized human activities" (Schatzki, 2005) and "any practice is an organized, open-ended spatial-temporal manifold of actions" (Schatzki, 2005, p. 471). Further, practice can be developed as social order (and consequential rule), while the way it is applied takes diverse forms. Schatzki (2011) contends that, at the basis of social order, lie social practices that govern both the importance of involved arranged entities and the actions that shape their arrangements. Arranged entities are called "material arrangements" (Schatzki, 1996), for example, configurations of machines and computers.

On the other hand, practices are constructed by arrays of actions (Schatzki, 2005), being organized by three phenomena: practical understandings of how to do things, rules, and teleo-affective structure (Schatzki, 2005, p. 471). Rules are "explicit formulations that prescribe, require, or instruct that such and such be done, said, or the case" (Schatzki, 2005, p. 241). The teleo-affective structure is constructed by teleological dimensions, representing an array of ends (objectives), projects, uses (of things), and emotional (affective) elements that are acceptable or prescribed for participants in practice.

The unique perspective of Schatzki's practice theory (1996) is that practices show intentionality within the teleo-affective structure. Extending the discussion of Davidson (1963), who highlights the role of desire and belief in shaping one's action, Schatzki (2011) argues that beliefs (understanding and expectation) and emotions are responsible for molding one's actions and behavior. Therefore, one's actions are constructed by his/her emotion (affective structure). However, this emotion is stimulated by practical intelligibility (Schatzki, 2011).

The affective structure (emotion) acts in two ways in shaping practice. First, it helps identify the direction of the meaning involved in practice. Emotions act as "determinants to shaping people's orientation toward ends" (Schatzki, 1996, p. 123), helping people determine their objectives. Second, emotions act directly on one's behavior, instead of following one's rational objectives. According to Schatzki (1996), "mattering can structure activity independently of an actor's ends and thereby overturn the teleological character of action" (Schatzki, 1996, p. 123). Therefore, emotion is observed as part of practice when "[people are] in particular moods and emotions or having particular feelings, affects, and passions" (Schatzki, 1996).

Therefore, the practice theory developed by Schatzki (1996) provides a theoretical account that cannot be fully explained by the teleological argument, through clarifying the aspect of emotion. By highlighting the concept of teleo-affectivity, Schatzki (1996) demonstrates that "the thing to do either derives from the actor's ends and projects, given particular states of affairs and how things matter, or reflects simply how things matter in a given situation" (Schatzki, 1996, pp. 123–124). In short, the application of practice theory on accounting practice clarifies its dimensions beyond the account of rationality and objectivity. Particularly, it helps us understand the mechanisms of practice by identifying the relationship between the chain of action and the goals or feelings caused and shared in practice. The subsequent section seeks to demonstrate how this relationship plays a key role in MFCA practices, having been sustained by observing the case study of a Japanese company, Naniwa.

## 4. Introducing and Sustaining MFCA Applications: Case Study of Naniwa Company

### 4.1 *Research method*

This chapter explores the case of Naniwa, a middle-sized manufacturing electronic equipment company with over 100 employees. Established in the 1970s in Osaka prefecture, the company sells products not only on the domestic market, but also exports them to Europe, North America, and other Asian countries. Naniwa is part of a supply chain for corporations within the factory automation market, in which Mitsubishi Electric and Panasonic act as key players.

Since its introduction in 2000, a collection of MFCA case studies has been published by METI (2009, 2011a, 2011b). We have reviewed these 144 case studies and contacted those companies that demonstrated the intention of adopting MFCA calculation practices and applying it for improving their activities. Naniwa is one of four companies that accepted to participate in our interview. At Naniwa, accounting and finance department played a leading role in the continuous practice of MFCA within the company.

Since the first visit to the company, in June 2016, we have conducted a series of interviews with their financial manager and maintained close contact with him. The financial manager has been with Naniwa since 2004 and has taken a decisive role in introducing MFCA. Drawing on the interviews, as well as official documents or reports used in company meetings, the case study below discusses the process by which MFCA was introduced and continuously practiced at Naniwa.

### 4.2 *Introduction of MFCA*

Naniwa introduced MFCA in the early 2000s, when an independent administrative agency, "Small and Medium Enterprise (SME) Infrastructure

Development Organization", started an MFCA joint research model for SMEs (METI, 2009). Naniwa applied for this outsourcing project due to their pressing need to grasp disposal costs. Their financial performance was declining and they attempted to determine the various costs and grasp what caused these problems. They found specific problems in waste management, in which they had applied a "non-adjusted rate" for the measurement and management of the production process. In this method, the production ratio was managed as the ratio of goods obtained from an input, excluding the number of recycling or return items. Basically, the application of the non-adjusted rate helps understand the percentage of items that went smoothly from the initial to the final processes. This means waste management was done based on the number of items. However, their cost varies depending on the location within the production process, and the prices also differ. Therefore, even if they achieve the same non-adjusted rate, the cost impact is different for the company. As such, for efficiency improvement, it would be more effective to prioritize the process with the highest losses. This was particularly important for Naniwa, which saw the urgency in improving costs by loss reduction. The company had chosen to apply MFCA, as it provides transparency to the loss rate by measuring the inputs and outputs of the process on a quantitative basis and multiplying them by cost.

MFCA was applied for a total of four production stages, including the processing stages of three parts of the electronic product and their assembly process. As a first step, a material flow model was created, illustrating the flow from receipt of materials to shipment. This flow chart shows not only the entire cost of defective items but also the amount of input materials that was not used for a product. This loss rate is important for creating an improvement plan at a later stage. As a result of the MFCA application, a total of 15 causes were identified (METI, 2011b). To improve these causes, each site (*genba*), including the design, purchasing, production technology, and manufacturing sites, needed to cooperate to reduce waste. At the same time, 20 improvement targets were presented, and the departments related to the respective improvement targets were specified (METI, 2011b). This was followed by specific improvement activities. For example, to eliminate material loss generated at the manufacturing stage, the optimum specification width was set by the cooperation between the design and manufacturing departments. Delivery of materials with optimum specification width was realized as a result of discussions with the supplier. Furthermore, by improving the design aspect, it was possible to reduce the number of steps, ultimately reducing edge material.

All these improvements became feasible because of the MFCA calculations, which allowed visualizing the rate of waste in monetary terms, thus enabling the company to evaluate the effects of equipment changes as numerical values (METI, 2009). This increase in visibility also lead to an improvement in their overall activity. Over the subsequent 10-year period, the company would gradually engage in 20 improvement objectives, which included changes in design and production technology (as explained during the interview). The measurement and visualization of the loss rate also continued in parallel. Specifically, the yield rate of each process was multiplied by the material cost and could be measured and tracked. As a result, it became possible to determine the cost of waste, which was not known at the non-adjusted rate. The products targeted in the introduction stage were transferred to overseas plants, where the waste assessment for each product was visualized and managed by MFCA. Therefore, at Naniwa, MFCA had been continuously practiced and successfully maintained throughout its supply chain. This raises the question of what has enabled the company to do so. The mechanism of this case could be explained not only by examining it teleologically, but also by exploring the teleo-affective structure sustaining the practice.

### 4.3 *Recognizing "how much we end up wasting": Teleo-affective structure of Naniwa*

Practice theory provides an effective angle to identifying the reasons why MFCA has continued being used as a method to evaluate rejected goods and waste at the production site of Naniwa. This process could be achieved by understanding the teleo-affective structure for the continuity of MFCA. We first discuss their ultimate goal by considering the semantic chain of introducing MFCA. This is further analyzed by determining the emotional structure behind it.

The financial manager explains the reasons why Naniwa introduced MFCA as follows:

"We were in the process of rebuilding many things from scratch to recover our poor performance. For this, it was important to think about the ways to understand the cost of discarded materials. To date, by using the non-adjusted rate, we managed the quantity of products compared to the number of inputs. In this calculation based on quantity control, the impact of one unit is deemed the same, no matter if the product is hundreds of yen or higher — it is calculated as the same one unit (product). But if expressed in monetary terms, the impact it gives to the company is totally different. The application of non-adjusted rate did not help us feel and think in this way. That is why I started to advocate introducing the different calculation method of grasping the amount of loss and manage the loss rate."

Applying the "signifying chain" (Schatzki, 1996, p. 122), the purpose for Naniwa's MFCA practice discussed above could be explained as follows:

1.  Corporate activities should raise profit.
2.  To gain profit, cost minimization is needed.
3.  For cost reduction, the measurement and management of invisible cost is necessary.
4.  Evaluation based on the number of items fails to recognize all costs; therefore, it needs to be changed.
5.  Losses need to be managed by physical quantity and monetary terms, not number of items.
6.  MFCA is an accounting technique that enables evaluation both quantitatively and in financial terms. Therefore, MFCA is effective for Naniwa.

The ultimate objective of the MFCA practice was "to manage profits." Naniwa introduced MFCA to improve its financial position and manage profits, which required a drastic effort for the improvement of business performance.

The way to maximize profits is either by raising the profit though increasing sales or by reducing cost, or both. For Naniwa, the latter took priority. While the effect of cost reduction could be demonstrated rapidly, MFCA was practiced within the manufacturing department, which shows greater concern over cost management. This leads to their next objective: minimizing expenses. For this, it was important to visualize and evaluate uncalculated cost. Until then, the non-adjustment rate had been their management philosophy, where the calculation was based on number of items instead of monetary terms. However, this calculation method does not demonstrate the cost and financial amount of loss, meaning it does not help with loss management.

Understanding that the non-adjusted rate method cannot fully recognize the cost of the production process, Naniwa was looking for a method that can visualize this cost:

"Basically, our urgent concern is to understand the method of collecting information. Once it is done, we can collect and organize information in the way we aim at."

Therefore, the above analysis on "signifying chains" demonstrates that the introduction of MFCA was the outcome of the need to visualize cost and manage it, which leads to the ultimate objective of increasing earnings. However, the continuous application of MFCA at Naniwa cannot be explained only by cost management, as several cost management methods exist besides MFCA. The question remains as to why MFCA has been continuously applied within the company.

To answer this, one could focus on the examination of changes in MFCA practice. Since its introduction, there have been changes in the way and format MFCA was applied at Naniwa. There are two main objectives of MFCA implementation: evaluate in monetary terms the amount of waste generated by the design and processing processes, and determine cost management in the production process. Although the company stopped updating the former processes since the final implementation in the first half of the 2000s, they continued to manage material loss by using the data gained from these outcomes:

"Above all, we wanted to see the whole picture. Some parts turn out to be products, and some unused materials as waste. Even for the materials that are 100% used, there are end materials. So, I made a flow chart to show the points in which end materials are produced. We followed what is flowing to the disposal waste and tracked data for a long time. By so doing, we can understand the amount of waste in the entire production process including disposal."

The major reasons they continued the MFCA practice lie in the management of material loss they conduct monthly. The data regarding the flows of input materials obtained by MFCA enables Naniwa to make long-term incremental improvements (*kaizen*) in reducing and managing production cost. Thus, once the data on material flow and its monetary evaluation are obtained, the company stops tracking the data:

"We could understand the amount of cost by grasping all the expenses involved and used there, not by simply stacking ordinary material parts. Once we get the outcome after a number of simulations, we terminate this process."

Therefore, the major reason for the sustained MFCA application at Naniwa lies in the waste value evaluation of cost management. The importance of cost minimization has led to their choice of MFCA instead of other methods, such as yield management. However, why they see it as important to evaluate the value of defective products and waste materials remains unanswered. One of the important reasons is related to the importance of visualizing the loss and the shared notion of what is "wasted" at the production site:

"The most important thing for us is to help workers in manufacturing site critically recognize 'how large amount we end up throwing away'. By changing the unit from a number of items to the monetary evaluation, it is expected that our employees have a more critical awareness of the loss we are incurring."

Applying practice theory, Naniwa's sustained MFCA practice could be teleologically explained by its effectiveness in cost evaluation. However, this function could be realized only when the company enthusiastically commits to expressing the cost in monetary terms of input materials, both for the end products and those "wasted". This objective is achieved when the "feeling" associated with loss is understood and shared at the manufacturing site. This is not a teleological structure but an emotional one. By enhancing the shared feeling associated with the monetary amount of how much "we are throwing away", MFCA helps the company achieve its purpose of enhancing profits, but also "determine doing by shaping people's orientation toward ends" (Schatzki, 1996, p. 123). In other words, Naniwa's sustained MFCA practice is explained not only by the teleological dimension in terms of rationality, but also underpinned by the affective (emotional) dimension, which creates a shared awareness within the organization with the scope to reduce waste.

## 5. Emotion Matters for Strategizing Sustainability: Discussion and Conclusions

People, things, and technologies are connected through the repetitive activities of accounting practices. Therefore, context matters in the way accounting practices are embedded and operate (Burchell, Clubb & Hopwood, 1985). While helping create a globally impactful local practice, the distinctive Japanese context creates limitations for the existing MFCA academic knowledge to "travel" beyond local contexts and be shared in the international accounting academic arena (Komori, 2015). However, it must be emphasized that the exploration of MFCA provides important insights into understanding how accounting played a role in the ways in which the sustainability and environmental agendas are dealt with. By applying practice theory, this chapter illustrates the ways in which MFCA has been continuously practiced in the organizational context of a Japanese manufacturing company. This would help broaden our understanding of the ways of achieving the SDGs, which tend to currently be argued from a Eurocentric perspective.

This study highlights that Naniwa's continuous MFCA practices cannot be explained only from the teleological perspective of achieving the economy-driven objective of enhancing profit. MFCA has played an important role in managing their material loss within the production process. It does so by awakening workers' feeling of "throwing away a lot of things" through the quantitative visualization of waste. The capacity of accounting to visualize (wasted) values numerically has helped shape emotions to "determine doing by shaping people's orientation toward ends" (Schatzki, 1996, p. 123). By working on the emotional dimension, accounting helps create balance between the economy and the environment within the production processes itself, thereby helping shape sustainable production.

The significance of emotion in everyday accounting practice provides important implications for "strategizing" (Jørgensen & Messner, 2010; Sawabe, Yoshikawa & Shinohara, 2010) the SDG agenda. In response to the ecological responsibility and shaping accountability processes of endangered species, for example, attention could be paid on how numerical visibility can trigger human beings' empathy and compassion to non-human species at the risk of extinction (Atkins *et al.*, 2018). Such emotional emphasis could even help create a more salient non-Western epistemology that underpins the human–nature relationship that has yet to be fully discussed in the Western accounting literature (Birkin & Polesie, 2011), which would bring balanced socio-cultural epistemic values (Hines, 1992). These values are the products of non-Western socio-cultural contexts. Asian accounting scholars have both the opportunities and important roles of introducing such dimensions, which are still waiting to be discovered and rediscovered.

## Acknowledgments

This chapter forms the basis of the SUMS–Kobe Research Partnership and was discussed at the SUMS–Kobe International Partnership Seminar, "Integrating Sustainability with Management Practice: A Role of Material Flow Cost Accounting", delivered by Professor Katsuhiko Kokubu at the Sheffield University Management School (June 2018). This research was supported by the Environment Research and Technology Development Fund (S-16) of the Environmental Restoration and Conservation Agency Japan and JSPS KAKENHI Grant numbers JP18K18577 and JP17H07206.

## References

Ahrens, T. and Chapman, C. (2007). Management accounting as practice. *Accounting, Organizations and Society 32*(1–2), 1–27.

Atkins, J. F., Maroun, W., Atkins, B. and Barone, E. (2018). From the Big Five to the Big Four? Exploring extinction accounting for the rhinoceros. *Accounting, Auditing and Accountability Journal 31*(2), 674–702.

Bebbington, J. and Unerman, J. (2018). Achieving the United Nations Sustainable Development Goals: An enabling role for accounting research. *Accounting, Auditing and Accountability Journal 31*(1), 2–24.

Belal, A., Spence, C., Carter, C. and Zhu, J. (2017). The Big 4 in Bangladesh: Caught between the global and the local. *Accounting, Auditing and Accountability Journal 29*(8), 145–163.

Birkin, F. and Polesie, T. (2011). An epistemic analysis of (un)sustainable business. *Journal of Business Ethics 103*(2), 239–253.

Burchell, S., Clubb, C. and Hopwood, A. G. (1985). Accounting in its social context: Towards a history of value added in the United Kingdom. *Accounting, Organizations and Society 10*(4), 381–413.

Burritt, R. and Schaltegger, S. (2010). Sustainability accounting and reporting: Fad or trend? *Accounting, Auditing and Accountability Journal 23*(7), 829–846.

Davidson, D. (1963). Actions, reasons and causes. *Journal of Philosophy 60*(23), 685–700.

Fujimoto, T. (1999). *The Evolution of Manufacturing System at Toyota.* Oxford: Oxford University Press.

Higashida, A. (2008). Material Flow Cost Accounting Expansion beyond supply chain. *Accounting 60*(1), 122–129 (in Japanese).

Higashida, A. (2010). Environmental management accounting supports green-supply-chain-management. In *Studies of Environmental Management Decision Making and Accounting System.* Japan Accounting Association special association, pp. 135–215 (in Japanese).

Higashida, A. and Kokubu, K. (2014). The relationship between the environment and the economy in corporate management. Special Issue Social and Environmental Accounting. *The Kokumin-keizai zasshi 210*(1), 87–100 (in Japanese).

Hines, R. (1992). Accounting: Filling the negative space. *Accounting, Organizations and Society 17*(3–4), 313–341.

Humphrey, C. and Gendron, Y. (2015). What is going on? The sustainability of accounting academia. *Critical Perspectives on Accounting 26*, 47–66.

International Federation of Accountants (2016). *The 2030 Agenda for Sustainable Development: A Snapshot of the Accountancy Profession's Contribution.* New York, NY: International Federation of Accountants.

ISO 14051 (2011). *Environmental management — Material flow cost accounting — General framework.* ISO.

Jørgensen, B. and Messner, M. (2010). Accounting and strategizing: A case study from new product development. *Accounting, Organizations and Society 35*, 184–204.

Kimura, A. and Nakajima, M. (2013). Subjects to establish low-carbon supply Chain with MFCA: Findings from material efficiency questionnaire research in Japan. *Research in Corporate Social Accounting and Reporting* (25), 13–28 (in Japanese).

Kitada, H. (2011). Expansion of management practice by material flow cost accounting. *The Journal of Cost Accounting Research 35*(2), 12–25 (in Japanese).

Kamla, R. and Komori, N. (2018). Diagnosing translation gap: The politics of translation and the hidden contradiction in interdisciplinary accounting research. *Accounting, Auditing and Accountability Journal*, 31(7), 1874–1903.

Komori, N. (2015). Beneath the globalization paradox: Towards the sustainability of cultural diversity in accounting research. *Critical Perspectives on Accounting 26*, 141–156.

Kokubu, K. (2007). The significance and future prospect of material flow cost accounting. *Accounting 59*(11), 18–23 (in Japanese).

Kokubu, K. (2010). The essence of MFCA: From the viewpoint of material flow and money flow. *Management Systems: A Journal of Japan Industrial Management Association 20*(1), 3–7 (in Japanese).

Kokubu, K. (2011). Production and environmental management by material flow cost accounting. *Journal of Information and Management 31*(2), 4–10 (in Japanese).

Kokubu, K. and Kitada, K. (2015). Material flow cost accounting and existing management perspectives. *Journal of Cleaner Production 108*, 1279–1288.

METI (2009). *Material Flow Cost Accounting (MFCA) Case Study Collection Version 2*. METI (in Japanese).

METI (2011a). *Case Collection of Promotion Collaboration of Supply Chain Resource Conservation Project*. METI (in Japanese).

METI (2011b). *Material Flow Cost Accounting MFCA Case Study 2011*. METI (in Japanese).

Nakajima, M. (2009). Practical material flow cost accounting (43) Significance of supply chain management by material flow cost accounting: possibilities of an environment-conscious 'Keiretsu'. *Environmental Management 45*(4), 348–353 (in Japanese).

Nakajima, M. and Kokubu, K. (2003). Usefulness of material flow cost accounting in management accounting. *The Journal of Cost Accounting Research* *27*(2), 12–20 (in Japanese).

Nakajima, M. and Kimura, A. (2012). Promotion of innovative improvement integrated MFCA with budgeting. *The Journal of Cost Accounting Research* *36*(2), 15–24 (in Japanese).

Nakajima, M. and Kimura, A. (2014). Challenges to implement material flow cost accounting (MFCA) in supply chain management: Case study on a buyer–supplier workshop. *The Journal of Cost Accounting Research 38*(1), 59–69 (in Japanese).

Okada, K. and Kokubu, K. (2018). Introduction of MFCA in supply chain. In Nakajima, M. and Kokubu, K. (eds.) *Material Flow Cost Accounting Theory and Practice*. Dobunkan-Shuppan, pp. 78–93 (in Japanese).

Sawabe, N., Yoshikawa, K. and Shinohara, K. (2010). Accounting and Emotion: A Case Study of a Financial Institution. Kyoto University Graduate School of Economics Research Project Center Discussion Paper. Kyoto University (in Japanese).

Schatzki, T. (1996). *Social Practices: A Wittgensteinian Approach to Human Activity and the Social*. Cambridge University Press.

Schatzki, T. (2002). *The Site of the Social: A Philosophical Account of the Constitution of Social Life and Change*. Pennsylvania State University Press.

Schatzki, T. (2005). The site of organizations. *Organization Studies 26*(3), 465–484.

Schatzki, T. (2011). *The Timespace of Human Activity: On Performance, Society, and History as Indeterminate Teleological Events*. Toposphia: Sustainability, Dwelling, Design. Lexington Books.

Wagner, B. (2015). A report on the origins of Material Flow Cost Accounting (MFCA) research activities. *Journal of Cleaner Production 108*, Part B, 1255–1261.

Weber, H. (2017). Politics of 'leaving no one behind': Contesting the 2030 Sustainable Development Goals agenda. *Globalizations 14*(3), 337–342.

## Chapter 8

# Material Flow Time Costing: New Management Accounting Concept Consistent with Toyota Production System and Material Flow Cost Accounting

Noriyuki Imai

*Graduate School of Business, Meijo University, Nagoya*
*Aichi Prefecture, Japan*

## 1. Introduction

In recent years, with the rise in environmental awareness in corporate management, the practice of environmental management accounting is on the rise. In particular, material flow cost accounting (MFCA) for corporate production and logistics processes is developing in both theory and practice. On the other hand, the environmental contribution of the Toyota Production System (TPS), which is an efficient production system developed in Japan, has been pointed out in the past. In this chapter, we discuss the relationship between TPS and MFCA, the concept of material flow time costing (MFTC) as a new management accounting concept consistent with TPS and MFCA, and action research on MFTC.

## 2. Generation and Development of MFCA

Since the latter half of the 20th century, many companies have aggressively promoted environmental conservation activities. Further,

environmental accounting as external reporting accounting and environmental management accounting as internal reporting accounting have
been introduced by the management of companies. Environmental management accounting sprouted from pioneering research in the United
States and Germany in the 1990s. In Japan, the Ministry of Economy,
Trade and Industry (2002) organized the environmental management
accounting system as follows: (1) environmentally conscious target
costing, (2) life cycle costing, (3) environment-friendly capital investment
decisions, (4) MFCA, (5) environmental cost matrix, and (6) environment-conscious performance evaluation.

MFCA is an environmental management accounting method that
induces improvements at the company's site by the accounting visualization of waste material loss, and simultaneously reduces environmental
burden and manufacturing cost. According to Nakajima and Kokubu
(2008), MFCA tracks the flow of materials in corporate production and
logistics processes from input to output and measures the materials on a
physical quantity basis and on a monetary basis. In addition, MFCA calculates the exact cost of both good products (positive products) and material loss (negative products) output from a process. There are three
subjects of cost calculation: (1) material cost (raw material cost, energy
cost), (2) system cost (processing costs such as labor cost, depreciation
cost), and (3) cost of material loss processing.

MFCA is distinguished from traditional cost accounting by identifying
material losses that have been neglected in the latter as independent environmental costs. Traditional cost accounting that focuses on earning profit
in the market is a collection value calculation of manufacturing costs of
good products and has been elaborated from the viewpoint of how to pass
costs to good products. On the other hand, MFCA accurately calculates the
value of both a positive product, referred to as good product, and a negative
product, referred to as material loss, by grasping the material loss as a negative product. Therefore, under MFCA, incentives for improvement will
occur at the company site, because calculating the cost of a negative product has a potential economic effect of reducing the material loss.

Based on these characteristics, MFCA has been increasingly attracting
international attention and is being practiced by many Japanese companies that have achieved results.

## 3. Environmental Contribution of TPS

TPS is an efficient production system developed in Japan. According to Ohno (1978), the founder of TPS, the basic idea of TPS is a thorough elimination of waste, and the two pillars of the TPS production technique are (1) Just-in-Time (JIT) and (2) Jidoka. JIT refers to producing the necessary amount when necessary. Jidoka means that if there is an abnormality or malfunction in a machine or manual work, we stop the production line immediately and investigate the cause and prevent its reoccurrence to prevent the mass production of defective products in the production line.

The major key performance indicators (KPIs) of the production and logistics processes operated by TPS are (1) lead time, (2) on-time delivery rate, and (3) inventory (retention) (Imai, 2004). In other words, TPS is a production technique aimed at the ultimate improvement of the three major KPIs: (1) lead time, (2) on-time delivery rate, and (3) inventory (retention), thus pursuing the two pillars of TPS: (1) JIT and (2) Jidoka.

The environmental contribution of TPS has been pointed out in the past. For example, Johnson and Bröms (2000) pointed out the following five points in the essence of TPS's environmental contribution: (1) The long-term success of Toyota can be explained by the fact that people are not motivated to achieve quantitative goals, and that balanced, cyclical, and unbroken flow patterns are formed in all the work carried out in the organization. (2) The TPS scheme has allowed Toyota to produce far more with less resources compared with other carmakers for decades. (3) The discipline attribute of the TPS scheme produces higher performance than repeatedly encouraging employees toward the financial goal of final profit. (4) The biggest reason for the success of the Toyota system is that each worker has an ideal limit of using only the minimum resources necessary to finish an order at a time. (5) Another reason for the success of Toyota's system is the spirit of employees taking improvement activities seriously and pursuing them on a sustainable basis.

Points (2) and (4) mentioned by Johnson and Bröms (2000) provide a useful suggestion. In other words, TPS is one of the environmental systems oriented toward the creation of maximum value with minimum resources, by eliminating waste thoroughly and reducing resource loss, as suggested by Ohno (1978). Therefore, the pursuit of the two pillars of TPS — JIT and Jidoka — aiming at ultimately improving the three main

KPIs — lead time, on-time delivery rate, and inventory (retention) — can lead to corporate environmental conservation activities of improving resource productivity (reducing environmental burden). In other words, it can be said that TPS is a production technique that has a latent function of integrating the economic activities and environmental conservation activities of an enterprise.

## 4. Relationship between TPS and MFCA

As mentioned earlier, MFCA is a form of environmental management accounting for the company's production and logistics processes, and TPS is an efficient production method that contributes to the environment. Further, considering the relationship between TPS and MFCA, one of the important views is that TPS's Jidoka contributes to the reduction of material loss by eliminating abnormalities and malfunctions in the production line and preventing mass production of defective products; that is, through TPS's Jidoka, it is possible to reduce material loss due to damage, failure, human error, etc. by investigating the cause and preventing the recurrence of the abnormality and malfunction. Thus, it contributes to the reduction of the difference between the standard value (normal reference value) and the actual value for production control and quality control, that is, the improvement of yield.

On the other hand, in MFCA, the physical quantity and monetary value of material loss are always measured and visualized regardless of the classification of normal and abnormal loss. In other words, MFCA visualizes and improves the overall picture of material loss including material loss hidden in regular work (normal state) (for example, material yield permitted as an error width at the time of designing, consumption necessary for inspections in operation procedures, and quality control), in addition to the reduction in material loss by TPS's Jidoka.

Therefore, from the viewpoint of reducing material loss, it can be said that the improvement achieved by implementing MFCA subsumes the improvement achieved by implementing TPS's Jidoka. In this regard, there is a certain affinity between TPS and MFCA.

However, MFCA does not have a time axis (lead time) in its calculation structure. Therefore, MFCA cannot directly contribute to lead time reduction using TPS's JIT.

In other words, MFCA takes a target production/logistics process as one flow and tracks and measures the material from the input (start point) to the output (end point) of the flow. MFCA then calculates the cost of good products (positive products) and material loss (negative products) and aims to reduce material losses throughout the flow. However, in MFCA, the amount of lead time required for a material to move in the flow is excluded from the cost calculation. Originally, the flow through which objects, such as materials, flow is composed of three dimensions: (1) unit price, (2) physical quantity, and (3) lead time. However, because the computational structure of MFCA is based on the two dimensions of (1) unit price and (2) physical quantity, it can be said that MFCA cannot subsume improvement by JIT in the (3) lead time dimension. In this respect, there are certain limitations of MFCA in relation to TPS.

In the following discussion, to overcome the above limitations, we will introduce MFTC as a new management accounting concept to incorporate the time axis (lead time) into MFCA and contribute to lead time reduction through TPS's JIT.

## 5. Concept of MFTC

Previous studies of management accounting consistent with TPS were carried out in the United States where attention given to TPS increased as a result of the reversal of the competitiveness of the Japanese and American manufacturing industries, including the automobile industry in the 1980s, and then spread to Japan.

O'Brien and Sivaramakrishnan (1994) devised the Cycle Time System concept to incorporate TPS's perspective into cost difference analysis of standard costing. Maskell and Baggaley (2004) and Stenzel (2007) grasped the production process operated by TPS as a value stream and advocated lean accounting to measure performance using direct costing while promoting improvements to eliminate waste and create customer value.

In Japan, Tanaka (2004) proposed the concept of J-Cost, which refers to the multiplier of the amount of money and the lead time of materials input to the production and logistics process, and proposed to use it for profitability evaluation based on TPS. Kawada (2008) proposed the concept of Profit Potential, which refers to the ratio of profit and opening stock as a comprehensive profitability management index consistent with TPS.

These previous studies are conscious of the consistency with the two pillars of TPS's production technique, especially JIT. However, these concepts of management accounting cannot directly measure the lead time reduction effect achieved through TPS's JIT. Among them, the concept of J-Cost by Tanaka (2004) encompasses lead time itself, which is one of the main KPIs of TPS. However, J-Cost in itself is not an accounting concept, as evidenced by the measurement unit of J-Cost being the multiplier of the amount of money and time.

Therefore, in this chapter, by using the concept of weighted average cost of capital (WACC) from the finance theory, J-Cost is converted to an accounting concept by incorporating it into the MFCA framework. In other words, the material input to the production/logistics process is regarded as one of the elements of capital, and the cost of the lead time required for the material as the capital to move through the flow is measured by WACC (pre-tax basis). This measured cost is the MFTC. In addition to (1) material cost, (2) system cost, and (3) material loss processing cost, the MFTC is included in the framework of MFCA as the fourth cost of MFCA. As a result, the time axis (lead time) is incorporated in MFCA, and MFCA can contribute to lead time reduction through TPS's JIT.

Here, the MFTC is measured according to the following equations:

Material Flow Time Cost
  = (material cost + system cost + material loss processing cost)
    × lead time × WACC (pre-tax basis)

WACC (pre-tax basis)
  = [debt cost × total debt/(total debt + total market capitalization)]
    + [shareholders' equity cost/(1–tax rate) × total market capitalization/
    (total debt + total market capitalization)]

Here, the example of calculation of MFTC is presented in Fig. 1 and Table 1.

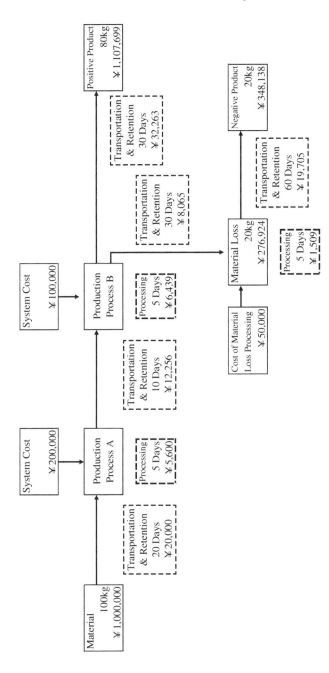

**Fig 1.** MFTC calculation example 1.

**Table 1.** MFTC calculation example 2.

|  | Material cost | System cost | Cost of material loss processing | Material flow time cost | Total |
|---|---|---|---|---|---|
| Good Product (Positive Product) | ¥800,000 | ¥240,000 | — | ¥67,699 | ¥1,107,699 |
| Material Loss (Negative Product) | ¥200,000 | ¥60,000 | ¥50,000 | ¥38,138 | ¥348,138 |
| Total | ¥1,000,000 | ¥300,000 | ¥50,000 | ¥105,837 | ¥1,455,837 |

In this example, we assume a simple flow in which 100 kg of one kind of material is the input, and 80 kg of positive product and 20 kg of negative product are the output after going through two production processes, A and B.

The three costs that conventional MFCA calculates are (1) material cost = ¥1,000,000, (2) system cost = ¥300,000 (¥200,000 + ¥100,000), and (3) material loss processing cost = ¥50,000. The sum of these three costs is ¥1,350,000. Among them, (1) material cost and (2) system cost are distributed to good products (positive products) and material loss (negative products) at a physical quantity ratio of 80:20. In addition, (3) material loss processing cost is included in material loss (negative product). As a result, the cost of good products (positive products) is ¥1,040,000, and the cost of material loss (negative product) is ¥310,000.

However, in reality, to move through the flow while capturing the system cost and the material loss processing cost, the input material requires lead time such as transportation time between processes, retention time, and material loss processing time. As a result, the MFTC is generated as an opportunity cost equivalent to the lead time for the material to flow; however, as mentioned above, the conventional MFCA cannot reflect this.

In this example, assuming WACC (pre-tax basis) at an annual interest rate of 36.5%, the total of MFTC is measured as ¥105,837. As a result, the cost of good products (positive products) is ¥1,107,699, and the cost of material loss (negative products) is ¥348,138.

## 6. Significance of MFTC

The significance of MFTC from the management accounting perspective is stated below.

The first point is the contribution of MFTC to corporate value creation. In other words, MFTC triggers lead time reduction through TPS's JIT in corporate production/logistics processes, contributing to the creation of corporate value by reducing opportunity cost. In recent years, the finance theory, especially the concepts of Economic Value Added (EVA) and WACC have greatly contributed to the creation of corporate value in both theory and practice. However, both the concepts were somewhat general, their unit of time was undifferentiated, and they had the disadvantage of not being directly applicable to the corporate value creation activity at the company site. In this chapter, we considered MFTC for focusing on measuring and visualizing the cost (opportunity cost) of the lead time of material by segmenting the time unit of WACC to the inside of the flow of production/logistics process. In that sense, it can be said that MFTC is a concept of management accounting having a latent function of integrating corporate sites and capital markets/stakeholders by inducing corporate value creation activities at the company site.

The second point is the enhancement of MFCA as an environmental management accounting method. As mentioned above, both TPS and MFCA are targeted at improving corporate production and logistics processes. TPS and MFCA retain mutual affinity by the fact that improvement by MFCA subsumes improvement owing to TPS's Jidoka from the viewpoint of reducing material loss. However, MFCA has certain limitations in that it cannot directly contribute to lead time reduction through TPS's JIT because the concept of management accounting that can directly measure the lead time reduction effect through TPS's JIT does not exist as a link between TPS and MFCA. A new management accounting concept that overcomes the limitations of MFCA and can promote the integrated evolution of TPS and MFCA is MFTC, which has been envisioned in this chapter. MFCA further refines the calculation of material loss and will be a management framework that encompasses improvement by both JIT and Jidoka of TPS by positioning the MFTC as one of the objects of cost calculation. As a result, MFCA can improve functionality as an environmental management accounting method.

## 7. Action Research of MFTC

In this chapter, we considered the relationship between TPS and MFCA so far and conceived MFTC as a new management accounting concept consistent with TPS and MFCA. Section 7.1 discusses MFTC's action research.

In promoting the action research in this chapter, we developed the MFTC model as a mesoscopic model (and a simulation module implementing it) applicable for practical use. The MFTC model is based on GD.findi, which is a production system simulator of LEXER RESEARCH Inc. in Japan. Further, the MFTC model incorporates the costing model of Nagasaka (2015), a simplified calculation function of MFCA, and the calculation function of MFTC. Also, GD.findi is a production system simulator that can optimize a large number of variables constituting the production system at the production preparation stage before entering the mass production stage. Here, the variables are the production process layout, the order of execution of the production work, the performance/capability of the production facility, the inventory storage space, the route and method of conveying products/work in progress/parts, the worker organization, and the like. In addition, GD.findi can do simulation work flexibly and quickly while visually checking in the virtual three-dimensional space without incurring a heavy load by performing conventional programming. By using GD.findi as the basis, the MFTC model is a mesoscopic model and can simultaneously be a simulation module applicable immediately to the production line site. The MFTC model calculates the manufacturing cost and creates the production cost table in a form linked with the production system simulation by GD.findi, given the conditions such as production planning, parts procurement, productivity, and defect rate. At the same time, the MFTC model can feedforward control the occupancy rate and operating time ratio of the production equipment, the time course of the inventory volume between processes, the occurrence of material loss, production lead time, and the MFTC.

Utilizing the above MFTC model, we conducted action research on three major Japanese manufacturing companies.

## 7.1 *Action research — Case of company Y*

Company Y is a leading automobile manufacturer representing Japan. For company Y, we adopted the approach to verify the effectiveness of the MFTC model later by applying the MFTC model to previous improvement cases at the time of production reduction in the final assembly line of the mass production factory in Japan. The vehicle type W produced in the assembly line is one of the finest car models (sedans) among the product line of company Y. At the time of structural changes of the Japanese automobile market after the collapse of the bubble in the 1990s, the production volume of vehicle type W decreased by half from its peak in the 1980s, and accordingly, the tact time and lead time in the assembly line doubled. In response to such a situation, as shown in Fig. 2, the improvement in production work by the operator's multiprocess handling and the improvement in the production process by shortening the line length (layout change) were achieved in the assembly line. As a result, significant improvements were realized, such as the reduction in both the number of workers and the lead time by half the original numbers. Based on a certain assumption, the effect of this improvement was measured by the MFTC model, and it was confirmed that the MFTC reduction effect was 25 yen per product and 2,250,000 yen per year.

The main evaluations of the action research at company Y by the person in charge of the production engineering department of company Y were the following two items: (1) The MFTC model has high consistency with company Y's production and logistics operation strategy, such that the MFTC directly links to the lead time, which is one of the major KPIs of TPS. (2) From the experience of company Y's long-term cost improvement activities, the improvement effect per product is significant, and the MFTC as a concept of management accounting has certain effectiveness.

## 7.2 *Action research — Case of company D*

Company D is a leading industrial machine manufacturer representing Japan. For company D, we adopted an approach that considers the contribution of the MFTC model in the framework of company-wide cost-reduction activities carried out by the head office's accounting department. From the demonstration of the MFTC model conducted for the

< Before Improvement >

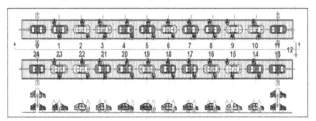

- Production volume: 7,500 units per month (at the peak of 15,000 units per month)
- Tact time: 180 seconds (at the peak of 90 seconds)
- Worker: 40 people
- Lead time: 180 seconds × 24 = 4,320 seconds

< After Improvement >

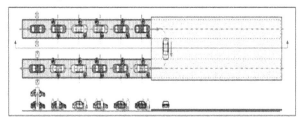

- Production volume: 7,500 units per month
- Tact time: 180 seconds
- Worker: 20 people
- Lead time: 180 seconds × 12 = 2,160 seconds

**Fig. 2.**   Improvement case in company Y.

department manager at the site of the production line and implementation of the study at the head office's accounting department based on the demonstration, the following two items were shown as main evaluations: (1) By utilizing the MFTC model in the framework of company-wide cost-reduction activities, it is possible to expect to find new cost-reduction measures including the reduction of material loss. (2) By evaluating the lead time-reduction effect through the MFTC model by the amount of money, it becomes possible to evaluate the efforts for improving the production lead time reduction within the framework of company-wide cost-reduction activities, and it is expected that the incentive for improving on-site production lead time reduction will increase.

## 7.3 *Action research — Case of company S*

Company S is a leading automotive parts manufacturer in Japan. For company S, we adopted the approach to actually apply the MFTC model to the current production line of a mass production factory in Japan and verify its effectiveness. The production line to which the MFTC model was applied comprises a continuous process of forging the main parts of Company S (fuel system precision part of automobile engine) using manufacturing machines. This process involves disposal of the end material resulting from cutting (occurrence of material loss), occurrence of stagnation such as waiting for transportation due to the inclusion of an outsourced process and waiting for processing due to the inclusion of a heat treatment step, periodic cutting tool change of manufacturing machines, and quality inspection by extracting by workers. Applying the MFTC model to the relevant production line revealed that an MFTC of 1.6 yen per product was incurred mainly due to the occurrence of stagnation under certain premises. As a result, the necessity of countermeasures against stagnation such as the optimization of the delivery cycle to the subcontractor in the outsourced process (small lot of carry-out) was clarified as a study subject. In addition, the optimization of the cutting tool change cycle of manufacturing machines and accurate visualization of material loss including MFTC were also clarified as a continuing study topic.

The main evaluations of the action research at company S by the person in charge of the production engineering department of the company were the following two items: (1) The MFTC model has high consistency with the company's production and logistics operation strategy, such that the MFTC directly links to the lead time, which is one of the major KPIs of TPS. (2) To evaluate the reduction of MFTC at the site of the production line within the framework of the cost-reduction activity of the head office's accounting department, it is necessary to reach a certain in-house consensus on the fact that MFTC is an opportunity cost.

## 8.  Conclusion

In this chapter, we take up the recent increase in adoption of environmental management accounting, especially the generation and development of MFCA, and consider the relationship between TPS with environmental contribution and MFCA. In addition, MFTC is conceived as a new management accounting concept consistent with TPS and MFCA, and its action research is conducted. The results indicate that the MFTC as a concept of management accounting has a certain level of effectiveness.

The following three points are mentioned as future research areas in the field of MFTC conceived by this chapter.

The first point is the establishment of a more reliable and systematic measurement, recording, collection, and aggregation method of material lead time information. As pointed out by Nakajima and Kokubu (2008), the physical quantity information and cost information necessary for MFCA are scattered at the site of the production and logistics process, but generally, they are not systematically managed. The same case of scattered information is seen for lead time. In this chapter, we developed the MFTC model based on the production system simulator to solve the problem of scattered information in a certain way; however, deepening the practical method on this point remains a future research subject.

The second point is the study of the extensibility of the target cost range of the MFTC. In this chapter, the cost of the lead time required for a material to move through the flow is measured by WACC (pre-tax basis) as the opportunity cost equivalent to the lead time. However, there are various lead time costs such as transportation costs during the transportation time between processes, depreciation expenses of storage facilities, labor costs of storage workers, and rents for storage places when the inventory is stored. The possibility of inclusion of these costs in the MFTC may be a future research subject.

The third point is the realization of enhancement of MFCA as an environmental management accounting method using MFTC. Although the measurement of MFTC has been realized in this action research (in the case of company S), a breakthrough improvement of the functionality as an environmental management accounting method, such as elaboration of the material loss calculation as MFCA, is not realized. This point is also a future research subject.

In the global economy of the 21st century, sustainability from the perspective of balancing the environment and the economy will be strongly demanded, along with the growth and development of emerging countries, mainly in Asia. At the same time, the importance of TPS with environmental contribution, MFCA as an environmental management accounting method, and MFTC conceived by this chapter is expected to increase in the future.

## References

Imai, N. (2004). Process-KPI Management System: Towards challenging and evolving organizations, *The Meijo Review 5*(1), 53–63 (in Japanese).

Johnson, H. T. and Bröms, A. (2000). *Profit Beyond Measure: Extraordinary Results through Attention to Work and People*. New York, NY: Free Press.

Kawada, M. (2008). Accounting link approach for TPS introduction. *Accounting 60*(9), 27–36 (in Japanese).

Ministry of Economy, Trade and Industry (2002). *Environmental Management Accounting Method Workbook*. Tokyo: Ministry of Economy, Trade and Industry (in Japanese).

Maskell, B. H. and Baggaley, B. (2004). *Practical Lean Accounting: A Proven System for Measuring and Managing the Lean Enterprise*. New York, NY: Productivity Press.

Nagasaka, Y. (2015). A Study on Mesoscopic Model for Management Control. Industry–Academia Joint Research Group Report in the Japanese Association of Management Accounting, 2013–2014, pp. 2–14 (in Japanese).

Nakajima, M. and Kokubu, K. (2008). *Material Flow Cost Accounting: An Innovative Approach of Environmental Management Accounting*. Tokyo: Nihon Keizai Shinbun Shuppansha (in Japanese).

O'Brien, J. and Sivaramakrishnan, K. (1994). Accounting for JIT: A cycle time-based approach. *Journal of Cost Management,* November/December, 63–70.

Ohno, T. (1978). *Toyota Production System: Beyond Large-Scale Production*. Tokyo: Diamond Inc. (in Japanese).

Stenzel, J. (eds). (2007). *Lean Accounting: Best Practices for Sustainable Integration*. Hoboken, NJ: John Wiley & Sons.

Tanaka, M. (2004). A study on profitability evaluation method with time axis: J-Cost theory, *IE Review 234*, 85–92 (in Japanese).

# Part 3

# Sustainability Management in Asia

Chapter 9

# Comprehensive Environmental Management Control System and Stakeholder Influences: Evidence from Thailand

Katsuhiko Kokubu*, Qi Wu†, Kimitaka Nishitani‡, Jittima Tongurai* and Pakpong Pochanart§

*Graduate School of Business Administration,
Kobe University, Kobe, Japan
†Faculty of Economics and Business Administration,
Kyoto University of Advanced Science, Kyoto, Japan
‡Research Institute for Economics and Business Administration,
Kobe University, Kobe, Japan
§National Institute of Development Administration, Bangkok, Thailand

## 1. Introduction

To implement practices of sustainable management on a global scale, corporate environmental conservation is essential, not only in developed countries, but also in developing countries. As many manufacturing companies in developed countries conduct their operations in developing countries, corporate environmental management in developing countries has become a critical issue. However, research on effective environmental management strategies for developing countries has hitherto been inadequate.

Much of the past research on environmental management for developing countries has centered on the effectiveness of environmental

131

management systems (EMSs), such as ISO 14001. For example, Ann, Zailani and Abd Wahid (2006), Nguyen and Hens (2015), and Singh, Brueckner and Padhy (2015) have investigated the effectiveness of the ISO 14001 certification in Malaysia, Vietnam, and India, respectively. However, since the ISO 14001 certification aims at mitigating specific environmental influences mainly originating from factories, it is not designed to foster comprehensive environmental management control on a company-wide scale. The current research on environmental management in developed countries predominantly focuses on the effectiveness not of ISO 14001, but on comprehensive environmental management control systems (EMCSs) (Guenther, Endrikat & Guenther, 2016).

In light of these developments, the primary objective of this study is to determine, via a questionnaire-based survey, whether comprehensive EMCS exists in Thailand, a developing country in Asia that is currently in the midst of brisk industrialization. Assuming that its existence can be confirmed, this study's second objective is to analyze stakeholder influence on it, and its third objective is to validate the efficacy of a comprehensive EMCS in bolstering environmental performance.

Although there are various definitions of management control systems, this study adopts the framework of Merchant and Van der Stede (2012), comprising four control categories: results controls, actions controls, personnel controls, and cultural controls. When these controls are utilized for environmental management, this system is referred to as a "comprehensive EMCS", to differentiate it from the EMS represented by ISO 14001.

After describing the background of environmental management in Thailand, we analyze the results of our survey.

## 2. Environmental Management in Thailand: A Background

The deterioration of environment and depletion of natural resources have increased social pressure on companies in Thailand and other ASEAN countries to address environmental issues. We have witnessed an increasing number of companies in Thailand, which have adopted and practiced environmental management. On the one hand, the practices of corporate environmental management in Thailand are carried out in compliance with the laws and regulations (for example, The Environment Act of 1992, The Environmental Protection Law of 1992, and regulations imposed by the Ministries of Industry, Natural Resources and Environment, and Science and Technology). On the other hand, some companies have voluntarily set up an EMS to increase operational efficiency and to gain stronger competitive positions in the marketplace. Since the adoption of corporate environmental management depends significantly on firm capability, know-how, and resources, multinational and large companies are the first group to implement it. The concept of corporate environmental management has been increasingly adopted and practiced countrywide, but is still limited to large firms.

Companies in Thailand, especially leading firms listed in the Stock Exchange of Thailand (SET), have implemented the global practice of environmental management such as environmental standard ISO 14001 (Techamontrikul, 1997). Some companies have integrated the concept of sustainability and environmental management, such as more efficient energy consumption, waste reduction, zero waste, eco-production, and green supply chain into their corporate strategies (Seetharaman, Ismail & Saravanan, 2007). A number of Thai companies focus on reducing energy consumption and greenhouse gas emission (Petcharat & Mula, 2013). Basic material management is also quite popular among Thai companies (Yagi & Kokubu, 2018).

An increasing number of companies are adopting environmental management accounting, and voluntarily disclosing environmental information. For example, some of these measures include making contributions to environmental projects or foundations, reporting and auditing corporate environmental management, awards received in relation to environmental performance, production system related to environmental management, and achievements, such as ISO 14001 accreditation, in their annual or supplementary reports (Techamontrikul, 1997; Setthasakko, 2010; Ratanasongtham, Phornlaphatrachakorn & Janjarasjit, 2017). From 1997 onward, SET has imposed requirements on listed companies to disclose environmental information — such as the impact of the companies' production and unused raw materials on the environment, to disclose the name of the authorities that control the companies' environmental management, to disclose the operations carried out in reality as against the maximum allowed limit in accordance with the law, and to disclose the history of environmental mistakes and policies or plans to remedy those mistakes (Techamontrikul, 1997). However, it is said that environmental information provided in company reports in Thailand intends to show good environmental policy and creates a good image of being environment-friendly in response to the concerns raised by stakeholders and the public (Connelly & Limpaphayom, 2004; Yongvanich & Guthrie, 2006; Kongpunya, Ussahawanitchakit & Khankaew, 2011; Silalertruksa & Gheewala, 2012; Petcharat & Mula, 2013).

Rewards and recognition (e.g., Sustainability Awards by SET, Thailand Sustainable Investment (THSI List) by SET, and ESG100 for Good Environmental, Social, and Governance Firms by Thaipat Institute) have played an important role in promoting the implementation of corporate environmental management in Thailand. They are increasingly important, as SET promotes responsible investment, encouraging stakeholders of the capital market to focus on sustainability in business processes, and to consider environmental, social, and governance (ESG) factors in their investment decisions.

Although Thai companies, particularly listed ones, have thus continued to exhibit progress in addressing specific environmental issues, it is still an open question as to whether a comprehensive EMCS has been achieved or not. This study explores that question.

## 3. Research Design

In order to examine the comprehensive EMCS in Thailand, we conducted a questionnaire-based survey in Thailand from October 2017 to December 2017. The survey was administered to 596 firms, which were all listed on the SET (466 firms) and the Market for Alternative Investment (MAI, 130 firms). Financial institutions and insurance companies were excluded. Finally, 101 firms participated in our survey. It resulted in a satisfactory response rate of 16.95% (SET: 78 firms; MAI: 23 firms). Table 1 shows the classification of the industries of the respondents and the response rate.

We prepared the questionnaire items on the comprehensive EMCS based on Widener (2007) and Goebel and Weissenberger (2017), which modify the four controls framework of Merchant and Van der Stede (2012) into environmental management.[1] The result controls consisted of financial and/or non-

---

[1]This method is based on our joint research project with Professors Edel Guenther and Thomas Guenther at Technische Universität Dresden.

**Table 1.** Industries of respondents and response rate.

| Industries | Agriculture and food | Consumer products | Industrials | Property and construction | Resources | Services | Techonology | Total |
|---|---|---|---|---|---|---|---|---|
| Sample population | 59 | 50 | 124 | 112 | 60 | 143 | 48 | 596 |
| Respondents | 8 | 8 | 37 | 11 | 17 | 15 | 5 | 101 |
| Respondents/total respondents | 7.92% | 7.92% | 36.63% | 10.89% | 16.83% | 14.85% | 4.95% | 100.00% |
| Respondents/sample population | 13.56% | 16.00% | 29.84% | 9.82% | 28.33% | 10.49% | 10.42% | 16.95% |

financial target indicators, which were used to define expected results, and to monitor and evaluate employees' performance. Action controls ensured that the employees conducted themselves to benefit the organization. On the other hand, personnel controls were applied to foster individual motivation levels. Cultural controls were used to define expected norms and values. We conducted an exploratory factor analysis (EFA) and confirmatory factor analysis (CFA) using the data gathered by the questionnaire in order to examine comprehensive EMCS of Thai companies.

With respect to stakeholder influence, we asked the respondents which stakeholder they thought was most important to their companies. We analyzed the impact of the stakeholders on a comprehensive EMCS using OLS (ordinary least squares). Table 2 shows the rankings of the most important stakeholders, listed from most to least important.

As for the index of environmental performance on the analysis of the impact of comprehensive EMCS, we asked the respondents "in

**Table 2.**   The most important stakeholders.

|      |                         | Frequency | Percent |
|------|-------------------------|-----------|---------|
| 1    | Community               | 28        | 27.7    |
| 2    | Consumers               | 20        | 19.8    |
| 3    | Buyers                  | 14        | 13.9    |
| 4    | Employees               | 10        | 9.9     |
| 5    | Governments             | 6         | 5.9     |
| 6    | Investors/shareholders  | 5         | 5.0     |
| 7    | Competitor              | 3         | 3.0     |
| 8    | Suppliers               | 1         | 1.0     |
| 9    | Banks                   | 1         | 1.0     |
| 10   | Labor unions            | 1         | 1.0     |
| 11   | NGOs                    | 1         | 1.0     |
| 12   | Industrial associations | 1         | 1.0     |
| N/A  |                         | 10        | 9.9     |
| Total |                        | 101       | 100.0   |

comparison with average firms in your industry, how would you evaluate the performance of your firm over the last three years" using a 5-point Likert Scale (5 representing the best). We employed the results for resource efficiency and pollution reduction in the above question, and the impact of a comprehensive EMCS and the stakeholders on these environmental performances was examined using an ordered probit analysis.

## 4. Analysis of Comprehensive EMCS

With respect to a comprehensive EMCS, we measured the result controls, action controls, personnel controls, and cultural controls by relying on a construct that was used by Widener (2007), and Goebel and Weissenberger (2017) to represent the package of EMCS. Before conducting an EFA, we checked the ceiling and floor factors, excluding inappropriate items.

Table 3 reports the results of an EFA of the items in our questionnaire. We used the principal components with promax rotation to extract all factors with an eigenvalue > 1.0, KMO ≥ 0.5 (Cerny & Kaiser, 1977), communality ≥ 0.5 (Fabrigar, Porter & Norris, 2009), and factor loading ≥ 0.5.

Table 4 reports the descriptive statistics, the results of EFA and CFA, and reliability measures. All factor loadings were significant ($p < 0.01$), and standardized factor loadings were above 0.60. The common threshold of Cronbach's alpha was 0.70. Individual item reliability exceeded the conventional threshold of 0.40 (Bagozzi & Baumgartner, 1994). Composite reliability measures went above the typical threshold of 0.60 (Bagozzi & Yi, 1988). The average variance extracted exceeded the threshold of 0.50 for latent constructs. The minimum set of fit statistics consisted of a model test statistic and three approximate fit indexes (Kline, 2016). These indexes were the Root Mean Square Error of Approximation (RMSEA) and its 90% confidence interval (Steiger, 1990); the Comparative Fit Index (CFI) which was better than 90% and was the baseline model (Bentler, 1990); the Standardized Root Mean Square Residual (SRMR) = 0, which was indicated as the perfect model; and increasingly higher values indicate a worse fit.

From the above analysis, action control, result control, cultural control, and personnel control can be extracted as EMCS factors in Thai

**Table 3.** Results of EFA.

| Item | Action controls | Result controls | Cultural controls | Personnel controls |
|---|---|---|---|---|
| J | | | | |
| 1. Superiors monitor and evaluate necessary steps regarding their subordinates' achievement of environmental performance goals. | 0.772 | | | |
| 2. Superiors define the most important work steps for routine environmental tasks. | 0.876 | | | |
| 3. Superiors provide subordinates with information on the most important steps regarding the achievement of environmental performance goals. | 0.906 | | | |
| 4. Policies and procedures manuals define the fundamental course of environmental activities. | 0.615 | | | |
| 5. Subordinates discuss the necessary work steps for achieving their environmental targets with their superiors. | 0.575 | | | |
| K | | | | |
| 1. Specific environmental performance goals are established for subordinates | | 0.576 | | |
| 2. Subordinates' achievement of environmental performance goals is controlled by their respective superiors. | | 0.792 | | |
| 3. Potential deviations from environmental performance goals have to be explained by the responsible subordinates. | | 0.734 | | |
| 4. Subordinates receive feedback from their superiors concerning the extent to which they achieved their environmental performance goals. | | 0.798 | | |

| | | |
|---|---|---|
| H | 1. Traditions, values and norms play a major role in our firm for dealing with environmental management. | 0.667 |
| | 2. Our mission statement clearly communicates the firm's environment-related core values | 0.909 |
| | 3. Top managers communicate the firm's environment-related core values to our workforce. | 0.875 |
| | 4. Our workforce is aware of the firm's environment-related core values. | 0.85 |
| I | 1. Our workforce is carefully selected whether it fits to our firm's environmental values and norms | 0.772 |
| | 2. Much effort has been put into establishing the best-suited recruiting process for an environmental job position. | 0.672 |
| | 3. The environmental goal achievement is regarded as important condition for promotion. | 0.929 |

*Note: N = 101.*

**Table 4.** Results for descriptive statistics, confirmatory factor analysis, and reliability measures.

| Item | Theoretical range | Mean | Standard deviation | Standardized regression weight (λ) | Individual item reliability | Composite reliability | Average variance extracted | Cronbach's alpha |
|---|---|---|---|---|---|---|---|---|
| **Second-order construct: EMCS** | | | | | | 0.925 | 0.757 | 0.960 |
| *First-order construct: Action control* | | | | | | 0.942 | 0.766 | 0.946 |
| J_1 | 1–5 | 3.85 | 1.014 | 0.936[a] | 0.877 | | | |
| J_2 | 1–5 | 3.81 | 0.997 | 0.908[a] | 0.825 | | | |
| J_3 | 1–5 | 3.63 | 1.008 | 0.909*** | 0.827 | | | |
| J_4 | 1–5 | 3.93 | 1.061 | 0.794*** | 0.631 | | | |
| J_5 | 1–5 | 3.89 | 0.999 | 0.876*** | 0.768 | | | |
| | | | | 0.884*** | 0.781 | | | |
| *First-order construct: Result control* | | | | | | 0.940 | 0.798 | 0.934 |
| K_1 | 1–5 | 3.88 | 1.080 | 0.939*** | 0.882 | | | |
| K_2 | 1–5 | 3.83 | 0.981 | 0.914[a] | 0.835 | | | |
| K_3 | 1–5 | 3.68 | 1.049 | 0.865*** | 0.747 | | | |
| K_4 | 1–5 | 3.65 | 1.014 | 0.875*** | 0.765 | | | |
| | | | | 0.918*** | 0.843 | | | |

| | | | | | | | | |
|---|---|---|---|---|---|---|---|---|
| *First-order construct: Cultural control* | | | | 0.788*** | 0.621 | 0.913 | 0.727 | 0.906 |
| H_1 | 1–5 | 3.98 | 0.927 | 0.655[a] | 0.429 | | | |
| H_2 | 1–5 | 3.89 | 1.019 | 0.935*** | 0.874 | | | |
| H_3 | 1–5 | 3.97 | 1.061 | 0.971*** | 0.942 | | | |
| H_4 | 1–5 | 3.82 | 0.994 | 0.814*** | 0.663 | | | |
| *First-order construct: Personnel control* | | | | 0.805*** | 0.649 | 0.849 | 0.654 | 0.849 |
| L_1 | 1–5 | 3.52 | 1.035 | 0.807[a] | 0.651 | | | |
| L_2 | 1–5 | 3.74 | 0.945 | 0.911*** | 0.829 | | | |
| L_4 | 1–5 | 3.10 | 0.964 | 0.694*** | 0.482 | | | |

*Fit indicies:*

$X^2 = 136.868$; $df = 94$ ; $P = 0.003$; RMSEA $= 0.068$; CFI $= 0.973$; NFI $= 0.921$

*Notes*: [a]Reference indicators; $*p < 0.10$; $**p < 0.05$; $***p < 0.01$.

companies. Since CFA demonstrates that our model has a good fit, it can be said that a comprehensive EMCS has been built.

## 5. The Impact of Stakeholders on Comprehensive EMCS

In this section, we examine how various stakeholders influence comprehensive EMCS by OLS. The dependent variable was "comprehensive EMCS", which was constructed from the results of factor analysis and evaluated by factor score. Independent variables are "Community", "Consumers", "Buyers", "Employees", "Government", and "Investors/shareholders." They were all dummy variables. The question asked was, "Is this stakeholder the most important?" "1" denotes "Yes", while "0" means "No". Referring to previous studies, we included firm size by the natural logarithm of total assets, profitability by return on assets (ROA), and "industry dummy" (Manufacturing: 1, Others: 0) as control variables. The descriptive statistics and the results are shown in Tables 5 and 6, respectively.

The estimation results in Table 6 reveal that there is no significant positive stakeholder impact on comprehensive EMCS. However, "Government" and "Investors/shareholders" exerted a negative influence at the 10% significance level. Despite ESG investments being on the rise in Thailand,

**Table 5.** Descriptive statistics.

| Variables | Obs | Mean | S.D. | Min | Max |
|---|---|---|---|---|---|
| EMCS | 83 | −0.048 | 0.913 | −2.943 | 1.271 |
| Community | 83 | 0.325 | 0.471 | 0 | 1 |
| Consumers | 83 | 0.241 | 0.430 | 0 | 1 |
| Buyers | 83 | 0.157 | 0.366 | 0 | 1 |
| Employees | 83 | 0.120 | 0.328 | 0 | 1 |
| Government | 83 | 0.060 | 0.239 | 0 | 1 |
| Investors/shareholders | 83 | 0.048 | 0.215 | 0 | 1 |
| ROA | 83 | 6.171 | 8.483 | −23.140 | 32.270 |
| ln(total assets) | 83 | 18.558 | 1.468 | 15.954 | 22.665 |
| Industry dummy | 83 | 0.361 | 0.483 | 0 | 1 |

**Table 6.** Regression results of the impact from stake-holders on comprehensive EMCS.

| | EMCS | |
|---|---|---|
| **Variables** | **Coef.** | **S.E.** |
| Community | 0.032 | 0.462 |
| Consumers | 0.065 | 0.477 |
| Buyers | −0.106 | 0.496 |
| Employees | −0.116 | 0.514 |
| Government | −1.133 | 0.582* |
| Investors/shareholders | −1.051 | 0.610* |
| ROA | 0.008 | 0.012 |
| ln(total assets) | 0.155 | 0.069** |
| Industry dummy | 0.211 | 0.208 |
| Constant | −2.928 | 1.398** |
| Observations | 83 | |
| R-squared | 0.209 | |

*** $p < 0.01$, **$p < 0.05$, *$p < 0.1$.

this result signals a tendency to treat environmental solutions lightly, due to enormous pressures to generate profits in terms of the capital market. Thai investors focus more on short-term profits, but the cost of CSR and ESG practices can be recovered only in the long term. Firms might feel pressure to pursue short-term profits to satisfy shareholders. Examining the reaction of investors to the announcements of the ESG 100 list by Thaipat Institution and the Thailand Sustainability Investment (TSI) list by SET during 2014–2015 using an event study (1-day, 5-day, 10-day, and 20-day window periods), Taechaubol (2016) finds significantly negative abnormal returns for stocks in the TSI list and the ESG 100 list. The government's negative impact may be ascribed to the fact that the current Thai government does not require comprehensive EMCS formation. It can be interpreted that because companies that deem the government as the most important stakeholder are prone to act only within the ambit of government policies.

## 6. The Effects of Stakeholders and Comprehensive EMCS on Environmental Performance

To examine the effects of stakeholders and comprehensive EMCS on environmental performance, we adopted the ordered probit analysis. The dependent variables were "resource efficiency" and "pollution reduction." We evaluated them using the questionnaire items. As independent variables, we employ the dummy variables of the six most influential stakeholders, which we presented in Section 5, and the comprehensive EMCS, which we evaluated using the same factor score as we used in the previous regression analysis. The descriptive statistics and the result are shown in Tables 7 and 8, respectively.

The results of our analysis indicate that a comprehensive EMCS has a significant positive impact on resource efficiency and pollution reduction, supporting its efficacy. However, none of the stakeholders impacted the environmental performance, clearly signifying that Thailand is not at a

**Table 7.** Descriptive statistics.

| Variables | Obs | Mean | S.D. | Min | Max |
|---|---|---|---|---|---|
| *Dependent variables* | | | | | |
| Resource efficiency | 80 | 3.663 | 0.856 | 1 | 5 |
| Pollution reduction | 79 | 3.769 | 0.821 | 1 | 5 |
| *Independent variables* | | | | | |
| EMCS | 80 | −0.016 | 0.876 | −2.943 | 1.271 |
| Community | 80 | 0.313 | 0.466 | 0 | 1 |
| Consumers | 80 | 0.250 | 0.436 | 0 | 1 |
| Buyers | 80 | 0.150 | 0.359 | 0 | 1 |
| Employees | 80 | 0.125 | 0.333 | 0 | 1 |
| Government | 80 | 0.063 | 0.244 | 0 | 1 |
| Investors/shareholders | 80 | 0.050 | 0.219 | 0 | 1 |
| *Control variables* | | | | | |
| ROA | 80 | 6.120 | 8.609 | −23.140 | 32.270 |
| ln (total assets) | 80 | 18.536 | 1.426 | 15.954 | 22.665 |
| Industry dummy | 80 | 0.375 | 0.487 | 0 | 1 |

**Table 8.**   Results of ordered probit regression.

| Variables | (1) Resource efficiency | | (2) Pollution reduction | |
|---|---|---|---|---|
| | **Coef.** | **S.E.** | **Coef.** | **S.E.** |
| EMCS | 0.432 | 0.169** | 0.450 | 0.182** |
| Community | 0.024 | 0.607 | −0.804 | 0.611 |
| Consumers | 0.638 | 0.626 | 0.008 | 0.626 |
| Buyers | 0.748 | 0.656 | −0.113 | 0.656 |
| Employees | 0.691 | 0.675 | −0.350 | 0.675 |
| Government | 0.466 | 0.794 | 0.112 | 0.846 |
| Investors/shareholders | 0.507 | 0.812 | 0.812 | 0.858 |
| ROA | 0.012 | 0.016 | 0.046 | 0.017*** |
| ln (total assets) | 0.083 | 0.099 | 0.202 | 0.101** |
| Industry dummy | −0.382 | 0.280 | −0.110 | 0.284 |
| Constant cut1 | −0.300 | 1.981 | 0.725 | 1.972 |
| Constant cut2 | 1.760 | 1.997 | 1.135 | 1.971 |
| Constant cut3 | 2.970 | 2.005 | 3.362 | 2.030* |
| Constant cut4 | | | 4.827 | 2.047** |
| Observations | 80 | | 79 | |
| Pseudo R2 | 0.101 | | 0.160 | |

***$p < 0.01$, **$p < 0.05$, *$p < 0.1$.

stage where stakeholders are the main influencers of environmental performance.

## 7.  Conclusions and Implications

In this study, we examined whether a comprehensive EMCS has taken shape among Thai companies, and, if it has, whether stakeholders wield any effective influence thereon. We also examined whether the EMCS and the stakeholders influences environmental performance or not. The results show that comprehensive EMCS factors based on Merchant and Van der Stede (2012) can be detected in Thai companies. However, no stakeholders exert a positive influence on the formation of EMCS. On the contrary, it was revealed that investors or shareholders and the government cast a negative influence. At the same time, it was clearly demonstrated that a comprehensive EMCS engenders a positive effect on environmental performance (resource efficiency and pollution reduction).

Based on the above results, this study shows that the progression in Thailand from EMS, such as ISO 14001, aimed at mitigating specific environmental influences to a comprehensive EMCS. The effectiveness of a comprehensive EMCS in Thailand is also confirmed. However, this study cannot show any positive stakeholder influence on a comprehensive EMCS. This means that comprehensive EMCS formation depends not on external factors but on internal factors led by corporate management.

Based on the positive effects of a comprehensive EMCS in Thailand, we can conclude that, in the future, even in developing countries, the policy for environmental management should go beyond the level of ISO 14001 and effectively pursue strategies for comprehensive environmental management. Particularly in Thailand, where reliance on government institutions negatively affects EMCS formation, government policy changes will be necessary. Moreover, by promoting ESG investments, pressures from the inordinate emphasis on profits by investors or shareholders will have to be moderated.

## Acknowledgments

This study was supported by JSPS KAKENHI Grant numbers JP16H03679 and 18K18577, and the Environmental Research and Technology Development Funds (S-16) of the Environment Restoration and Conservation Agency, Japan.

## References

Ann, G. E., Zailani, S. and Abd Wahid, N. (2006). A study on the impact of environmental management system (EMS) certification towards firms' performance in Malaysia. *Management of Environmental Quality: An International Journal 17*(1), 73–93.

Bagozzi, R. P. and Baumgartner, H. (1994). The evaluation of structural equation models and hypotheses testing. In Bagozzi, R. P. (ed.) *Principles of Marketing Research*. Blackwell Business.

Bagozzi, R. P. and Yi, Y. (1988). On the evaluation of structural equation models. *Journal of the Academy of Marketing Science 16*(1), 74–94.

Bentler, P. M. (1990). Comparative fit indexes in structural models. *Psychological Bulletin 107*, 238–246.

Cerny, C. A. and Kaiser, H. F. (1977). A study of a measure of sampling adequacy for factor-analytic correlation matrices. *Multivariate Behavioral Research 12*(1), 43–47.

Connelly, T. J. and Limpaphayom, P. (2004). Environmental reporting and firm performance: Evidence from Thailand. *Journal of Corporate Citizenship 13*, 137–149.

Fabrigar, L. R., Porter, R. D. and Norris, M. E. (2009). Some things you should know about structural equation modeling but never thought to ask. *Journal of Consumer Psychology 20*(2), 221–225.

Goebel, S. and Weissenberger, B. E. (2017). Effects of management control mechanisms: Towards a more comprehensive analysis. *Journal of Business Economics 87*, 185–219.

Guenther, E., Endrikat, J. and Guenther, T. W. (2016). Environmental management control systems: A conceptualization and a review of the empirical evidence. *Journal of Cleaner Production 136*, Part A, 147–171.

Kline, R. B. (2016). *Principles and Practice of Structural Equation Modeling*, 4th edn. The Guilford Press.

Kongpunya, P., Ussahawanitchakit, P. and Khankaew, C. (2011). Building accounting sustainability of listed firms in Thailand: How does it affect accounting disclosure and disclosure quality? *Journal of Academy of Business and Economics 11*(1), 93–107.

Merchant, K. A. and Van der Stede, W. A. (2012). *Management Control Systems: Performance Measurement, Evaluation and Incentives*, 3rd edn. Financial Times Prentice Hall.

Nguyen, Q. A. and Hens, L. (2015). Environmental performance of the cement industry in Vietnam: The influence of ISO 14001 certification. *Journal of Cleaner Production 96*, 362–378.

Petcharat, N. and Mula, J. (2013). Toward a conceptual model for sustainability financial reporting system. Paper presented at *the AFAANZ Conference*, Perth, Australia, 7–9 July.

Ratanasongtham, W., Phornlaphatrachakorn, K. and Janjarasjit, S. (2017). Antecedents of environmental management accounting capability: Empirical evidence from ISO 14000 firms in Thailand. *Journal of Innovative Management Science 10*(2), 12–26.

Seetharaman, A., Ismail, M. and Saravanan, A. S. (2007). Environmental accounting as a tool for environmental management system. *Journal of Applied Sciences and Environmental Management 11*(2), 137–145.

Setthasakko, W. (2010). Barriers to the development of environmental management accounting: An exploratory study of pulp and paper companies in Thailand. *EuroMed Journal of Business 5*(3), 315–331.

Silalertruksa, T. and Gheewala, S. H. (2012). Environmental sustainability assessment of palm biodiesel production in Thailand. *Energy 43*(1), 306–314.

Singh, M., Brueckner, M. and Padhy, P. K. (2015). Environmental management system ISO 14001: Effective waste minimisation in small and medium enterprises in India. *Journal of Cleaner Production 102*, 285–301.

Steiger, J. H. (1990). Structural model evaluation and modification: An interval estimation approach. *Multivariate Behavioral Research 25*, 173–180.

Taechaubol, K. (2016). *Investor Types and Trading of the Environment, Social and Governance Stocks in the Stock Exchange of Thailand*. Master Thesis, Department of Banking and Finance, Faculty of Commerce and Accountancy, Chulalongkorn University.

Techamontrikul, S. (1997). Environmental disclosures for companies listed in the Stock Exchange of Thailand: Guidelines and model. Dissertation for the Degree of Doctor of Business Administration, Graduate School, Chulalongkorn University.

Widener, S. K. (2007). An empirical analysis of the levers of control framework. *Accounting, Organizations and Society 32*, 757–788.

Yagi, M. and Kokubu, K. (2018). Corporate material flow management in Thailand: The way to material flow cost accounting. *Journal of Cleaner Production 198*, 763–775.

Yongvanich, K. and Guthrie, J. (2006). An extended performance reporting framework for social and environmental accounting. *Business Strategy and the Environment 15*(5), 309–321.

# Chapter 10

# Corporate Social and Environmental Reporting Research in Asia: A Structured Literature Review

Trong Q. Trinh

*School of Accounting and Auditing, National Economics University*
*Hanoi, Vietnam*

## 1. Introduction

Corporate social and environmental reporting (CSER) research in Asia is still rather new despite some notable publications in the 1980s and 1990s (Singh & Ahuja, 1983; Teoh & Thong, 1984; Foo & Tan, 1988; Yamagami & Kokubu, 1991). In the past decade, nonetheless, non-financial information has gained more attention from both academics and practitioners in the world's largest continent. Along with rapid economic growth, Asia also experiences severe social and environmental problems such as wealth inequality and high carbon emissions. In 2015, of the top 10 emitting countries in the world, which contribute over two-thirds of global emissions, six were in Asia (IEA, 2017). This rapid growth in many Asian countries has led to warnings by national and global authorities (IEA, 2017; IMF, 2017).

Corporate stakeholders in Asia are not only concerned with financial information, but also social and environmental disclosures (Shauki, 2011; Lee, Park & Klassen, 2015; Shen, Wu & Chand, 2017). On the academic side, the number of studies focusing on CSER practice in Asia has risen significantly in recent years; however, few review studies in the field specifically refer to the Asian context. Thus, to provide a more comprehensive picture of CSER research in Asian countries, this review investigates studies in the field from their origin until the present time. It has two main research objectives. First, it aims to explore the characteristics of CSER research in Asian countries. Second, it attempts to determine and systematize the factors driving corporate social and environmental disclosure in Asia by comprehensively reviewing studies in this topic.

The remainder of this chapter is structured as follows. Section 2 describes the research methodology. Then, the characteristics of CSER research in Asia are provided in Section 3. Section 4 discusses the disclosure determinants of CSER in Asia before ending with the discussion and conclusion in Section 5.

## 2. Research Method

To include as many relevant articles as possible, we combined several methods to collect CSER studies in the Asian context. First, a structured search for relevant work was conducted. The Web of Science (WoS) Social Science Citation Index and EBSCO Business Source Premier database were selected as they include all high-impact factor journals in the field (Hahn, Reimsbach & Schiemann, 2015). Then, the keywords for the search were identified by looking at the development history of non-financial reporting. In total, 20 keywords were used[1]: "social report*", "environment* report*", "sustainab* report*", "triple bottom line report*", "TBL report*", "CSR report*", "responsib* report*", "non-financ* report*", "carbon* report*", "greenhouse gas* report*", "social disclosure*", "environment* disclosure*", "sustainab* disclosure*", "triple bottom line disclosure*", "TBL disclosure*", "CSR disclosure*", "responsib* disclosure*", "non-financ* disclosure*", "carbon* disclosure*", and "greenhouse gas* disclosure*".

The time period for the search was set as 1970–2017. The starting year was considered to be the beginning of the adoption of CSER practices (Fifka, 2012). The keywords were searched "in topic" for the categories

---

[1]The asterisks "*" were used to expand the coverage of the keywords while using fewer of them.

of "Business", "Management", and "Business Finance." Only "article" was chosen from "Document Type", and the language was "English". This approach resulted in 767 articles in the WoS database and 2,771 articles in the EBSCOhost database. Then, these articles were manually screened to decide which were related to the CSER topic and conducted in Asia. This screening process resulted in 66 related articles from the WoS database and 84 articles from the EBSCOhost database. After a cross-check to eliminate duplicated articles, 123 studies remained.

Of those, 89 studies were conducted in China, Malaysia, Bangladesh, and India. Of the remaining 34 studies, 25 were conducted in six other countries/territories and nine in multiple Asian countries. To cover more CSER studies in Asia, a second search using the Emerging Source Citation Index (ESCI) on WoS was conducted. The ESCI by Clarivate Analytics (the owner of WoS) was launched in 2017 to extend relevant scholarly content (Clarivate Analytics, 2017). Therefore, the ESCI was chosen to cover more related studies across Asian countries.

The second search was conducted by using a similar approach; however, studies from China, Malaysia, India, and Bangladesh were excluded as a large volume of research from those countries was discovered in the initial search. The ESCI only holds studies for three years (2015, 2016, and 2017). Finally, this search process resulted in 14 more studies from eight countries.

Lastly, among the literature review studies in the field, only Fifka (2012) explicitly refers to Asia. Fifka (2012), however, does not provide rigorous methods or describe in detail how to choose the studies to review. In addition, Fifka (2012) only refers to 46 CSER studies in Asia, a low number compared with the studies identified in the two aforementioned search processes. On the contrary, many of the CSER studies in Asia mentioned in Fifka (2012) were not discovered by the two initial search processes in this review. Thus, to avoid missing relevant articles, we incorporated the studies in Asia mentioned in Fifka (2012) that were not picked up by our initial search processes. This resulted in another 27 articles. After these three search processes, 164 CSER studies in Asia were identified for the present review.

## 3. CSER Research in Asia

These 164 studies were published in 88 journals, with 12 articles in the *Journal of Business Ethics*, 11 in the *Managerial Auditing Journal*, nine in the *Journal of Cleaner Production*, and eight each in the *Accounting, Auditing & Accountability Journal* and *Social Responsibility Journal*. The distribution of CSER studies across journals reflects the growing interest in this topic in Asia.

## 3.1 *Chronology and geography*

The history of CSER began in the early 1970s when companies provided their first publications on non-financial-related issues (Fifka, 2012). However, the first Asian study of this topic (as identified in this review) did not appear until 1983 (Singh & Ahuja, 1983). During the 1980s and early 1990s, only a few notable CSER studies were conducted in Asia (Singh & Ahuja, 1983; Foo & Tan, 1988; Andrew *et al.*, 1989; Yamagami & Kokubu, 1991; Lynn, 1992). The number of studies rose significantly in the late 2000s, peaking in 2017 with 24 studies (Fig. 1).

The distribution of CSER studies diverges considerably across Asia. Of the 164 studies identified in this review, 153 were conducted in 18 single Asian countries and 11 studies used samples from multiple Asian countries. East Asia and Southeast Asia have 49 articles each, followed by South Asia with 44 CSER studies. West Asia lags behind with only 16 articles and no studies were found in Central Asia. Some countries contribute largely to CSER research in their area; for instance, China and Malaysia constitute around 65% of the CSER research in East and Southeast Asia, respectively, while Bangladesh and India contribute around 85% of CSER studies in South Asia.

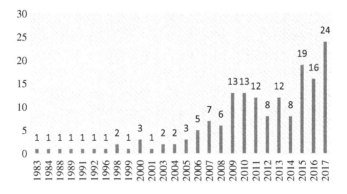

**Fig. 1.**   Number of CSER studies in Asia by year.

## 3.2 *Theories employed*

Note that 49 studies, approximately 30% of the identified studies, did not refer to or explicitly adopt any particular theories. Among the remains, legitimacy theory and stakeholder theory appeared in 40 and 36 studies, respectively.

Legitimacy theory refers to the general perceptions of society on the appropriateness of a company's behavior based on the notion of a "social contract", while stakeholder theory relates to the impact on the firm for particular stakeholder groups (Yu & Rowe, 2017). The next most common theory is institutional theory, which was used in 20 studies. Institutional theory employs three isomorphic processes (coercive, mimetic, and normative) to explain the process when organizations become similar to others in the field. Agency theory, which concerns the relationship between principals and agents, was employed in 16 studies, while other theories such as political economy theory, signaling theory, and resource dependence theory were referred to in 43 studies. A significant number of studies ($n = 26$) adopted multiple theories (Table 1).

The distribution of theories used also diverges significantly by region. Among CSER research-intensive countries, the proportions of non-theoretical framework studies in Bangladesh and India are much higher than those in other countries such as China or Malaysia. Legitimacy theory is the most common theory employed; however, in East and Southeast Asia, stakeholder theory has been more prevalently adopted, while legitimacy theory is dominant in South Asia and West Asia. This phenomenon is further investigated and discussed in Section 5.

## 4. Determinants of Disclosure

The determinants of CSER practices are most commonly discussed among the reviewed studies, which typically examine the variables affecting the quantity/quality of social and environmental information and the decision to disclose. In addition to common variables widely discussed in the literature (see Section 4.1), unique determinants exist for Asia (Section 4.2).

## 4.1 *Frequently discussed determinants*

Previous literature review studies in the field (Fifka, 2013; Hahn & Kühnen, 2013; Dienes, Sassen & Fischer, 2016; Ali, Frynas & Mahmood, 2017) have

**Table 1.** Distribution of studies by region and theory employed.

| Region and country | Number of studies | Theory employed | | | | | |
|---|---|---|---|---|---|---|---|
| | | None | LT | ST | IT | AT | Others |
| Across regions | 6 | 3 | 1 | — | 1 | 1 | 1 |
| East Asia | 49 | 13 | 7 | 13 | 7 | 1 | 19 |
| *China* | 32 | 5 | 5 | 9 | 7 | 1 | 14 |
| *Hong Kong* | 5 | 3 | 1 | 1 | — | — | 2 |
| *Japan* | 7 | 3 | 1 | 1 | — | — | 1 |
| *Korea (South)* | 3 | 2 | — | — | — | — | 1 |
| *Taiwan* | 2 | — | — | 2 | — | — | 1 |
| Southeast Asia | 49 | 11 | 12 | 12 | 7 | 3 | 12 |
| *Multiple nations* | 4 | 3 | — | — | 1 | — | — |
| *Indonesia* | 8 | 2 | 2 | 3 | 1 | — | — |
| *Malaysia* | 32 | 5 | 7 | 9 | 5 | 3 | 10 |
| *Singapore* | 3 | 1 | 2 | — | — | — | — |
| *Thailand* | 2 | — | 1 | — | — | — | 2 |
| South Asia | 44 | 18 | 14 | 6 | 4 | 4 | 6 |
| *Bangladesh* | 23 | 10 | 7 | 4 | 3 | 1 | 2 |
| *India* | 15 | 8 | 5 | 2 | — | 2 | 1 |
| *Pakistan* | 3 | — | 2 | — | — | 1 | 1 |
| *Sri Lanka* | 3 | — | — | — | 1 | — | 2 |
| West Asia | 16 | 4 | 6 | 4 | 1 | 7 | 5 |
| *Multiple nations* | 1 | — | 1 | — | 1 | — | — |
| *Jordan* | 2 | 1 | — | — | — | — | 1 |
| *Lebanon* | 1 | — | — | — | — | 1 | — |
| *Qatar* | 2 | 1 | 1 | 1 | — | 1 | 1 |
| *Saudi Arabia* | 2 | — | 1 | 1 | — | 2 | 1 |
| *Turkey* | 8 | 2 | 3 | 2 | — | 3 | 2 |
| Total | 164 | 49 | 40 | 36 | 20 | 16 | 43 |

*Notes*: LT: Legitimacy theory; ST: Stakeholder theory; IT: Institutional theory; AT: Agency theory.

shown that internal determinants are more likely than external factors to affect non-financial reporting practices. Internal factors can thus serve as drivers of social and environmental disclosure, especially corporate governance, ownership structure, and financial performance.

### 4.1.1 *Corporate governance*

Board size, measured by the number of directors on the board, can be considered to have a positive effect on non-financial disclosure, as a larger board may comprise more experienced and knowledgeable directors (Barakat, Pérez & Ariza, 2015); hence, different ideas including on social and environmental issues, can be included in discussions, especially in times of crisis and regulatory change (Ahmed Haji, 2013). Indeed, the empirical results strongly support this line of thought (e.g., Ahmed Haji, 2013; Majeed, Aziz & Saleem, 2015; Akbas, 2016; Trireksani & Djajadikerta, 2016), as only two studies show no significant relationship between board size and non-financial disclosure (Said, Zainuddin & Haron, 2009; Kiliç, Kuzey & Uyar, 2015).

Turning to board independence, measured by the proportion of non-executive directors to total directors on the board, agency theory suggests a positive relationship, as the existence of non-executive directors (outsiders) reinforces the quality of environmental disclosure and closes the information gap among managers, shareholders, and other stakeholders (Iatridis, 2013). The empirical results, nonetheless, are rather mixed. A number of studies reveal a positive association (e.g., Rashid & Lodh, 2008; Lattemann *et al.*, 2009; Khan, 2010), whereas many others show no correlation (e.g., Ahmed Haji, 2013; Akbas, 2016) or even a negative relationship (e.g., Haniffa & Cooke, 2005; Cahaya *et al.*, 2017).

The presence of a board audit committee, which often requires the presence of independent directors, is also predicted to positively affect CSR disclosure. The existence of an audit committee provides a means for companies to review processes on internal control, thus reducing agency costs and producing higher-quality reporting (Said, Zainuddin & Haron, 2009). This prediction is proven by the sample of CSER studies in Asia, most of which reveals a positive association between board audit committees and CSR disclosure (e.g., Rouf & Abdur, 2011; Iatridis, 2013;

Barakat, Pérez & Ariza, 2015; Alotaibi & Hussainey, 2016). Indeed, only one study shows no significant relationship (Akbas, 2016).

### 4.1.2 *Ownership structure*

In this category, the most frequently examined determinants are state ownership, foreign ownership, and managerial ownership. Stakeholder theory suggests that government ownership is the dominant factor that influences corporate governance disclosure, especially in developing countries (Alotaibi & Hussainey, 2016). Government interventions may pressure voluntary disclosure by companies, as the government is a public body (Said, Zainuddin & Haron, 2009); therefore, it is predicted that government shareholdings increase the level of CSR disclosure. The majority of the reviewed studies support this prediction (e.g., Zeng *et al.*, 2010, 2012; Ahmed Haji, 2013; Habbash, 2016; Cheng *et al.*, 2017); nonetheless, some reveal no significant association (e.g., Cahaya *et al.*, 2017) or an inverse impact (e.g., Li *et al.*, 2013).

In terms of foreign ownership, based on legitimacy theory, companies with a higher percentage of foreign ownership are expected to report more information on social and environmental issues as a kind of proactive legitimacy strategy to satisfy foreign investors and gain more capital from foreigners (Khan, Mutakin & Siddiqui, 2012). Teoh and Thong (1984), Lynn (1992), Haniffa and Cooke (2005), Zeng *et al.* (2010), and Khan, Mutakin and Siddiqui (2012) confirm this argument, whereas Amran and Susela Devi (2008), Said, Zainuddin and Haron (2009), and Cahaya *et al.* (2017) reveal no significant association.

Concerning managerial ownership, scholars present two opposite perspectives. Alotaibi and Hussainey (2016) argue for a positive relationship on the grounds that the interests of managers in firms with a high proportion of managerial ownership are aligned with the interests of shareholders; thus, managers are motivated to reduce the agency problem (agency theory) and report more vital information to meet stakeholders' needs (stakeholder theory). On the contrary, Khan, Mutakin and Siddiqui (2012), based on legitimacy theory, contend that concentrated managerial ownership allows managers to have an overwhelming say on the organization's policies and strategies; hence, public accountability and corporate disclosure might be less of an issue as outsiders' interest and pressure is small. A high number of the reviewed studies support the latter argument (Mohd Ghazali, 2007; Khan, Mutakin & Siddiqui, 2012; Ahmed Haji, 2013), while two studies confirm the former (Iatridis, 2013; Alotaibi & Hussainey, 2016) and another two reveal no significant relationship (Rashid & Lodh, 2008; Said, Zainuddin & Haron, 2009).

### 4.1.3 *Financial performance*

Profitability, represented by return on assets, return on equity, profit margin, or sales, is also a common driver of CSER in the Asian setting. A significant positive relationship between profitability and CSER, which indicates that companies with better financial performance disclose more non-financial information, is a popular result in the reviewed studies (e.g., Rashid & Lodh, 2008; Rouf & Abdur, 2011; Batra, 2013; Khalil & O'Sullivan, 2017). Khan, Mutakin and Siddiqui (2012) explain that profitability allows managers the freedom and flexibility to undertake more extensive social responsibility activities and report them to stakeholders. Moreover, profitable companies tend to demonstrate their contribution to society's well-being and legitimize their existence by disclosing social information.

## 4.2 *Unique determinants of CSER in Asia*

### 4.2.1 *Religion*

In Asian culture, religion plays an important role, not only in daily life, but also in the business world. In the non-financial reporting field, some scholars have investigated religion as an underlying driver of CSER practices. Kamla and Rammal (2013) use content analysis to examine the annual reports and websites of 19 Islamic banks[2] across Asia and find that one of the drivers encouraging social disclosure is Sharia (Islamic law) teachings. Similarly, Sobhani *et al.* (2011) and Sobhani, Amran and Zainuddin (2012) posit that Islamic principles have a significant influence

---

[2]One of the 19 banks was based in the United Kingdom.

on the CSER practices of Islamic banks in Bangladesh. Nonetheless, Mohammed, Alwi and Jamil (2010), investigating Sharia-compliant listed companies in Malaysia, find that those companies do not clearly disclose items under the Sharia compliance index and call for mandatory rules for disclosing sustainability-related information. Khalil and O'Sullivan (2017) also find no clear relationship between the religion of the main owners and level of CSR disclosure.

Du *et al.* (2014) examine whether and how Buddhism, China's most influential religion, affects corporate environmental responsibility. To measure the independent variable, they calculate the number and distance of Buddhist monasteries in the area from the sample companies, finding strong and robust evidence that Buddhism is significantly positively associated with corporate environmental reporting. Buddhism in Sri Lanka also shows a degree of influence on managers' beliefs to engage in sustainability reporting practices (Thoradeniya *et al.*, 2015). Nonetheless, Abeydeera, Tregidga and Kearins (2016) reveal surprisingly little evidence of Buddhist principles and values in corporate sustainability reporting by award-winning corporations in Sri Lanka.

### 4.2.2 *Government connections*

The political system in Asian countries such as China is different from those in other countries. In addition, as the majority of countries in Asia are developing nations, the connections between governments and corporations are usually strong and comprise various forms. Cheng *et al.* (2017) and Kuo and Yu (2017) determine the influence of political connections on a firm's environmental information disclosure level in China by measuring the number of (Communist) Party members on the company's executive board. They show that political connections can influence companies to more actively disclose environmental information; however, they can also mask political rent-seeking in the guise of protecting the environment. On the other side, Amran and Devi (2007) measured the dependence on the government of Malaysian corporations by the sales for the government over total sales of the companies. The study shows that companies depending on the government or with significant government shareholdings are institutionalized by the government's aspiration and vision of social and environmental issues. Similarly, Thompson and Zakaria (2004), Amran and Susela Devi (2008), Amran and Haniffa (2011), and Ahmed Haji (2013) also find a positive relationship between political connections and CSER practices.

### 4.2.3 *Pressure from Western buyers*

Many companies in Asia participate in the supply chains of multinational corporations from Western countries. Hence, the customers of those companies are Western buyers, and they serve as a motivating factor for adopting CSER practices. Islam and Deegan (2008) study companies in the clothing sector in Bangladesh and find that one of the drivers for employing CSER practices in those companies is to satisfy and respond to the pressure from foreign buyers. Rahman Belal and Owen (2007) also make similar findings for a sample of various sectors in Bangladesh.

## 5. Discussion and Conclusion

### 5.1 *Social and environmental reporting research in Asia*

The present study identifies and reviews 164 CSER studies in the Asian context, distributed over four regions and 18 countries/territories. More studies are identified in China, Malaysia, and Bangladesh than in other nations for various reasons. In China, owing to its increasing economic liberalization and subsequent social and environmental issues such as wealth inequality, work safety, and a high level of emissions, the literature has recently experienced an explosion of CSER research. The case is different for Malaysia. Although a similar number of CSER studies were identified ($n = 32$), CSR disclosure research in Malaysia has a much longer history, with some studies appearing in the 1980s such as Teoh and Thong (1984), Foo and Tan (1988), and Andrew *et al.* (1989). These works can be considered to be the earliest research on this topic in Asia. Bangladesh, a developing country that specializes in labor-intensive industries, has gained much negative publicity for its human rights abuses, employment of child labor, and inadequate health and safety measures, which result in frequent accidents and deaths (Islam & Deegan, 2008).

Thus, CSER in Bangladesh has been motivated by powerful stakeholders such as multinational buying companies, non-government organizations, and the media. The numbers of studies found in other countries are small or moderate; nonetheless, this review study only covers works published in English. Hence, publications in other languages were ignored.

Regarding the theoretical framework, 49 studies, accounting for nearly 30% of all reviewed studies, did not refer to or explicitly adopt any theories. As the majority of countries in Asia are developing and new emerging economies, this finding is consistent with those of Belal and Momin (2009) and Ali, Frynas and Mahmood (2017), who indicate that CSR disclosure research in developing and emerging countries is undertheorized. Among the remaining studies, legitimacy theory and stakeholder theory are the prevalent theoretical frameworks, used in 40 and 36 studies, respectively. However, there are regional differences in the theories employed. In East and Southeast Asia, stakeholder theory has been more prevalently adopted, whereas in South Asia and West Asia, legitimacy theory is dominant. This distinction can be explained by the difference in economic status. The economies in East Asia and some Southeast Asian countries such as Japan, China, South Korea, Thailand, and Malaysia are more developed than those in South and West Asia; thus, the enterprises in these areas have to respond to various stakeholder groups, which normally appear with economic development. On the contrary, in the less-developed economies in West and South Asia, enterprises spend their resources on legitimizing their existence and continuing operation. Hence, in these regions, legitimacy theory seems to be more suitable for explaining the practice of CSR disclosure.

## 5.2 *Determinants of social and environmental reporting in Asia*

Studies of the determinants of CSR disclosure in Asia focus on internal drivers rather than external ones. Of those factors, only a few variables receive attention and provide sufficiently consistent results to illustrate a clear trend of influence on corporate social and environmental disclosure. Board size, board audit committee, and profitability appear to have significant and positive effects on the practice of CSR disclosure, while other variables such as board independence, board diversity, state ownership, and managerial ownership demonstrate mixed findings on the relationship with CSER. These findings imply that companies in Asia with larger boards and board audit committees as well as more profitable companies disclose more non-financial information than others.

In addition to the determinants widely discussed in the literature, the reviewed studies also present some unique drivers of CSER practices in Asia. One of them is religion, which plays an important role in culture and directly affects people's behavior in many Asian countries. In contrast to the Western context, where Christianity is more popular, CSER research in Asia focuses on the effects of Islam and Buddhism on CSR practices. Overall, the findings illustrate the significant and positive impact of moral principles from both Islam (Sobhani *et al.*, 2011; Sobhani, Amran & Zainuddin, 2012; Kamla & Rammal, 2013) and Buddhism (Du *et al.*, 2014; Thoradeniya *et al.*, 2015) on the level of non-financial information disclosure, although some studies find no clear relationship (e.g., Mohammed, Alwi & Jamil, 2010; Khalil & O'Sullivan, 2017). The number of studies that examine the relationship between religion and CSR disclosure, nevertheless, is still insignificant compared with those of internal determinants.

## 5.3 *Suggestions for future research*

This study, in addition to reviewing research on social and environmental disclosure, also points out some directions for future research. First, as discussed above, the impact of religion on social and environmental disclosure can be considered to be a unique characteristic of Asian countries. Several scholars have focused on this topic; however, this number is still limited. Moreover, the methods used to measure the impact of religion were relatively simple, with most studies employing content analysis or the religion of corporate managers for the analysis; however, the effects of religion are not always explicitly stated in company reports or directly related to the beliefs of managers. Religions sometimes have effects at deeper layers and need more sophisticated methods to explore and discover their impacts. Hence, future research could explore the relationship between religions, and corporate social and environmental disclosure by using more sophisticated measurement methods to provide meaningful results on this relationship.

Another direction for CSER research in Asia is to emphasize other independent variables than the quantity of information disclosed. Studies of the determinants of CSER practices could be expanded to investigate the drivers of information quality or the decision to engage in CSER. This would link to the presented research method as well. More exploratory and confirmatory analysis methods might also be used rather than content analysis only.

## References

Abeydeera, S., Tregidga, H. and Kearins, K. (2016). Sustainability reporting — More global than local? *Meditari Accountancy Research 24*(4), 478–504.

Ahmed Haji, A. (2013). Corporate social responsibility disclosures over time: Evidence from Malaysia. *Managerial Auditing Journal 28*(7), 647–676.

Akbas, H. E. (2016). The relationship between board characteristics and environmental disclosure: Evidence from Turkish listed companies. *South East European Journal of Economics and Business 11*(2), 7–19.

Ali, W., Frynas, J. G. and Mahmood, Z. (2017). Determinants of corporate social responsibility (CSR) disclosure in developed and developing countries: A literature review. *Corporate Social Responsibility and Environmental Management 24*, 273–294.

Alotaibi, K. and Hussainey, K. (2016). Determinants of CSR disclosure quantity and quality: Evidence from non-financial listed firms in Saudi Arabia. *International Journal of Disclosure and Governance 13*(4), 364–393.

Amran, A. and Devi, S. S. (2007). Corporate social reporting in Malaysia: A political theory perspective. *Malaysian Accounting Review 6*(1), 19–44.

Amran, A. and Haniffa, R. (2011). Evidence in development of sustainability reporting: A case of a developing country. *Business Strategy and the Environment 20*(3), 141–156.

Amran, A. and Susela Devi, S. (2008). The impact of government and foreign affiliate influence on corporate social reporting. *Managerial Auditing Journal 23*(4), 386–404.

Andrew, B. H., Gul, F. A., Guthrie, J. E. and Teoh, H. Y. (1989). A note on corporate social disclosure practices in developing countries: The case of Malaysia and Singapore. *The British Accounting Review 21*(4), 371–376.

Barakat, F. S. Q., Pérez, M. V. L. and Ariza, L. R. (2015). Corporate social responsibility disclosure (CSRD) determinants of listed companies in

Palestine (PXE) and Jordan (ASE). *Review of Managerial Science 9*(4), 681–702.

Batra, G. S. (2013). Environment management and environmental disclosures: A comparison of corporate practices across Malaysia, Singapore and India. *South Asian Journal of Management 20*(1), 62–96.

Belal, A. R. and Momin, M. (2009). Corporate social reporting (CSR) in emerging economies: A review and future direction. *Research in Accounting in Emerging Economies 9*, 119–143.

Belal, A. R. and Owen, D. L. (2007). The views of corporate managers on the current state of, and future prospects for, social reporting in Bangladesh. *Accounting, Auditing and Accountability Journal 20*(3), 472–494.

Cahaya, F. R., Porter, S., Tower, G. and Brown, A. (2017). Coercive pressures on occupational health and safety disclosures. *Journal of Accounting in Emerging Economies 7*(3), 318–336.

Cheng, Z., Wang, F., Christine, K. and Bai, Y. (2017). Will corporate political connection influence the environmental information disclosure level? Based on the panel data of a-shares from listed companies in Shanghai stock market. *Journal of Business Ethics 143*(1), 209–221.

Clarivate Analytics (2017). *Web of Science*. [Online] Available at: http://wokinfo. com/media/pdf/ESCI_Fact_Sheet.pdf [Accessed 20 October 2017].

Dienes, D., Sassen, R. and Fischer, J. (2016). What are the drivers of sustainability reporting? A systematic review. *Sustainability Accounting, Management and Policy Journal 7*(2), 154–189.

Du, X., Jian, W., Zeng, Q. and Du, Y. (2014). Corporate environmental responsibility in polluting industries: Does religion matter? *Journal of Business Ethics 124*(3), 485–507.

Fifka, M. S. (2012). The development and state of research on social and environmental reporting in global comparison. *Journal für Betriebswirtschaft 62*(1), 45–84.

Fifka, M. S. (2013). Corporate responsibility reporting and its determinants in comparative perspective: A review of the empirical literature and a meta-analysis. *Business Strategy and the Environment 22*(1), 1–35.

Foo, S. L. and Tan, M. S. (1988). A comparative study of social responsibility reporting in Malaysia and Singapore. *Singapore Accountant*, 12–15.

Habbash, M. (2016). Corporate governance and corporate social responsibility disclosure: Evidence from Saudi Arabia. *Social Responsibility Journal 12*(4), 740–754.

Hahn, R. and Kühnen, M. (2013). Determinants of sustainability reporting: A review of results, trends, theory, and opportunities in an expanding field of research. *Journal of Cleaner Production 59*, 5–21.

Hahn, R., Reimsbach, D. and Schiemann, F. (2015). Organizations, climate change, and transparency: Reviewing the literature on carbon disclosure. *Organization and Environment 28*(1), 80–102.

Haniffa, R. M. and Cooke, T. E. (2005). The impact of culture and governance on corporate social reporting. *Journal of Accounting and Public Policy 24*(5), 391–430.

Iatridis, G. E. (2013). Environmental disclosure quality: Evidence on environmental performance, corporate governance and value relevance. *Emerging Markets Review 14*(1), 55–75.

International Energy Agency (2017). *$CO_2$ Emissions from Fuel Combustion Highlights*, Paris: IEA Publications.

IMF (2017). *World Economic Outlook: October 2017, Seeking Sustainable Growth: Short-term Recovery, Long-term Challenges, International Monetary Fund*. IMF.

Islam, M. A. and Deegan, C. (2008). Motivations for an organization within a developing country to report social responsibility information. *Accounting, Auditing and Accountability Journal 21*(6), 850–874.

Kamla, R. and Rammal, H. (2013). Social reporting by Islamic banks: Does social justice matter? *Accounting, Auditing and Accountability Journal 26*(6), 911–945.

Khalil, S. and O'Sullivan, P. (2017). Corporate social responsibility: Internet social and environmental reporting by banks. *Meditari Accountancy Research 25*(3), 414–446.

Khan, A. R., Mutakin, M. B. and Siddiqui, J. (2012). Corporate governance and corporate social responsibility disclosures: Evidence from an emerging economy. *Journal of Business Ethics 114*(2), 207–223.

Khan, H. (2010). The effect of corporate governance elements on corporate social responsibility (CSR) reporting. *International Journal of Law and Management 52*(2), 82–109.

Kiliç, M., Kuzey, C. and Uyar, A. (2015). The impact of ownership and board structure on Corporate Social Responsibility (CSR) reporting in the Turkish banking industry. *Corporate Governance: The International Journal of Business in Society 15*(3), 357–374.

Kuo, L. and Yu, H.-C. (2017). Corporate political activity and environmental sustainability disclosure. *Baltic Journal of Management 12*(3), 348–367.

Lattemann, C., Fetscherin, M., Alon, I., Li, S. and Schneider, A. M. (2009). CSR communication intensity in Chinese and Indian multinational companies. *Corporate Governance: An International Review 17*(4), 426–442.

Lee, S. Y., Park, Y. S. and Klassen, R. D. (2015). Market responses to firms' voluntary climate change information disclosure and carbon communication. *Corporate Social Responsibility and Environmental Management 22*(1), 1–12.

Li, Q., Luo, W., Wang, Y. P. and Wu, L. S. (2013). Firm performance, corporate ownership, and corporate social responsibility disclosure in China. *Business Ethics 22*(2), 159–173.

Lynn, M. (1992). A note on corporate social disclosure in Hong Kong. *The British Accounting Review 24*(2), 105–110.

Majeed, S., Aziz, T. and Saleem, S. (2015). The effect of corporate governance elements on corporate social responsibility (CSR) disclosure: An empirical evidence from listed companies at KSE Pakistan. *International Journal of Financial Studies 3*(4), 530–556.

Mohammed, R., Alwi, K. and Jamil, C. Z. M. (2010). Sustainability disclosure among Malaysian Shari'ah-Compliant listed companies: Web reporting. *Issues in Social and Environmental Accounting 3*(2), 160–179.

Mohd Ghazali, N. A. (2007). Ownership structure and corporate social responsibility disclosure: Some Malaysian evidence. *Corporate Governance: The International Journal of Business in Society 7*(3), 251–266.

Rashid, A. and Lodh, S. C. (2008). The influence of ownership structures and board practices on corporate social disclosures in Bangladesh. *Research in Accounting in Emerging Economies 8*, 211–237.

Rouf, D. and Abdur, M. (2011). The corporate social responsibility disclosure: A study of listed companies in Bangladesh. *Business and Economics Research Journal 2*(3), 19–32.

Said, R., Zainuddin, Y. H. and Haron, H. (2009). The relationship between corporate social responsibility disclosure and corporate governance characteristics in Malaysian public listed companies. *Social Responsibility Journal 5*(2), 212–226.

Shauki, E. (2011). Perceptions on corporate social responsibility: A study in capturing public confidence. *Corporate Social Responsibility and Environmental Management 18*(3), 200-208

Shen, H., Wu, H. and Chand, P. (2017). The impact of corporate social responsibility assurance on investor decisions: Chinese evidence. *International Journal of Auditing 21*(3), 271–287.

Singh, D. R. and Ahuja, J. M. (1983). Corporate social reporting in India. *International Journal of Accounting 18*(2), 151–169.

Sobhani, F. A., Zainuddin, Y., Amran, A. and Baten, M. A. (2011). Corporate sustainability disclosure practices of selected banks: A trend analysis approach. *African Journal of Business Management 5*(7), 2794–2804.

Sobhani, F. A., Amran, A. and Zainuddin, Y. (2012). Sustainability disclosure in annual reports and websites: A study of the banking industry in Bangladesh. *Journal of Cleaner Production 23*(1), 75–85.

Teoh, H.-Y. and Thong, G. (1984). Another look at corporate social responsibility and reporting: An empirical study in a developing country. *Accounting, Organizations and Society 9*(2), 189–206.

Thompson, P. and Zakaria, Z. (2004). Corporate social responsibility reporting in Malaysia. *Journal of Corporate Citizenship 2004*(13), 125–136.

Thoradeniya, P., Lee, J., Tan, R. and Ferreira, A. (2015). Sustainability reporting and the theory of planned behavior. *Accounting, Auditing and Accountability Journal 28*(7), 1099–1137.

Trireksani, T. and Djajadikerta, H. G. (2016). Corporate governance and environmental disclosure in the Indonesian mining industry. *Australasian Accounting, Business and Finance Journal 10*(1), 18–28.

Yamagami, T. and Kokubu, K. (1991). A note on corporate social disclosure in Japan. *Accounting, Auditing and Accountability Journal 4*(4), 32–39.

Yu, S. and Rowe, A. L. (2017). Emerging phenomenon of corporate social and environmental reporting in China. *Sustainability Accounting, Management and Policy Journal 8*(3), 386–415.

Zeng, S. X., Xu, X. D., Dong, Z. Y. and Tam, V. W. Y. (2010). Towards corporate environmental information disclosure: An empirical study in China. *Journal of Cleaner Production 18*(12), 1142–1148.

Zeng, S. X., Xu, X. D., Yin, H. T. and Tam, C. M. (2012). Factors that drive Chinese listed companies in voluntary disclosure of environmental information. *Journal of Business Ethics 109*(3), 309–321.

## Chapter 11

# Which Factors Influence Sustainability Reporting in Indonesia? A Literature Review

Nurhayati Soleha

*Faculty of Economics and Business*
*University of Sultan Ageng Tirtayasa, Banten, Indonesia*

## 1. Introduction

Sustainability reporting (SR) has become an important aspect for businesses. Companies have shown a growing interest in reporting their social and environmental initiatives. This study investigates SR in a developing country, namely Indonesia. While many studies have investigated SR in developed countries (Eugénio, Lourenço & Morais, 2010; Goyal, Rahman & Kazmi, 2013), there is a scarcity of research in developing countries (Pisani *et al.*, 2017). This study explores the factors that drive SR for Indonesian companies and thus contributes to the literature on developing countries.

Indonesia had a population of 260 million and its economic growth was around 5% in 2016 (Indonesia's Statistics Agency/BPS, 2016). The Indonesian government formally regulates corporate social responsibility (CSR) practices and reporting by Law No. 40 (2007) on Limited Liability Companies, which states that companies in the field of and/or related to natural resources are obliged to be socially and environmentally responsible. The adoption of this law has created significant debate over the nature (voluntary or mandatory) of SR, as this law does not impose any sanctions on or supervise CSR disclosure (Waagstein, 2011; Shahib & Irwandi, 2016; Pujiyono, Wiwoho & Sutopo, 2017). Consequently, CSR regulation in Indonesia still raises many issues in practice and creates confusion regarding the contents and procedures.

Based on the Global Reporting Initiative (GRI), during 2007–2015, SR showed only a small percentage increase, proving the low motivation on the part of companies as well as weak influence of stakeholders (Rofelawaty, 2014; Muqodim & Susilo, 2013; Hadiningtiyas & Mahmud, 2017). Some corporations only perform SR because of external pressure from international buyers, foreign investors, and international regulatory bodies (Ali *et al.*, 2017; Waagstein, 2011; Famiola & Adiwoso, 2016; Bartley & Egels-Zanden, 2016; Park *et al.*, 2015). In particular, this research addresses the following question: what makes SR applicable in Indonesian companies? To answer this question, we carry out a literature review to analyze which determinants influence SR in Indonesian companies.

## 2. Background of SR in Indonesia

Since 1995, the government of Indonesia has encouraged CSR and environmental responsibility through the Program for Pollution Control, Evaluation and Rating (PROPER) issued by the Ministry of Environment and Forestry. Target participants of PROPER are companies that have an important environmental impact, export-oriented products, or have products that are used by the public at large. Under PROPER, a polluter is assigned one of five color ratings that correspond to environmental performance: gold (excellent), green (good), blue (adequate), red (poor), or black (very poor). The number of companies participating in PROPER has continued to grow steadily (Ratmono, Purwanto & Cahyonowati, 2014), reaching 2,076 in 2015 from only 82 in 2002. Clarkson *et al.* (2008) and Moser and Martin (2012) stated that many companies are eager to make a good impression with regard to their environmental performance.

The foundations of SR in Indonesia are Law No. 40 (2007) on Limited Liability Companies, Law No. 25 (2007) on Investment and Government Regulation, and Government Regulation No. 47 (2012) on Corporate Social Responsibility and the Environment for Limited Companies. All these laws compel companies to participate in sustainable economic development to improve the quality of life and the environment, which will benefit not only the company itself but also the local community and society in general (Pujiyono, Wiwoho & Sutopo, 2017). However, there is no standard for SR. Companies conduct SR in different forms such as SR based on the GRI, integrated reporting, stand-alone reports, and CSR disclosure in annual reports. In 2016, 55 of the companies that conducted SR based on the GRI were participants in the Indonesian Sustainability Reporting Award.

## 3. Research Method

This study employed the method of literature review based on the prior literature on SR in Indonesian companies. We selected relevant papers from EBSCOhost, Web of Science, and Indonesian publications accredited by the Directorate General of the Higher Education of Indonesia (journals in economics and management fields). The keyword search performed in March 2018 included "corporate social responsibility", "CSR", "sustainability report*", "disclosure*", "global reporting initiative", "GRI", and "Indonesia". We used "*" in a term as a wildcard to match any sequence of characters (e.g., "report*" would match documents containing "reporting" as well as "reports"). We limited the search criteria to a published date until 2017, a document type of article, and a source type of academic journal. After the screening process, we were left with 117 studies; 40 papers were from both EBSCO and Web of Science, and the remaining 77 papers were derived from Indonesian publications. For the last screening process, we selected studies examining the determinants of SR (Dienes, Sassen & Fischer, 2016), which reduced the number of studies to 45 (12 papers from EBSCO or Web of Science, and 33 papers from Indonesian publications). Also, 21 papers employed English and 24 papers used Indonesian. To obtain the results for this study, we classified the papers according to the theory employed, determinants/factors, and main findings (Lodhia & Hess, 2014; Hahn & Kühnen, 2013; Pisani *et al.*, 2017; Dienes, Sassen & Fischer, 2016; Ali *et al.*, 2017).

Following the literature in the field of SR, we structure the presentation in two parts. First, we provide a descriptive analysis that offers general information. Second, we summarize and analyze the determinants and main findings concerning SR in Indonesian companies.

## 4. Results

### 4.1 *Theories employed*

Of the studies, eight employed agency theory, six studies employed stakeholder theory, six studies used legitimacy theory, and four studies did not have an explicit theory. The remaining studies employed more than one theory. Hence, stakeholder theory was deployed by 23 (51.1%) studies, agency theory was adopted by 22 (48.9%) studies, and legitimacy theory was adopted by 20 (44.4%) studies (Table 1).

Under the stakeholder theory approach (Freeman, 1984; cited in Roberts, 1992), a stakeholder is any group or individual who can affect or is affected by the achievement of the firm's objectives. Stakeholders thus influence corporate decisions. The company aims to meet the expectations of stakeholders. If social reporting is an effective management strategy for dealing with stakeholders, stakeholder power has a positive influence on social reporting (Roberts, 1992; Ullmann, 1985; Chiu & Wang, 2015). Agency theory explains that the agency relationship is a contract between a principal and an agent doing the work on behalf of the principal, who gives authority to the agent to make the best decision for the principal (Jensen & Meckling, 1976; cited in Hadiningtiyas & Mahmud, 2017). Legitimacy theory (Deegan & Islam, 2014) asserts that organizations continually seek to ensure that they are perceived as operating within the bounds and norms of their respective societies, that is, they attempt to ensure that their activities are perceived by outside parties as legitimate. Suchman (1995) states that legitimacy is socially constructed in that it reflects a congruence between the behaviors of the entity and the social group. Legitimacy theory therefore assumes that the company will disclose SR to legitimize its activities or improve public responses.

### 4.2 *Dependent variable*

We examined the dependent variable of SR. This study found different approaches for measuring SR such as its extent, quality, and adoption of

**Table 1.** Theories employed by the sample studies.

| Theory | Study |
|---|---|
| Agency | Wijantini (2006), Nuryaman (2009), Cahyaningsih and Martina (2011), Jaffar, Mardinah and Ahmad (2013), Faizal and Probohudono (2013), Lukito and Susanto (2013), Widyadmono (2014), Hapsoro and Fadhilla (2017) |
| Stakeholder | Susi (2009), Rahardja *et al.* (2011), Shauki (2011), Nussy (2013, 2014), Handoyo and Jakasurya (2017) |
| Legitimacy | Rahman and Widyasari (2008), Kartika and Puspa (2013), Ratmono, Purwanto and Cahyonowati (2014), Nasution and Adhariani (2016), Nugraheni and Permatasari (2016), Shahib and Irwandi (2016) |
| Institutional | Cahaya *et al.* (2015) |
| Agency, stakeholder | Frendy and Kusuma (2011), Pujiningsih and Utami (2011), Sari, Sutrisno and Sukoharsono (2013), Ibrahim, Solikahan and Widyatama (2015) |
| Stakeholder, legitimacy | Gunawan (2007, 2015), Yuliana, Purnomosid and Sukoharsono (2008), Kiswanto (2016), Anggraeni and Djakman (2017), Sinaga and Fachrurrozie (2017) |
| Agency, signaling | Almilia (2008, 2010) |
| Agency, legitimacy | Solikhah and Winarsih (2016) |
| Agency, stakeholder, legitimacy | Wardani (2012), Riantani and Nurzamzam (2015), Anggiyani and Yanto (2016), Krisna and Suhardianto (2016), Taufik (2016), Hadiningtiyas and Mahmud (2017), Junita and Yulianto (2017) |
| No explicit theory | Margaretha and Isnaini (2014), Nugraheni and Anuar (2014), Susilawati, Tin and Agustina (2014), Trireksani and Djajadikerta (2016) |

reporting. The measurement of the extent of SR considers whether the items are disclosed in an annual report, sustainability report, integrated report, or environmental performance report (score = 1) or not disclosed (score = 0). Then, the number of SR items disclosed by the company is divided by the total number of SR disclosure items. The quality of disclosure is the provision of information ranging from narrative or descriptive disclosure to a description of monetary and non-monetary data. The adoption of SR mainly deals with the decision to engage in reporting from the perspective of the stakeholders. Most studies ($n = 36$) adopted the content analysis method to measure the extent of SR.

## 4.3 *Independent variables*

### 4.3.1 *Firm size*

Firm size was used in 25 studies. Note that 16 studies found a positive significant influence of firm size on SR, eight studies did not find any influence of firm size on SR, and one study found a negative influence. Therefore, firm size tends to influence SR positively, suggesting that large companies have sufficient resources to carry out SR (Table 2).

### 4.3.2 *Profitability*

Profitability was used in 24 studies as a determinant, where 10 studies found a positive significant influence of profitability on SR, 13 studies detected no significant influence on SR, and one study indicated a negative influence. Empirical research on this determinant thus provides

**Table 2.**  Independent variable of firm size.

| Firm size | Study |
|---|---|
| Number of employees | Yuliana, Purnomosid and Sukoharsono (2008) (0), Ibrahim, Solikahan and Widyatama (2015) (−) |
| Total assets | Wijantini (2006) (+), Almilia (2008) (+), Susi (2009) (+), Almilia (2010) (+), Frendy and Kusuma (2011) (+), Wardani (2012) (+), Faizal and Probohudono (2013) (+), Kartika and Puspa (2013) (+), Lukito and Susanto (2013) (+), Nugraheni and Anuar (2014) (+), Widyadmono (2014) (+), Riantani and Nurzamzam (2015) (+), Anggiyani and Yanto (2016) (+), Krisna and Suhardianto (2016) (+), Taufik (2016) (+), Junita and Yulianto (2017) (+), Gunawan (2007) (0), Rahman and Widyasari (2008) (0), Cahyaningsih and Martina (2011) (0), Sari, Sutrisno and Sukoharsono (2013) (0), Nussy (2014) (0), Susilawati, Tin and Agustina (2014) (0) |
| Total sales | Nuryaman (2009) (+) |

*Notes*: (+) = positive influence on the dependent variable; (−) = negative influence; (0) = no significant influence.

**Table 3.**   Independent variable of profitability.

| Profitability | Study |
| --- | --- |
| Return on assets | Gunawan (2007) (+), Almilia (2008) (+), Wardani (2012) (+), Frendy and Kusuma (2011) (+), Kartika and Puspa (2013) (+), Taufik (2016) (+), Kiswanto (2016) (+), Handoyo and Jakasurya (2017) (+), Susi (2009) (0), Yuliana, Purnomosid and Sukoharsono (2008) (0), Almilia (2010) (0), Riantani and Nurzamzam (2015) (0), Krisna and Suhardianto (2016) (0), Anggiyani and Yanto (2016) (0), Shahib and Irwandi (2016) (0) |
| Return on equity | Sari, Sutrisno and Sukoharsono (2013) (+), Almilia (2008) (0), Shahib and Irwandi (2016) (0), Lukito and Susanto (2013) (0), Junita and Yulianto (2017) (0) |
| Profit margin | Nussy (2014) (+), Sinaga and Fachrurrozie (2017) (–), Rahman and Widyasari (2008) (0), Susilawati, Tin and Agustina (2014) (0) |

*Notes*: (+) = positive influence on the dependent variable; (–) = negative influence; (0) = no significant influence.

contradictory results, suggesting that companies with large or small profits are still required to disclose information to shareholders and the public (Table 3).

### 4.3.3 *Industry type*

Industry type was a determinant used in 13 studies. Nine studies exhibited a positive influence of industry type on SR, three studies did not find an effect of industry type on SR, and one study found a negative influence. Therefore, industry type tends to have a positive influence on SR. Companies in high-profile industries can have a direct impact on the environment (Table 4).

### 4.3.4 *Corporate governance structure*

Corporate governance structure, which was used in 18 studies, can be proxied by six variables. One study used more than one independent variable. The number of members of the board of commissioners (BoC) and board of directors (BoD) as well as the number of board meetings were used as determinants in seven studies. Five studies found a positive

Table 4.  Independent variable of industry type.

| Industry type | Study |
|---|---|
| High/low-profile company, dummy variable (high = 1, low = 0) | Rahman and Widyasari (2008) (+), Yuliana, Purnomosid and Sukoharsono (2008) (+), Susi (2009) (+), Almilia (2010) (+), Frendy and Kusuma (2011) (+), Susilawati, Tin and Agustina (2014) (+), Widyadmono (2014) (+), Solikhah and Winarsih (2016) (+), Sinaga and Fachrurrozie (2017) (+), Nugraheni and Anuar (2014) (−), Gunawan (2007) (0), Kartika and Puspa (2013) (0), Hadiningtiyas and Mahmud (2017) (0) |

*Notes*: (+) = positive influence on the dependent variable; (−) = negative influence; (0) = no significant influence.

influence of the number of members of the BoC and BoD on SR, while two studies did not find any influence on SR. Hence, the number of board members and board meetings tend to positively influence SR, perhaps because BoC and BoD members encourage SR.

Thirteen studies used the number of independent members on the BoC. Four studies detected a positive relationship between independent commissioners and SR. Eight studies did not find a relationship between independent commissioners and SR, and only one study found a negative relationship. According to the results, the number of independent commissioners had little relationship with SR. Likewise, the number of female members on the board had no relationship with SR. Only one study examined the presence of family members on the BoC and the results showed a negative influence on SR (Table 5).

According to Law No. 40 (2007), a company is a separate legal entity with two tiers of boards (i.e., the BoC and the BoD). Each member of the BoC and BoD is appointed by shareholders during the company's General Meeting. The BoC consists of affiliated and independent commissioners. Affiliated commissioners are family members of major shareholders or business associates of the major shareholders or the company, while independent commissioners are members with no family or business ties with the major shareholders or the company. All BoC members are non-executives as they cannot hold any executive duties in an organization. The role of the BoC is to supervise and advise the BoD on the running of the company, assisted by supporting committees. The audit committee is

**Table 5.**    Independent variable of corporate governance structure.

| Corporate governance structure | Study |
| --- | --- |
| Number of BoC/BoD members | Solikhah and Winarsih (2016) (+), Trireksani and Djajadikerta (2016) (+), Hapsoro and Fadhilla (2017) (+), Yuliana, Purnomosid and Sukoharsono (2008) (0), Krisna and Suhardianto (2016) (0) |
| Number of board meetings | Junita and Yulianto (2017) (+), Sinaga and Fachrurrozie (2017) (+) |
| Number of independent members on the BoC | Jaffar, Mardinah and Ahmad (2013) (+), Nussy (2013) (+), Trireksani and Djajadikerta (2016) (+), Hapsoro and Fadhilla (2017) (+), Solikhah and Winarsih (2016) (−), Nuryaman (2009) (0), Cahyaningsih and Martina (2011) (0), Frendy and Kusuma (2011) (0), Pujiningsih and Utami (2011) (0), Sari, Sutrisno and Sukoharsono (2013) (0), Margaretha and Isnaini (2014) (0), Kiswanto (2016) (0), Sinaga and Fachrurrozie (2017) (0) |
| Number of audit committee members | Nussy (2013) (+), Krisna and Suhardianto (2016) (+), Kiswanto (2016) (+) |
| Number of female members on the board | Margaretha and Isnaini (2014) (−), Solikhah and Winarsih (2016) (0), Nugraheni and Permatasari (2016) (0), Trireksani and Djajadikerta (2016) (0), Anggraeni and Djakman (2017) (0) |
| Percentage of family members on the BoC | Jaffar, Mardinah and Ahmad (2013) (−) |

*Notes*: (+) = positive influence on the dependent variable; (−) = negative influence; (0) = no significant influence.

responsible for reviewing and assessing the company's risk management. By contrast, the BoD is fully responsible for the management of the company. However, when dominant BoC members are family members, it weakens the position of independent commissioners. BoC members are not truly independent, as commissioner members cannot function and monitor properly. Proposed family members can have easier access to internal information. Agency conflict is not visible and this affects the lack of encouragement of management to conduct SR (Cahyaningsih & Martina, 2011; Sinaga & Fachrurrozie, 2017).

### 4.3.5 *Capital structure*

Sixteen studies analyzed capital structure by using total debt over total equity and total debt over total assets. One study found a positive influence on SR and five studies found a negative influence. Ten studies found no effect. According to these findings, most studies find that a capital structure derived from debt does not affect SR. It appears that companies with high or low leverage provide SR to show the openness of management, which creates a positive image of the company. This openness of management is expected to generate the trust of creditors and other stakeholders (Table 6).

### 4.3.6 *Ownership structure*

Ownership structure was proxied by four variables: percentage of shares held by the institution/majority shareholder, percentage of shares held by the management over total shareholders, percentage of shares held by foreign shareholders over total shareholders, and government ownership. Ownership structure was used in 27 studies. Eight studies found a positive influence of institutional shareholders on SR, whereas eight studies found no effect and one study found a negative effect of institutional shareholders on SR. The findings on the influence of institutional shareholders on SR are thus inconsistent. Inconsistent results are also observed for foreign

**Table 6.** Independent variable of capital structure.

| Capital structure | Study |
|---|---|
| Total debt over total equity | Widyadmono (2014) (–), Anggiyani and Yanto (2016) (–), Nugraheni and Permatasari (2016) (–), Wijantini (2006) (0), Rahman and Widyasari (2008) (0), Cahyaningsih and Martina (2011) (0), Wardani (2012) (0), Susilawati, Tin and Agustina (2014) (0), Riantani and Nurzamzam (2015) (0), Krisna and Suhardianto (2016) (0) |
| Total debt over total assets | Handoyo and Jakasurya (2017) (+), Frendy and Kusuma (2011) (–), Lukito and Susanto (2013) (–), Almilia (2008) (0), Almilia (2010) (0), Kartika and Puspa (2013) (0) |

*Notes*: (+) = positive influence on the dependent variable; (–) = negative influence; (0) = no significant influence.

**Table 7.** Independent variable of ownership structure.

| Ownership structure | Study |
|---|---|
| Percentage of shares held by institution/ majority shareholder over total shareholders | Almilia (2008) (+), Yuliana, Purnomosid and Sukoharsono (2008) (+), Nuryaman (2009) (+), Almilia (2010) (+), Faizal and Probohudono (2013) (+), Nussy (2013) (+), Sari, Sutrisno and Sukoharsono (2013) (+), Ibrahim, Solikahan and Widyatama (2015) (+), Frendy and Kusuma (2011) (−), Cahyaningsih and Martina (2011) (0), Pujiningsih and Utami (2011) (0), Kartika and Puspa (2013) (0), Lukito and Susanto (2013) (0), Nugraheni and Anuar (2014) (0), Solikhah and Winarsih (2016) (0), Kiswanto (2016) (0), Hapsoro and Fadhilla (2017) (0) |
| Percentage of shares held by management over total shareholders | Kiswanto (2016) (+), Rahman and Widyasari (2008) (0), Jaffar, Mardinah and Ahmad (2013) (0), Nussy (2013) (0), Hapsoro and Fadhilla (2017) (0), Hadiningtiyas and Mahmud (2017) (0), Junita and Yulianto (2017) (0) |
| Percentage of shares held by foreign shareholders over total shareholders | Faizal and Probohudono (2013) (+), Susilawati, Tin and Agustina (2014) (+), Hapsoro and Fadhilla (2017) (−), Lukito and Susanto (2013) (0), Handoyo and Jakasurya (2017) (0) |
| Government ownership | Cahaya *et al.* (2015) (0) |

*Notes*: (+) = positive influence on the dependent variable; (−) = negative influence; (0) = no significant influence.

ownership. By contrast, the dominant determinant of managerial owner-ship has an insignificant influence on SR. Six studies found no effect of managerial ownership on SR. Only one study showed a positive influence on SR. However, most of the results of ownership structure are found to have an insignificant influence on SR (Table 7).

### 4.3.7 *Auditor use, media, firm age, and environmental performance*

Five studies examined the correlation between the use of auditors and SR. Four studies found a positive relationship between auditor usage and SR (Kartika & Puspa, 2013; Jaffar, Mardinah & Ahmad, 2013; Nuryaman, 2009; Solikhah & Winarsih, 2016), while Nugraheni and Anuar (2014) observed no effect. The findings suggest a positive influence on SR. Two studies adopted media (proxied by the number of articles or magazines) as a determinant. Junita and Yulianto (2017) found a positive correlation, while Solikhah and Winarsih (2016) did not. Five studies used firm age. Susilawati, Tin and Agustina (2014) and Kiswanto (2016) observed a positive influence of firm age on SR, whereas Gunawan (2007) and Kartika and Puspa (2013) found no effect and Wardani (2012) found a negative effect. Inconsistent results also occur for environmental performance. Ratmono, Purwanto and Cahyonowati (2014) found a positive correlation between environmental performance and SR. Kiswanto (2016) and Hadiningtiyas and Mahmud (2017) did not find any effect. Auditor use, media, firm age, and environmental performance are all underrepresented as determinants.

## 5. Discussion and Conclusion

This study carried out a literature review of 45 studies and analyzed the factors that drive SR in Indonesian companies. The results showed that the most frequently examined determinants are corporate governance structure, ownership structure, firm size, profitability, capital structure, and industry type. Three of these factors, namely firm size, industry type (high-profile industries), and corporate governance structure (proxied by the number of board members), tend to have a positive influence on SR. High-profile companies use natural resources and/or have a direct impact on the environment, thereby affecting SR. The findings show that high-profile companies, larger companies, and board members are more active in reporting higher social responsibility. Larger companies are more vulnerable to high political costs as well. Furthermore, under Law No. 40 (2007) and Government Regulation No. 47 (2012), companies having a direct impact on the environment and listed companies are required to disclose SR.

By contrast, ownership structure, capital structure, and corporate governance structure (proxied by the number of independent commissioners) were found to be insignificant for SR. This finding indicates that a company perceives little pressure from shareholders to conduct SR, which is similar to a managerial ownership structure. When managers have considerable ownership of a company, they are less inclined to provide detailed SR, as the required information is directly accessible from the organization. In addition, companies that have high or low leverage usually carry out SR to demonstrate their positive image, as this boosts the trust of creditors and other stakeholders.

Other determinants such as profitability, auditor use, media, firm age, and environmental performance showed inconsistent results because the measurements used in the reporting are diverse. Indeed, there is no uniformity in the disclosure of SR, with most studies finding that companies include such reports in their annual reports; a small number deliver SR in accordance with GRI standards. Owing to the different forms of sustainability reports, the researchers also used different measurement indicators.

The studies covered in this literature review only examined companies listed on the Indonesia Stock Exchange (IDX). The sample is thus not representative of most of the companies in Indonesia. For example, the studies used a maximum sample size of 110 of the 500 companies listed on the IDX, whereas the number of participating companies in PROPER was 2,076 in 2015.

Furthermore, the unique corporate governance framework in Indonesia has also been identified as one of the reasons for inconsistent results. Indonesia has one of the highest number of family-controlled firms in the world. Hence, in certain instances, members of the BoC in Indonesian companies may not be completely independent since they are appointed owing to their affiliation with major shareholders or with the company itself. The presence of family members on the board is believed to affect the practice of SR. Since family members have access to internal information, the need for additional reporting may be lower.

Regarding the theories employed to explain SR, the majority of studies used stakeholder theory and agency theory, perhaps because the ownership structure and corporate governance structure are the dominant determinants. These theories thus seem relevant because stakeholder power is the major influence on SR.

Several suggestions for future research follow from the presented findings. First, it is crucial to examine the effect of family ownership on the level of SR in a country with such a large proportion of family-controlled firms. Second, examining SR behavior in foreign firms might also be an interesting topic. Indeed, even when SR regulations are weak, foreign companies can still conduct SR.

These findings have practical implications. To encourage companies to implement SR, especially family firms, the Indonesian government has conducted socialization and seminars on the importance of SR. The role of directors and commissioners is crucial in the decision to implement SR. Furthermore, independent commissioners need to use their authority and power within corporate governance structures to encourage the company to legitimize its corporate social and environmental activities.

## References

Ali, W., Frynas, J. G. and Mahmood, Z. (2017). Determinants of CSR disclosure in developed and developing countries: A literature review. *Corporate Social Responsibility and Environmental Management 24*(4), 273–294.

Almilia, L. S. (2008). The factors influence on Internet Financial and Sustainability Reporting (IFSR). *Journal of Indonesian Audit and Accounting 12*(2), 117–131.

Almilia, L. S. (2010). Factors of financial and non-financial influence on IFSR in Indonesia Stock Exchange. *Journal of Indonesian Economy and Business 25*(2), 201–221.

Anggiyani, S. W. and Yanto, H. (2016). The determinant of SR on companies listed in IDX. *Accounting Analysis Journal 5*(2), 1–10.

Anggraeni, D. Y. and Djakman, C. D. (2017). Slack resources, board's feminism, and the quality of corporate social responsibility disclosure. *Indonesian Journal of Accounting and Finance 14*(1), 94–118.

Bartley, T. and Egels-Zanden, N. (2016). Beyond decoupling: Unions and the leveraging of corporate social responsibility in Indonesia. *Norsk Geografisk Tidsskrift/Norwegian Journal of Geography 68*(5), 282–290.

Cahaya, R., Porter, S., Tower, G. and Brown, A. (2015). The Indonesian Government's coercive pressure on labour disclosures: Conflicting interests or government ambivalence? *Sustainability Accounting, Management and Policy Journal 6*(4), 475–497.

Cahyaningsih and Martina, V. Y. (2011). The influence of corporate governance mechanisms and firm characteristics on CSR disclosure. *Jurnal Siasat Bisnis/Journal of Business Tactics 15*(2), 171–186.

Chiu, T.-K. and Wang, Y.-H. (2015). Determinants of social disclosure quality in Taiwan: An application of stakeholder theory. *Journal of Business Ethics* *129*(2), 379–398.

Clarkson, P. M., Li, Y., Richardson, G. D. and Vasvari, F. P. (2008). Revisiting the relation between environmental performance and environmental disclosure: An empirical analysis. *Accounting, Organizations and Society Journal 33*, 303–327.

Deegan, C. and Islam, M. A. (2014). An exploration of NGO and media efforts to influence workplace practices and associated accountability within global supply chains. *The British Accounting Review 46*, 397–415.

Dienes, D., Sassen, R. and Fischer, J. (2016). What are the drivers of sustainability reporting? A systematic review. *Sustainability Accounting, Management and Policy Journal 7*(2), 154–189.

Eugénio, T., Lourenço, I. C. and Morais, A. I. (2010). Recent developments in social and environmental accounting research. *Social Responsibility Journal 6*(2), 286–305.

Faizal, R. P. and Probohudono, A. N. (2013). The factors affected the voluntary disclosure in IFSR. *Journal of Bank and Finance 17*(1), 87–101.

Famiola, M. and Adiwoso, S. A. (2016). CSR diffusion by multinational subsidiaries in Indonesia: Organisational dynamic and institutional effect. *Social Responsibility Journal 12*(1), 117–129.

Frendy and Kusuma, I. W. (2011). The impact of financial, non-financial, and corporate governance attributes on the practice of GRI based environmental disclosure. *Gadjah Mada International Journal of Business 13*(2), 143–159.

Goyal, P., Rahman, Z. and Kazmi, A. A. (2013). Corporate sustainability performance and firm performance research: Literature review and future research agenda. *Management Decision 51*(2), 361–379.

Gunawan, J. (2007). Corporate social disclosures by Indonesian listed companies: A pilot study. *Social Responsibility Journal 3*(3), 26–34.

Gunawan, J. (2015). Corporate social disclosures in Indonesia: Stakeholders' influence and motivation. *Social Responsibility Journal 11*(3), 535–552.

Hadiningtiyas, S. W. and Mahmud, A. (2017). Determinant of environmental disclosure on companies listed in IDX. *Accounting Analysis Journal 6*(3), 380–393.

Hahn, R. and Kühnen, M. (2013). Determinants of sustainability reporting: A review of results, trends, theory, and opportunities in an expanding field of research. *Journal of Cleaner Production 59*, 5–21.

Handoyo, S. and Jakasurya, T. (2017). Analyze the factors influencing disclosure level of CSR. *Jurnal Manajemen, Strategi Bisnis dan Kewirausahaan/ Journal of Entrepreneurship, Business Strategic and Management 11*(2), 178–187.

Hapsoro, D. and Fadhilla, A. F. (2017). Relationship analysis of corporate governance, corporate social responsibility disclosure and economic consequences. *South East Asian Journal of Management 11*(2), 164–182.

Ibrahim, M., Solikahan, E. Z. and Widyatama, A. (2015). The characteristics of the company, CSR disclosure and corporate value. *Jurnal Akuntansi Multiparadigma/Journal of Paradigm Accounting 6*(1), 99–106.

Jaffar, R., Mardinah, D. and Ahmad, A. (2013). Corporate governance and voluntary disclosure practices. *Jurnal Pengurusan/Journal of Management 39*, 83–92.

Junita, N. L. and Yulianto, A. (2017). Determinants influence on environmental disclosure in high profile in Indonesian companies. *Accounting Analysis Journal 6*(3), 420–431.

Kartika and Puspa (2013). Company characteristics as the IFSR determinants. *Journal of Bank and Finance 17*(2), 181–191.

Kiswanto, T. A. (2016). The determinant of carbon emission disclosures. *Accounting Analysis Journal 5*(4), 326–336.

Krisna, A. D. and Suhardianto, N. (2016). The factors influence CSR disclosures. *Journal of Finance and Accounting 18*(2), 119–128.

Lodhia, S. and Hess, N. (2014). Sustainability accounting and reporting in the mining industry: Current literature and directions for future research. *Journal of Cleaner Production 84*, 43–50.

Lukito, Y. P. and Susanto, Y. K. (2013). The factors that affected the voluntary disclosure of IFSR. *Journal of Bank and Finance 17*(1), 61–70.

Margaretha, F. and Isnaini, R. (2014). Board diversity and gender composition on CSR. *Journal of Entrepreneurship and Management 16*(1), 1–8.

Moser, D. V. and Martin, P. R. (2012). A broader perspective on corporate social responsibility research in accounting. *The Accounting Review 87*(3), 797–806.

Muqodim and Susilo, J. (2013). Triple bottom line reporting in the annual report in Indonesia. *Jurnal Akuntansi dan Audit Indonesia/Journal of Indonesian Audit and Accounting 17*(2), 31–42.

Nasution, R. M. and Adhariani, D. (2016). Symbolic or substantive? Analysis of CSR reporting practices and the quality of disclosure. *Indonesian Journal of Accounting and Finance 13*(1), 23–51.

Nugraheni, P. and Anuar, H. A. (2014). Implications of Shariah on the voluntary disclosure in Indonesian listed companies. *Journal of Financial Reporting and Accounting 12*(1), 76–98.

Nugraheni, P. and Permatasari, D. (2016). The sharia compliant companies provide and corporate social responsibility disclosure. *Jurnal Akuntansi dan Audit Indonesia/Journal of Indonesian Audit and Accounting 20*(2), 136–146.

Nuryaman (2009). The effect of ownership concentration, firms size, and corporate governance mechanisms on voluntary disclosure. *Journal of Indonesian Finance and Accounting 6*(1), 89–116.

Nussy, T. M. (2013). The effect of corporate governance and ethnicity on the CSR disclosure. *Journal of Bank and Finance 17*(1), 1–10.

Nussy, T. M. (2014). CSR disclosure in Indonesian banking. *Jurnal Keuangan dan Perbankan/Journal of Bank and Finance 18*(2), 329–334.

Park, Y. R., Song, S., Choe, S. and Baik, Y. (2015). Corporate social responsibility in international business: Illustrations from Korean and Japanese electronics MNEs in Indonesia. *Journal of Business Ethics 129*, 747–761.

Pisani, N., Kourula, A., Kolk, A. and Meijer, R. (2017). How global is international CSR research? Insights and recommendations from a systematic review. *Journal of World Business 52*, 591–614.

Pujiningsih, S. and Utami, H. (2011). GCG on CSR disclosure. *Journal of Bank and Finance 15*(2), 168–177.

Pujiyono, P., Wiwoho, J. and Sutopo, W. (2017). Implementation of Javanese traditional value in creating the accountable corporate social responsibility. *International Journal of Law and Management, 59*(6), 964–976.

Rahardja, E., Zain, D. J., Salim, U. and Rahayu, M. (2011). Implementation of CSR and implication in perspective stakeholder theory. *Jurnal Aplikasi Manajemen/Journal of Management Application 9*(2), 535–544.

Rahman, A. and Widyasari, K. N. (2008). The analysis of company characteristic influence toward CSR disclosure. *Journal of Indonesian Audit and Accounting 12*(1), 25–35.

Ratmono, D., Purwanto, A. and Cahyonowati, N. (2014). The relationship between CSR performance and CSR disclosure and earnings management. *Journal of Finance and Accounting 16*(2), 63–73.

Riantani, S. and Nurzamzam, H. (2015). Analysis of company size, financial leverage, and profitability and its effect to CSR disclosure. *Jurnal Dinamika Manajemen/Journal of Management Dynamics 6*(2), 203–213.

Roberts, R. W. (1992). Determinants of corporate social responsibility disclosure: An application of stakeholder theory. *Accounting, Organizations and Society 17*(6), 595–612.

Rofelawaty, B. (2014). A practical analysis of sustainability reporting on companies listed on the Indonesia stock exchange. *Jurnal Aplikasi Manajemen/ Journal of Management Application 12*(2), 258–268.

Sari, A. R., Sutrisno and Sukoharsono, E. G. (2013). The effect of institutional ownership, the composition of the board of commissioners, firm performance toward the extent CSR disclosure in the SR on manufacture companies listed in IDX. *Jurnal Aplikasi Manajemen/Journal of Management Application 11*(3), 481–491.

Shahib, H. B. and Irwandi, S. A. (2016). Violation regulation of financial services authority (FSA), financial performance, and corporate social responsibility disclosure. *Journal of Economics, Business, and Accountancy Ventura 19*(1), 141–154.

Shauki, E. (2011). Perceptions on corporate social responsibility: A study in capturing public confidence. *Corporate Social Responsibility and Environmental Management 18*(3), 200–208.

Sinaga, K. J. and Fachrurrozie (2017). The effect of profitability, activity analysis, industrial type and GCG mechanism on the SR. *Accounting Analysis Journal 6*(3), 347–358.

Solikhah, B. and Winarsih, A. M. (2016). The effect of media coverage, industry sensitivity and corporate governance structure on environmental disclosure quality. *Journal of Indonesian Finance and Accounting 13*(1), 1–22.

Suchman, M. C. (1995). Managing legitimacy: Strategic and institutional approaches. *Academy of Management Review 20*(3), 571–610.

Susi (2009). The occurrence of environmental disclosures in the annual reports. *Journal of Indonesian Audit and Accounting 13*(1), 29–42.

Susilawati, C. D. K., Tin, S. and Agustina, L. (2014). The fundamental factors and types of industries to CSR and their impact on stock prices. *Jurnal Keuangan dan Perbankan /Journal of Bank and Finance 18*(3), 384–395.

Taufik (2016). The mediating effect of profitability on the relationship of GCG and firm size on corporate social responsibility. *Jurnal Ilmiah Manajemen/ Journal of Management Science VI*(3), 399–415.

Trireksani, T. and Djajadikerta, H. G. (2016). Corporate governance and environmental disclosure in the Indonesian mining industry. *Australasian Accounting Business and Finance Journal 10*(1), 17–28.

Ullmann, A. A. (1985). Data in search of a theory: A critical examination of the relationship among social performance, social disclosure, and economic performance of U.S. Firms. *The Academy of Management Review 10*(3), 540–557.

Waagstein, P. R. (2011). The mandatory corporate social responsibility in Indonesia: Problems and implications. *Journal of Business Ethics 98*, 455–466.

Wardani, R. P. (2012). The affecting factors of voluntary disclosure. *Journal of Finance and Accounting 14*(1), 1–15.

Widyadmono, V. M. (2014). The impact of industry type, company size and leverage on the disclosure of corporate social responsibility. *Jurnal Siasat Bisnis/ Journal of Business Tactics 18*(1), 118–132.

Wijantini (2006). Voluntary disclosure in the annual reports of financially distressed companies in Indonesia. *Gadjah Mada International Journal of Business 8*(3), 343–365.

Yuliana, R., Purnomosid, B. and Sukoharsono, E. G. (2008). The effect of firm characteristics on CSR disclosure and the impact on the investors reactions. *Journal of Indonesian Finance and Accounting 5*(2), 245–276.

# Part 4

# Advanced Topics

## Chapter 12

# Pricing Strategy and Cost Compensation of the Platforms of a Two-sided Market — With a Case Study of Amazon Online Shopping

Yasuhiro Monden

*University of Tsukuba 1 Chome 1 – 1 Tennodai, Tsukuba*
*Ibaraki Prefecture 305-8577, Japan*

## 1. Background and Research Theme

Amazon appeared in 1995 in the United States, when the "internet shopping" phenomenon started, spreading throughout the world due to smartphone popularization since 2010.

However, the barrier between real stores and internet shopping became lower and their mutual cooperation has increased the popularity of both.

In the academic world, the concept of the "two-sided market" is often used to describe the market operated by *platforms* such as Amazon or Google that mitigate the activities of two sets of economic entities or participants in the virtual market. The concept of the two-sided market was first advocated by Rochet and Tirole (2003, 2006).

As shown in Fig. 1, participant $C$ is the consumer of the goods provided by participant $S$ in the platform. Both participants $C$ and $S$ must pay for their use of the market (i.e., platform) to enjoy the services provided by the platform.

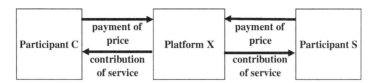

**Fig. 1.**   Conceptual framework of a two-sided market of platform *X*.

Such payment must be made to compensate for use of the services (i.e., "contribution") endowed by the platformer. The question of *the determination of the amount to be paid by participants C and S to compensate for the contributions endowed by the platformer* is *the main theme of this chapter*. Such payments could be interpreted as the "payments of incentives" to induce or motivate cooperation by the platformer.

## 2. "Indirect Network Effect" of Amazon as the Two-sided Market

In terms of the participants in the network, there are two types of "network effects". The first is referred to as the "direct network effect", which is the effect that appears among the users of participant *C*'s network. That is, the effect on participants when the number of participants in *C* increases. An example of such an effect is the increase in the number of users of Microsoft personal computers.

The second effect is referred to as the "indirect network effect", which is the effect that causes an increase in the number of members in *S* to occur when there is an increase in the number of members in *C*. That is, there is an indirect relationship between the increase in the number of members in *S* and the increase in number of participants *C*.

It is due to the indirect network effect that the platform business model has the peculiar characteristic of a "two-sided market", though most of their features can be found in conventional supply chains, such as the relationship between the parts suppliers and the assembler of automobile. (For more details of the indirect network effect, see Odagiri (2016, p. 227).)

Let us consider participants *C* and *S* and the network effect of Amazon as an example of a platform business model. Amazon is "market provider *X*" in the internet shopping business or the "virtual shopping street", where the "consumers $C$" are the retrievers or searchers on the internet via the site of Amazon, or the buyers of goods or services in the shops on the virtual shopping street, and the "sellers $S$" are the real shops that sell goods or services and also act as real advertisers of various goods.

It would be better for real advertiser $S$ to show their business on platform $X$, which receives a greater number of searchers $C$, so that the larger "indirect network effect" could be received.

## 3. How should the Prices to be Paid by Participants $C$ and $S$ be Determined in the Two-sided Market?

Figure 1 illustrates this issue. The price to be charged to retriever $C$ in the platform is referred to as $P^C$, while the price to be charged to advertiser $S$ is called $P^S$. Thus, the aim of this chapter is to investigate how such prices ($P^C$ and $P^S$) will be determined. To understand this problem, it is necessary to explain the concepts of "imperfect competition market" or "monopolistic market."

### 3.1 *Characteristics of the imperfect competition market*

There are many platformers (i.e., platform providers) in a certain market (e.g., a real estate market). They are competing with each other to attract as many consumers $C$ and sellers $S$ as possible.

Each real estate agent (realtor) proposes his/her own price $P^C$ to buyer $C$ and price $P^S$ to seller $S$. Although such realtors are competing with each other, the market is not in perfect competition and therefore some larger realtor often has some market governing power.

The reason why the market is so imperfect lies in the fact that the goods or service they provide is not identical, but "differentiated" in some aspect. E. H. Chamberlin referred to this as a *monopolistic competition market*, but it is now often referred to as an "imperfect competition market". In addition, since the "critical mass", which is the minimum volume needed to successfully enter the platform market, is in many cases hard to achieve, the market will be imperfect.

Thus, in the two-sided market under imperfect competition, the equality between the price and the marginal cost or the balance between supply and demand quantities would rarely be achieved, making price determination in the two-sided market complicated.

### 3.2 *Model of the price determination strategy of the platform*

The price setting and the profit of platformer $X$ are as follows:

The revenue of platformer $X$ when member $C$ and member $S$ only pay the basic registration fees (i.e., subscription fee) at the time of their entry into the platform will be similar to the subscription fee at the entry time of a newspaper buyer, for example.

Since the membership fee $P^C$ for subscriber $C$, and the advertising rate $P^S$ for promoting real company $S$ on the platform's website will be collected at the point of subscription, the following basic equation is formulated since the revenue will be price P multiplied by demand D.

Revenue of Platform $X$ = membership revenue $P^C D^C$ given by the
subscriber $C$ + advertising revenue $P^S D^S$ given
by the advertising real company $S$

Thus, the total profit of the platform = $(P^C D^C + P^S D^S)$ – total expenses, where the total expenses include the total amount of *fixed costs* as the initial investment and variable costs made by the platformer. A certain amount of such initial fixed costs might become "sunk cost" unless the "critical mass" (i.e., minimum necessary number of customer firms for the platform to be successful) is achieved.

### 3.2.1 *Unique characteristics of platform business*

Now the readers may be aware of the fact that companies such as Amazon or Google would charge a relatively *higher* amount of advertising rates from the real stores $S$, while they charge a relatively *lower* amount of subscription fee from visitors $C$ to their websites, and *most of the participants C would be non-fee paying customers*. Such a business model is a unique characteristic of the internet platform business.

Thanks to the aforementioned "indirect network effect", this is applicable as long as the number of visitors $C$ to the Amazon website or the market (platform) itself could increase and thus make the platform attractive for the real store $S$, attracting a greater number of real stores $S$ to participate in the platform (*TheNikkei* (2018 a)). As a result, the amount of $P^S D^S$ could be so large that the total cost of the platformer is compensated, even though the fee $P^C$ charged to the visiting consumers $C$ may be zero or very low.

## 4. Barriers Restricting Entry into the Two-sided Market and the Diversified Business

The factor that has a significant effect on the price level of the two-sided market is the level of competition or the difficulty of entry into the market.

There is also the aforementioned problem of "critical mass". Unless the critical mass of the number of participants $C$ was achieved, the opening investment made by platformer $X$ would be a "sunk cost", which is the amount of investment that could not be covered, and it will be the barrier restricting the entry into such a two-sided market.

One of the strategies for the platformer to solve such a barrier is to engage in "*diversified business*" for risk spreading. In other words, a company that entered the market to establish the platform $X_1$, which has attracted a certain number of customers $C_1$ may enter another platform $X_2$ while suggesting that the existing customers $C_1$ of $X_1$ utilize the new platform $X_2$ at the same time.

For example, a newspaper company may enter the broadcasting business as its second business or an electricity company may enter the gas business as its second business in addition to the existing electricity business. This type of diversified business model could be operated if the same customers are involved in both the former and latter businesses at the same time.

## 5. Three Patterns of the Amazon Business Model

How should the amount of payment, as incentives in the form of various shared costs, be determined to compensate for and motivate platformer's contribution in their services? This problem and its solution can be analyzed and verified using a case study of the Amazon business model.

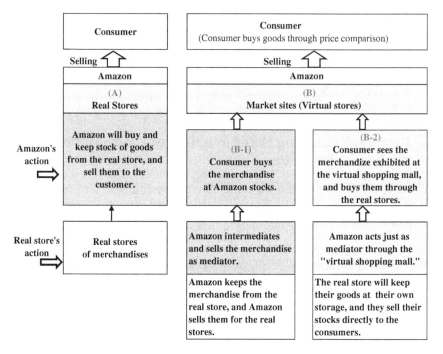

**Fig. 2.**   Three patterns of Amazon's business model.

In order to verify the aforementioned problem, we have to understand the three patterns of the Amazon business model, as shown in Models (B-1), (B-2) and (A) in Fig. 2.

## 6. Cost Sharing in the Online Shopping Ecosystem

As a typical case of Amazon's business, let us examine the Model (B) in Fig. 2. Amazon, as a platform in the online shopping business in the ecosystem, provides various services to the consumers $C$ and to the real stores $S$ in the virtual shopping mall. For such services, Amazon pays the costs $F$ for the benefit of participants $C$ and $S$, which must be compensated (or paid) by the service prices $P^C$ and $P^S$, respectively. Thus, the following equation must be maintained:

$$F \leqq P^C D^C + P^S D^S$$

The inequality sign ($\leqq$) implies that the amount of the cost as "contribution" $F$ given by Amazon should be *at least* compensated by the "incentive payments" to be extended by the consumers and real stores.

How can such a win–win relationship or the mutual cooperation between platformer $X$, real stores $S$, and consumers $C$ be maintained? Let us explore the structure of sharing such costs among the three parties. Again, this problem is the central theme of this chapter.[1]

There are four types of costs shared among Amazon, the real store, and the consumer:

(1) Subscription fee of premium subscribers (consumers).
(2) Sharing the advertising costs by Amazon and the real stores.
(3) Sharing the delivery costs between Amazon and real stores.
(4) Sharing the "system investment" costs between Amazon and real stores.

## 6.1 *Subscription fee of the "prime member" for Amazon*

A "prime member" is a subscriber who is granted free delivery when he or she purchases goods via Amazon.

Such free delivery service also includes the special benefit of "delivery within the day after tomorrow." As of May 2018, the number of target commodity items covered by this benefit is more than one hundred million. In the United States, foods sold by Whole Foods Market Inc., which is the high-end supermarket acquired by Amazon in 2017, are delivered within a few hours, depending on the area.

In Amazon Japan, when prime members pay an annual subscription of 3,900 yen, their privileges include free movies, music, games, and so on, in addition to the free 48-hour delivery service (see Fig. 3).

### 6.1.1 *Conflict between the increase in subscription fee of prime customers and the increase in service costs*

As long as the various free services shown in Fig. 3 are promoted, the number of prime subscribers (i.e., customers) will increase. Therefore, it can be said that the strategy to attract customers to the Amazon platform

---

[1] The theoretical analysis of such a relationship between the contribution and the payment of incentives was examined in Monden (2018) from the viewpoint of the "cooperative game theory" and Barnard's "organization equilibrium theory."

| Basic services (without additional charge) |
|---|
| ○ free delivery service also including the "delivery within the day after tomorrow." |
| ○ free movies such as drama, animation and game, etc. |
| ○ More than 100 free music |

**Fig. 3.** Main benefits for "Prime subscribers" in Japan (adapted from *The Nikkei* (2018e)).

has been successful. (In fact, as of 2018, Amazon has exceeded 10 million prime customers around the world.)

On the other hand, the cost of supporting such value or service benefits (i.e., the cost of IT technology and content departments) has also increased, and this phenomenon should not be overlooked. Thus, Amazon is now trying to charge prime members higher prices for such services.

In the United States, Amazon increased the annual prime membership fee by 20% to $119 in May 2018, four years after the previous fee increase. In addition, in order to encourage monthly fee-paying members to switch to the annual fee, the monthly prime fee was increased by 18% in January 2018.[2]

## 6.2 *Sharing the advertising costs between the platformer and the real stores*

In case of Google (or Amazon), the reason why their *charge rate* to the user C could be reduced to *zero* is due to their online advertising business

---

[2]Change in Amazon Japan: Amazon Japan introduced the prime member system in 2007. Prime members can select either a monthly (400 yen) or an annual fee (3,900 yen). Although the prime members in the world are about 30%, Japanese prime members are still about 10%, since internet shopping in Japan is now on the rise. There is therefore a strong need to attract fee-paying members. That is, most Japanese online shopping users are still non-fee paying members, and thus the platform still has stronger characteristics of a two-sided market. However, since Amazon Japan has also been increasing its service quality, it must also increase (a) the proportion of prime members, and at the same time increase (b) the prime fee, in order to cover the increased system cost. In addition, Amazon Japan is trying to increase (c) the advertising fee (which are referred to as "cooperation costs") for domestic real stores. This data on Amazon Japan was adapted from *The Nikkei* (2018e).

that gives both (a) enough "advertisement revenue linked to each visit by the consumer *C* to the store *S*" and (b) the sufficient "advertisement revenue as a reward linked to every actual purchase by the customer *C* to the store *S*". Thus, Google, on account of its advertising service, earns as much revenue as equivalent to 90% of its total revenue. (For more details, see Yoda (2018).)

## 6.3 *Sharing the delivery costs of the goods: (B-2) business model*

Amazon used to buy and stock goods from (small and medium) real stores, and sell them on their behalf, while the consumer purchases them from Amazon's online store.

For such agent services, Amazon used to collect commissions from real stores. However, since delivery costs have recently been increasing, Amazon decided to increase commission rates; for large items, the commission rate has been increased to a maximum of 20% (*The Nikkei* (2018c)).

The aim of increasing commission was to maintain better services to consumers, which include the "delivery on the day of actual order." Therefore, it is actually to "share" the delivery costs between Amazon and real stores.[3]

## 6.4 *Sharing the costs of "investment in the sales management" system using big data*

Amazon utilizes its own big data based sales management system for sales promotions, even for direct sales through real stores (see Model (A) in Fig. 2). For developing such systems, Amazon must have invested its fund, which also must be shared between Amazon and the real stores as well as manufacturers of such goods.

To develop the "big data"-based sales systems using the massive amount of consumers' personal data, Amazon must pay its fund

---

[3]Due to a serious driver shortage in the "Yamato Transport Co.", a 40% increase in the home delivery charge was agreed between Amazon and Yamato in fall 2017. Additionally, the commission for managing real stores' inventory stocked in Amazon's warehouse was also increased by 4%–10% after April 2018.

which will be a heavy burden on its "fixed costs." Such systems suggest goods that are similar to the goods the customer has recently purchased.[4]

Thus, Amazon charges real stores and/or the private brand (PB) manufacturers 1%–5% of the sales amount, the so-called "cooperation payment" *The Nikkei* (2018b)).

## 6.5 *Shared costs of the real stores will eventually shift to the final sales price*

Both the shared payment of the delivery cost (see Section 5.3) and the shared payment of the cost of system development (see Section 5.4) will eventually shift to the final sales price. The platform business model will not be sustained if this does not occur. Such shift, however, will eventually raise retail prices.

## 7. Conclusion: Relationships between "Contribution" and "Incentive Payments"

Various payments by Amazon must be interpreted as its "contribution" to the real stores $S$ and the consumers $C$ for their receipt of benefits. In order to provide "incentives" to Amazon's contribution, both the real stores and the consumers must pay for Amazon's contribution.

Now, let us first compute the *ratio of each shared cost of real store S* as follows:

---

[4]Such recommendation technology is called the "collaborative filtering". This system first prepares the matrix table whose rows show various customers and the columns show various books. On this table, the figures that show the "grades of interests" in each book by each customer will be assigned to each cell at all intersects in the matrix, depending on whether each book was "previously purchased" or "just inspected" by each customer on the row in question. Amazon's recommendation of books is based on the assumption (or hypothesis) that the customer whose numerical figure is similar (correlated) to other customers in terms of their "coefficient of correlation" will have similar purchase behavior as the other customers in question. Thus, Amazon will recommend such high correlated books in question. Since such data in the matrix table is so big, it is really called the "big data."

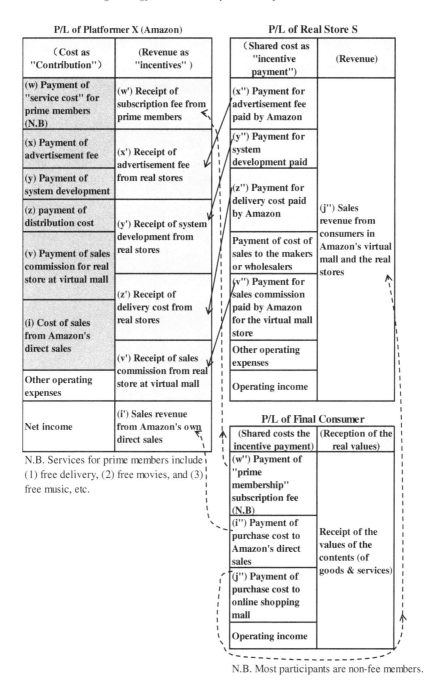

**Fig. 4.** Incentive payments by the real store and the consumers for the contribution by Amazon.

In the above P/L statement of Amazon the following relationships must hold:

The expenses $\leq$. The revenues,

or the Contribution by Amazon $\leq$ the Incentives to Amazon.

Therefore, it follows that

**w + x + y + z + v + i $\leq$ w' + x' + y' + z' + v' + i'**

Further, since the total payment (v') by the real store for the sales commission in the virtual mall must be equivalent to the summation ($\Sigma$) of the payments by each real store in Amazon's mall, it follows that: v' = $\Sigma$v".

Therefore it follows that:

**w' + x' + y' + z' + v' + i' = $\Sigma$(w" + x" + y" + z" + v" + i")**

Further, take (x), which is the payment of advertisement cost by Amazon, for example, it follows that: x' = x$\times$(1 + markup rate). Thus, for each cost item it follows that:

w'= w$\times$(1 + markup rate)

x' = x$\times$(1 + markup rate)

y'= y$\times$(1 + markup rate)

z' = z$\times$(1 + markup rate)

i' = i$\times$(1 + markup rate)

The above markup rate will be determined as follows: First the initial proposal of markup rate for each cost item will be proposed by the platformer to the real sores, and then the final value of each markup will be determined through the negotiation between both parties.

In case the proposed rate by the platformer was much higher or pressing, then the Fair Trade Commission will examine it and be arranged (*The Nikkei* (2018d)).

## References

Monden, Y. (2018). *Economics of Incentives for Inter-Firm Innovation.* Singapore: World Scientific Publishing Company.

Odagiri, H. (2016). *Competition Policy in the Innovation Age: Law and Economics for Research, Patents and Platform.* Tokyo: Yuhikaku (in Japanese).

Rochet, J.-C. and Tirole, J. (2003). Platform competition in two-sided markets. *Journal of the European Economic Association 1*, 990–1029.

Rochet, J.-C. and Tirole, J. (2006). Two-sided market: A progress report. *RAND Journal of Economics 37*, 645–667.

*The Nikkei* (2018a). Alliance with Amazon increased in the real stores, 10 February (in Japanese).

*The Nikkei* (2018b). Amazon demanded charge as cooperation costs to the real stores by 1 or 5%, 28 February (in Japanese).

*The Nikkei* (2018c). Amazon demanded to raise the delivery costs for the net real stores, 1 March (in Japanese).

*The Nikkei* (2018d). How the excellence will be judged: Amazon checked by Fair Trade Commission, 16 March (in Japanese).

*The Nikkei* (2018e). Amazon aggressive price raise: Prime membership fee was raised by 20%, 28 April (in Japanese).

Yoda, T. (2018). Platform and the two-sided market. *The Nikkei*, 9–18 May (in Japanese).

# Chapter 13

# Environmental Effect and Economic Analysis of Environmentally Conscious Capital Investment — Case of Small Chinese Steel Company A

Xuechao Meng and Shufuku Hiraoka

*Faculty of Business Administration, Soka University*
*1 Chome-236 Tangimachi, Hachioji, Tokyo 192-8577, Japan*

## 1. Introduction

Since 1991, the Chinese economy has developed at an annual growth rate of just under 10%. In 2010, China ranked second in the world for GDP, after Japan. However, the high growth of the Chinese economy and industrialization means that there are serious environmental problems. Because the worsening environmental problems began to influence the everyday life of the nation, the Chinese government expanded its authority to cope with these problems and strengthened responsibility. Under such a background, Chinese companies need to pursue economic benefits, as well as focus on environmental impact. Among them, not only large companies but also small- and medium-sized companies have begun to emphasize on environmental management.

This chapter focuses on the environmentally conscious capital investment's economic and environmental effect of a small Chinese steel company, company A. In order to analyze the economic effect of environmentally conscious capital investment, the annual cost reduction amount is calculated, and based on cash flow (CF), the profitability of company-wide investment is also calculated using internal rate of return (IRR) and net present value (NPV) methods. Furthermore, we will establish a consolidated model of environmentally conscious capital investment and MFCA, and numerically clarify the environmental effect of environmentally conscious capital investment.

## 2. Cost Reduction Effect Analysis on Environmentally Conscious Capital Investment

Manufacturing cost data for 15 months[1] before capital investment was collected (see Table 1). Monthly production volume and manufacturing cost are shown in the scatter diagram (see Fig. 1). The unit of production quantity was set as tons, as shown on the x-axis, and the manufacturing cost, yuan, CNY is shown the y-axis.

As can be seen in Fig. 1, it is assumed that the monthly production volume before manufacturing capital investment and the manufacturing cost have a certain relationship. To clarify the relationship, we estimate the variable manufacturing cost per unit and fixed manufacturing cost using Microsoft Excel and exclude the highest and the lowest values using the least-squares method.[2]

Since the multiple correlation coefficient of 15 observations is around 0.98,[3] it can be predicted that there is a relationship between monthly production and production cost. The intercept will be 906, 747, and the x value will be around 3,190. Therefore, the estimated equation is as follows:

$$y = 3,190x + 906,747$$

---

[1] In order to analyze the effect of capital investment from August 2014, data for 15 months from October 2012 to July 2014 before capital investment were collected. Among them, data on months when production stopped was excluded.

[2] The least squares method is a form of mathematical regression analysis that finds the line of best fit for a dataset, providing a visual demonstration of the relationship between the data points. Each point of data is representative of the relationship between a known independent variable and an unknown dependent variable.

[3] It depends on rounding.

**Table 1.** Production volume and manufacturing cost for 15 months before capital investment.

| Month | Production volume (*t*) | Cost of production (Yuan, CNY) |
|---|---|---|
| 10/2012 | 3,761 | 13,269,341 |
| 11/2012 | 7,918 | 27,472,944 |
| 01/2013 | 5,599 | 19,479,506 |
| 03/2013 | 7,271 | 25,956,115 |
| 04/2013 | 8,250 | 28,901,122 |
| 05/2013 | 5,997 | 20,943,378 |
| 09/2013 | 7,078 | 24,134,018 |
| 10/2013 | 3,575 | 11,840,068 |
| 11/2013 | 5,220 | 17,236,496 |
| 12/2013 | 7,393 | 24,803,424 |
| 01/2014 | 3,148 | 10,776,458 |
| 03/2014 | 9,079 | 27,900,418 |
| 04/2014 | 9,331 | 28,948,010 |
| 05/2014 | 5,188 | 16,507,610 |
| 06/2014 | 5,796 | 17,186,493 |

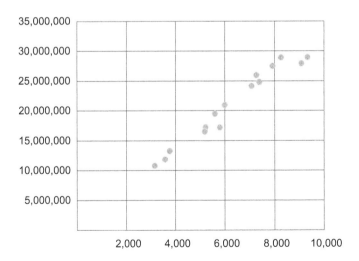

**Fig. 1.** Scatter diagram of monthly production volume and manufacturing cost before capital investment.

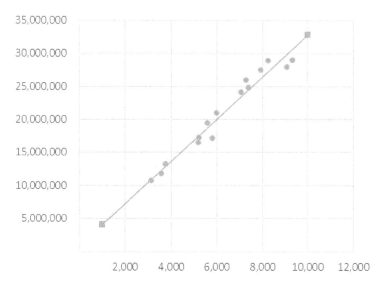

**Fig. 2.** Production cost estimate according to monthly production before capital investment.

Here, $x$ is the production volume, and $y$ is the manufacturing cost (see Fig. 2). That is, the variable manufacturing cost per ton is estimated at 3,190 (yuan, CNY), and the monthly fixed manufacturing cost is estimated at 906,747 (yuan, CNY). The straight line in Fig. 2 is the regression equation using the least-squares method, and the points are the actual values.

Next, we estimate the manufacturing cost assuming that we did not invest in capital, corresponding to the production volume from September 2014 to April 2015. In addition, compared with the actual annual manufacturing cost (see Table 2), it is possible to calculate the annual cash expenditure cost savings. That is, the actual annual manufacturing cost (excluding depreciation expense) is deducted from the annual manufacturing cost estimate after capital investment, and the annual cash expenditure cost savings are calculated (see the formula below).

Annual manufacturing cost estimate when assuming no capital investment

$$= 3{,}190 \times \text{Annual production} + 906{,}747 \times 12 \text{ months}$$
$$= 3{,}190 \times 89{,}019 + 906{,}747 \times 12$$
$$= 294{,}852{,}933 \text{ (yuan, CNY)}$$

**Table 2.** Annual production volume after capital investment and actual manufacturing cost of each month.

| Month | Production volume (*t*) | Cost of production (Yuan, CNY) | (Depreciation cost) |
|---|---|---|---|
| 09/2014 | 6,440 | 18,417,227 | 19,125 |
| 10/2014 | 8,662 | 23,413,835 | 192,027 |
| 11/2014 | 9,309 | 24,421,347 | 138,675 |
| 12/2014 | 6,743 | 16,350,388 | 131,027 |
| 01/2015 | 2,780 | 6,949,620 | 131,027 |
| 02/2015 | 0 | 0 | 0 |
| 03/2015 | 11,130 | 25,505,417 | 262,054 |
| 04/2015 | 13,765 | 30,428,277 | 0 |
| 05/2015 | 13,682 | 30,719,966 | 185,725 |
| 06/2015 | 7,899 | 16,701,154 | 185,725 |
| 07/2015 | 0 | 0 | 0 |
| 08/2015 | 0 | 0 | 0 |
| 09/2015 | 8,610 | 16,836,912 | 185,725 |
| Total | 89,019 | 209,744,143 | 1,431,110 |

Annual cash expenditure cost savings

= Annual manufacturing cost estimate – (Annual actual manufacturing cost after capital investment – Depreciation cost)
= 294,852,933 – (209,744,143 – 1,431,110) = 86,539,900 (yuan, CNY)

From 2014 to 2015, Company A saved cash expenditure cost of 86,539,900 yuan per year through capital investment.

In addition, the reduction rate per ton is calculated, and using these, the cost reduction effect after capital investment can be expressed numerically (see Table 3). As can be seen from Table 3, except for depreciation expenses, unit manufacturing costs for the seven months after capital investment gradually declined. Compared to the forecasts before capital investment, it was speculated that this time environmentally conscious capital investment can cut costs by around 10%–30% per unit. As a result,

**Table 3.**    Cost savings after capital investment.

| Month | Production (*t*) | Pre-investment forecast (Yuan/ton) | After investment (Yuan/ton) | Reduction rate |
|---|---|---|---|---|
| 9/2014 | 6,440 | 3,331 | 2,860 | 14% |
| 10/2014 | 8,662 | 3,295 | 2,703 | 18% |
| 11/2014 | 9,309 | 3,287 | 2,623 | 20% |
| 12/2014 | 6,743 | 3,324 | 2,425 | 27% |
| 1/2015 | 2,780 | 3,516 | 2,500 | 29% |
| 3/2015 | 11,130 | 3,271 | 2,292 | 30% |
| 4/2015 | 13,765 | 3,256 | 2,211 | 32% |

the economic effect of Capital Investment for Environment (hereinafter abbreviated as CIfE) was clarified by numerical examples.

## 3. CF Analysis of CIfE

IRR, NPV, and collection period methods can be used to analyze the economic effect of CIfE. In order to evaluate the company-wide economic effect including company CIfE effect by IRR, and NPV methods, with reference to CF data obtained from our company's annual P/L (Profit and Loss) and B/S (Balance Sheet), we first calculated the present value of the investment of Company A as of August 31, 2014. Next, we calculate the present value of CF as of August 31, 2015, one year later. Finally, we calculate the IRR and NPV of the investment at Company A as of August 31, 2014, assuming that the current value of CF at the end of August 2015 can be secured as CF for the next 10 years, using Microsoft Excel. Based on the CF, we clarify the profitability of the whole company including CIfE.

### 3.1 *Calculation of the present value of the investment at Company A on August 31, 2014*

Company A made capital investment in August 2014, December 2014, and August 2015. To calculate the present value of the investment as of

| Balance sheet | | | | | | | |
|---|---|---|---|---|---|---|---|
| The assets | | | | Liabilities | | | |
| | 8/2014 | 12/2014 | 8/2015 | | 8/2014 | 12/2014 | 8/2015 |
| I Current assets: | | | | I Current liabilities | | | |
| Cash deposit | 2,730,525 | 8,826,894 | 10,490,268.43 | Short-term debt | 15,952,800 | 17,408,800 | 12,511,480.00 |
| Other monetary funds | 109,120 | 0 | | Accounts payable | 566,950 | 1,692,437 | 977,436.13 |
| Accounts receivable | 149,959 | 799,697 | 188,810.39 | Advance payment | 1,527 | 1,527 | 1,526.80 |
| Advance payment | 7,600 | 7,469 | -146,760.00 | Accrued salary | 288,724 | 903,393 | 458,846.00 |
| Other accounts recen | 2,867,015 | 2,867,015 | 2,861,190.80 | Accrued expenses | 894,614 | 758,225 | 843,574.60 |
| Products | 485,518 | 4,457,271 | 768,151.52 | Total current liabilities | 17,704,614 | 20,764,381 | 14,792,864 |
| Prepaid expenses | 172,500 | 435,582 | 477,282.66 | II Long-term liabilities | | | |
| raw materials | 10,153,011 | 4,090,644 | 6,284,408.13 | Total fixed liabilities | 0.00 | 0.00 | 0.00 |
| Package | 115,457 | 75,257 | 12,070.45 | Net assets | | | |
| Low cost consumable | 246,180 | 381,653 | 300,257.49 | Paid-up capital | 17,800,000 | 17,800,000 | 17,800,000.00 |
| Total current asse | 17,036,884 | 21,941,481 | 21,235,680 | Undisclosed profit | -2,359,621 | -2,359,621 | -2,865,416.47 |
| II Fixed assets: | | | | Current profit | 2,235,783 | -505,796 | 5,288,174.63 |
| Fixed asset cost | 13,106,164 | 13,136,664 | 13,173,663.62 | | | | |
| Construction in progre | 766,163 | 620,820 | 606,278.00 | Total net assets | 13,204,596 | 14,934,584 | 20,222,758 |
| Total fixed assets: | 13,872,327 | 13,757,484 | 13,779,942 | | | | |
| Total assets | 30,909,210 | 35,698,965 | 35,015,622 | Total liabilities and net assets | 30,909,210 | 35,698,965 | 35,015,622 |

**Fig. 3.** Company A's monthly balance sheet (unit: yuan) for August 2014, December 2014, and August 2015.

August 31, 2014, we should calculate invested capital and the present value as of August 31, 2014 of the increase in invested capital[4] as of December 31, 2014, and the present value as of August 31, 2014, of the increase in invested capital as of August 31, 2015.

In addition, referring to the balance sheet of Company A in August 2014 (Fig. 3), the invested capital as of August 31 is the total of the current short-term borrowings and net assets. That is calculated using the following formula:

Invested capital as of August 31, 2014

= Short-term borrowings as of August 31, 2014 + Net asset
= 15,952,800 + 13,204,596
= 29,157,396 (yuan, CNY)

---

[4]The increase in invested capita = (Short-term borrowings in December 2014 + Net assets in December 2014) − (Short-term borrowings in August 2014 + Net assets in August 2014).

Then, annual capital cost is set to 10%.[5] In order to calculate the present value as of August 31, 2014, of the increase in invested capital as of December 31, 2014, we use one-third of the annual capital cost. This is calculated using the following formula:

Present value as of August 31, 2014 of the increase in invested capital as of December 31, 2014

= (Increase in invested capital + Depreciation expenses from September to December 2014) ÷ (1 + Annual capital cost × 1/3)
= (3,185,988 + 480,854) ÷ (1 + 0.1 × 1/3)
≈ 3,666,842/1.033
≈ 3,549,701 (yuan, CNY)

Finally, in order to calculate the present value as of August 31, 2014 of the increase in invested capital as of August 31, 2015, we calculated the present value when considering the increase in invested capital from January to August 2015 (see Fig. 3) and the depreciation expenses during that period (see Table 2) as 10% annual capital cost. This is calculated using the following formula:

Present value as of August 31, 2014, of the increase in invested capital as of August 31, 2015

= (Increase in invested capital + Depreciation expenses from January to August 2015) ÷ (1 + 0.1)
= (390,855 + 764,531) ÷ 1.1
= 1,155,386 / 1.1
≈ 1,050,351 (yuan, CNY)

Through the above calculation, the present value of the investment on August 31, 2014 is 33,757,448 (yuan, CNY).

## 3.2 Calculating the present value of CF as of August 31, 2015 (one year later)

To calculate the present value of CF as of August 31, 2015, we use the following expression.

---

[5]Since the annual interest rate of Company A's short-term borrowing is 10%, this chapter considers A's capital cost to be 10%.

Present value of CF as of the end of August 2015

= Total CF from September 2014 to August 2015 + present value of September 2015 for CF as of the end of August 2015.

In other words, it is the sum of the CF from September 2014 to August 2015 and the present value of September 2015[6] for CF as of the end of August 2015.

In addition, in order to calculate CF from September 2014 to August 2015, referring to the monthly "Profit and loss statement", we calculated the operating profit after tax from September 2014 to August 2015. However, since depreciation expenses are also included, the portion is multiplied by the corporate tax rate and added back. This is calculated using the following formula:

CF between September 2014 and August 2015

= Operating profit after tax from September 2014 to August 2015 + Depreciation expenses from September 2014 to August 2015 × Corporate tax rate[7]

= Operating profit[8] from September 2014 to August 2015 × (1 − 0.25) + Depreciation expenses from September 2014 to August 2015 × 0.25

= 6,885,032 × (1 − 0.25) + 1,245,386 × 0.25

= 5,475,121 (yuan, CNY)

In order to calculate the present value of CF in September 2015 as of the end of August 15, 2015, it multiplies 1/12 of the annual capital cost by CF as of the end of September 2015. This is calculated using the following formula:

Present value of CF as of the end of August 2015 in September 2015

= (Operating profit after tax in September 2015 + Depreciation expenses in September 2015 × Corporate tax rate) ÷ (1 + capital cost ÷ 12 months)

= {188,908 × (1 − 0.25) + 185,725 × 0.25} ÷ (1 − 0.1 ÷ 12)

≒ 186,619 (yuan, CNY)

---

[6]We obtained the Profit and Loss statement from September 2014 to September 2015, and also calculated the present value of CF as of the end of August 2015.

[7]Company A's corporate tax rate is 25%.

[8]Operating profit from September 2014 to August 2015 = Total operating profit for each month from September 2014 to August 15.

**Table 4.**  IRR and NPV of Company A.

| Investment in the first year | −33,757,448 | Investment in the first year | −33,757,448 |
|---|---|---|---|
| CF for the 1st year | 5,661,740 | NPV for the 1st year | 5,147,036.36 |
| CF for the 2nd year | 5,661,740 | NPV for the 2nd year | 4,679,123.97 |
| CF for the 3rd year | 5,661,740 | NPV for the 3rd year | 4,253,749.06 |
| CF for the 4th year | 5,661,740 | NPV for the 4th year | 3,867,044.6 |
| CF for the 5th year | 5,661,740 | NPV for the 5th year | 3,515,495.09 |
| CF for the 6th year | 5,661,740 | NPV for the 6th year | 3,195,904.63 |
| CF for the 7th year | 5,661,740 | NPV for the 7th year | 2,905,367.84 |
| CF for the 8th year | 5,661,740 | NPV for the 8th year | 2,641,243.49 |
| CF for the 9th year | 5,661,740 | NPV for the 9th year | 2,401,130.45 |
| CF for the 10th year | 5,661,740 | NPV for the 10th year | 2,182,845.86 |
| IRR = | **10.7%** | NPV = | **1,031,493** |

The present value of CF as of the end of August 2015 was about 5,661,740 yuan.

### 3.3 *IRR and NPV calculations using Excel*

Assuming that the present value of CF as of the end of August 2015 can be secured as CF for the next 10 years, the internal profit rate that satisfies the pension present value coefficient (33,757,448 yuan = 5,661,740 × 10 years) exceeds 10% of the capital cost; this investment can secure profitability. We then calculate IRR and NPV of Company A in Excel (see Table 4).

## 4. Environmental Effect Analysis of CIfE by MFCA

MFCA is a method of environmental management accounting aimed at simultaneously pursuing reduction of environmental burden and cost reduction. We aim to reduce the cost by reducing waste and consequently improving productivity. In MFCA, goods and material losses are captured by the quantity flow, and the cost is calculated proportionally by quantity. That is, since the "positive products" and the "negative products" are calculated in the same way according to the physical quantity, the cost of each product is more accurate and the cost of the "negative product" which could not be clarified by the conventional cost calculation method, can also be clarified. In addition, in MFCA, the cost of each product is classified into MC, SC, and EC[9]; therefore, EC is considered to have high use value as environmental load index. Therefore, according to MFCA, it is possible to clarify the environmental effectiveness of environmentally conscious investment, which could not be observed using conventional cost calculation.

Using the one-month data before and after the environmentally conscious investment (May 2014 and October 2014), we apply MFCA. In order to apply MFCA, we first build a material flow model of Company A. Using this model, we clarify the material input and the output of each manufacturing process (see Fig. 4). Next, in order to quantitatively capture the inputs and outputs, we prepared Table 5, which shows the quantity of inputs and outputs of each month before and after capital investment.

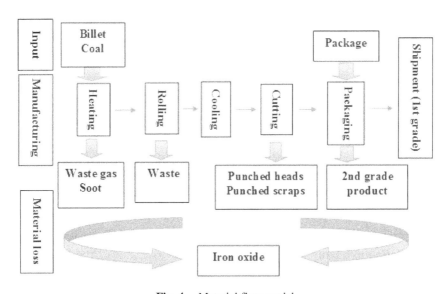

**Fig. 4.** Material flow model.

*Note*: We believe that materials other than the first grade are material loss. "Second-grade product" means products that are 50–100 centimeters shorter than first-grade products. Because second-grade product is not deliberately generated output, we consider it "material loss."

---

[9]MC: Material Cost, SC: System Cost, and EC: Energy Cost

**Table 5.**  Input and output (quantity, unit: ton).

|  | **05/2014** | **10/2014** |
|---|---|---|
| **Input** | **Before capital investment** | **After capital investment** |
| Billet | 5,621.01 | 9,221.69 |
| Coal | 727.24 | 892.06 |
| Package | 4.00 | 20.00 |
| **Total** | **6,352.25** | **10,133.75** |
| **Output** | | |
| Waste gas • Soot | 710.72 | 883.57 |
| Waste | 16.26 | 32.70 |
| Punched heads | 4.82 | 8.92 |
| Punched scraps | 190.52 | 271.15 |
| Iron oxide | 216.26 | 210.60 |
| Second-grade product | 25.91 | 65.11 |
| First-grade product | 5,187.76 | 8,661.69 |
| **Total** | **6,352.25** | **10,133.75** |

Here, the total quantity of inputs and outputs of each month are equal. Next, the total cost item was classified into MC, SC, and EC (see Table 6). Finally, a cost summary table for each output was created (see Table 7). In Table 7, the cost of each product is further classified into MC, SC, and EC. MC is calculated using the following formula. The calculation formulas of SC and EC are similar, so they are omitted.

> **Total MC = Amount of billet + Amount of packaged goods ... ①**
> **MC of each output = ① × the quantity of each output/the total quantity of output ... ②**

In this research, first-grade products are regarded as "positive products." Since the others are not deliberately generated outputs, they are regarded as "negative products" (material loss). In conventional costing, we subtract the value of the sale of products other than the first-grade

**Table 6.** Cost classification table (unit: yuan, CNY).

| | | 5/2014 | 10/2014 |
|---|---|---|---|
| | | **Before capital investment** | **After capital investment** |
| **MC** | Billet | 15,203,483.01 | 21,786,310.02 |
| | Package | 12,187.48 | 56,499.20 |
| | **Total** | **15,215,670.49** | **21,842,809.22** |
| **SC** | Salary | 280,600 | 382,480 |
| | Processing cost | 49,000 | 39,600 |
| | Repair cost | 25,818 | 43,585 |
| | Fixtures | 86,668 | 21,136 |
| | Auxiliary material | — | 3,000 |
| | Low cost consumables | 23,368.04 | 60,282.10 |
| | Work protection | — | 2,400 |
| | **Total** | **465,454.04** | **552,483.1** |
| **EC** | Coal | 449,427.07 | 507,798.55 |
| | Electric energy | 377,058.48 | 318,717.15 |
| | **Total** | **826,485.55** | **826,515.7** |

product from the total manufacturing cost; the rest is the manufacturing cost of the first-grade product. However, we subtract the apportioned cost from the total manufacturing cost of the products other than the first-grade product in the MFCA, and the rest is the manufacturing cost of the first-grade product. Therefore, the unit cost of each product calculated by traditional cost accounting and MFCA is also different (see Table 8).

In MFCA, the manufacturing cost of "negative products" is not selling price that is divided by the quantity, so the manufacturing cost of "negative products" is higher, the manufacturing cost of the first grade is lower. MFCA clarified the cost of "negative products" that could not be clarified by conventional cost accounting, and also clarified the cost of waste gas and soot that had not been visualized so far.

Furthermore, in order to analyze the environmental effect of CIfE, a comparison table of MFCA matrix before and after capital investment was prepared (see Table 9). Based on Table 9, first-grade products are

**Table 7.**　Cost table of each output (unit: yuan, CNY).

| | MC | | SC | | EC | | MC+SC+EC | |
|---|---|---|---|---|---|---|---|---|
| | Before | After | Before | After | Before | After | Before | After |
| **Waste gas · Soot** | — | — | 52,007 | 48,171 | 92,471 | 72,065 | 144,548 | 120,236 |
| **Waste** | 43,819 | 77,016 | 1,191 | 1,783 | 2,116 | 2,667 | 47,126 | 81,466 |
| **Punched heads** | 12,990 | 21,009 | 353 | 486 | 627 | 728 | 13,970 | 22,223 |
| **Punched scraps** | 513,437 | 638,628 | 13,960 | 14,783 | 24,788 | 22,115 | 552,185 | 675,527 |
| **Iron oxide** | 582,804 | 496,012 | 15,846 | 11,482 | 28,137 | 17,177 | 626,788 | 524,670 |
| **Second-grade product** | 69,886 | 153,771 | 1,899 | 3,550 | 3,371 | 5,310 | 75,156 | 162,631 |
| **First-grade product** | 13,992,735 | 20,456,374 | 380,127 | 472,228 | 674,975 | 706,454 | 15,047,837 | 21,635,056 |
| **Total** | 15,215,671 | 21,842,810 | 465,383 | 552,483 | 826,485 | 826,516 | 16,507,610 | 23,221,809 |

**Table 8.** Unit cost comparison of each output (unit: yuan/ton).

| | Conventional unit cost valuation | | Unit cost of MFCA | |
|---|---|---|---|---|
| | **Before** | **After** | **Before** | **After** |
| **Waste gas · Soot** | — | — | 203 | 136 |
| **Waste** | 2250 | 1870 | 2898 | 2491 |
| **Punched heads** | 2650 | 2180 | 2898 | 2491 |
| **Punched scraps** | 2270 | 1900 | 2898 | 2491 |
| **Iron oxide** | 800 | 640 | 2898 | 2491 |
| **Second-grade product** | 2670 | 2150 | 2901 | 2498 |
| **First-grade product** | 3042 | 2530 | 2901 | 2498 |

**Table 9.** MFCA matrix comparison before and after capital investment.

**MC, SC, EC, and MC + SC + BC of the good product · Material loss · Internal waste (before and after capital investment) ÷ Total MC, Total SC, Total EC, Total MC + SC + EC**

| Cost classification | MC | | SC | | EC | | MC + SC + EC | |
|---|---|---|---|---|---|---|---|---|
| | **Before** | **After** | **Before** | **After** | **Before** | **After** | **Before** | **After** |
| **Positive product** | 92.0% | 93.7% | 81.7% | 85.5% | 81.7% | 85.5% | 91.2% | 93.2% |
| **Material loss** | 8.0% | 6.3% | 18.3% | 14.5% | 18.3% | 14.5% | 8.8% | 6.8% |
| **Internal waste** | — | — | 11.2% | 8.7% | 11.2% | 8.7% | 0.9% | 0.5% |
| **Total** | 100% | 100% | 100% | 100% | 100% | 100% | 100% | 100% |

non-defective products — such as waste gas, soot, waste products, punched heads, punched scraps, and iron oxide — and second-grade produces are classed as material loss. Among them, waste gas and soot shall be used as wastes. This is calculated using the following formula.

As can be seen from Table 9, there was a change in the ratio of positive products and material loss before and after capital investment. After capital investment, the non-defective rate increased, and material loss and waste generation decreased. The overall positive product rate rose from 91.2% before capital investment to 93.2%. At the same time, the ratio of material loss fell from 8.8% before capital investment to 6.8%, among which the proportion of waste fell from 0.9% to 0.5%. Therefore, MC, SC, and EC of material loss and waste were reduced overall. The ratio of EC of material loss after capital investment fell from 18.3% to 14.5%, and the ratio of EC of internal waste also decreased from 11.2% to 8.7%. We believe that the change in the ratio of EC (mainly coal) can be used as an index of environmental load reduction. Through the above numerical examples, the environmental effect of CIfE was clarified.

## 5. Conclusion

In order to analyze the economic effect of CIfE at the Chinese steel Company A, we first calculated the annual cash expenditure cost savings using data of the 15 months before capital investment. Furthermore, using the IRR and NPV methods, the company-wide economic effect by CF, including the effect of CIfE, was evaluated. Finally, in order to analyze the environmental effect of CIfE, we introduced the MFCA method using data before and after capital investment. Environmental effectiveness could be evaluated numerically by the linkage model between MFCA and CIfE.

Environmentally conscious capital investment is a source for Chinese enterprises to create environmental and cost competitiveness regardless of their scale. We could also argue that combining MFCA with CIfE would be a more powerful tool, because CIfE and MFCA, which already have accumulated know-how in Japan, can observe the simultaneous achievement of environmental load reduction and economic effect. It is considered easy to introduce this into Chinese enterprises, and it will be a solution to part of the environmental problems in China.

## Bibliography

FEM/FEA (2003). *Guide to Corporate Environmental Cost Management.* Germany Federal Environmental Ministry and Federal Environment Agency.

Hiraoka, S. (2003). *Business Valuation and Management Accounting on EVA™ Organization Structure and Management Accounting*, ZEIMU KEIRI KYOKAI (in Japanese).

ISO14051 (2011). *Environmental Management — Material Flow Cost Accounting — General Framework.* ISO.

IFAC (International Federation of Accountants) (2005). *International Guidance Document: Environmental Management Accounting*. International Federation of Accountants.

Kokubu, K. (2004). *Introduction to Environmental Management Accounting*. Industry Environmental Management Association (in Japanese).

Kokubu, K. (2011). *Accounting System to Support Environmental Management Decision-making*. Chuokeizaisha (in Japanese).

Monden, Y. (2008). *Management Accounting Lecture*. Taxation Accounting Association (in Japanese).

Min, H. and Galle, W. P. (1997). Green purchasing strategies: Trends and implications. *Journal of Supply Chain Management* 33(2), 10–17.

Rooney, C. (1993). Economics of pollution prevention: How waste reduction pays. *Pollution Prevention Review summer*, 261–276.

Shields, M. D. (1995). An empirical analysis of firms' implementation experiences with activity-based costing. *Journal of Management and Accounting Research* 7(4), 148–166.

UNCTAD (United Nations Conference on Trade and Development) (2000). *Integrating Environmental and Financial Performance at the Enterprise Level: A Methodology for Standing Eco-efficiency Indicators*. UN.

UNDSD (United Nations Division for Sustainable Development) (2001). *Environmental Management Accounting: Procedures and Principles*. UN.

## Chapter 14

# Environmental Management to Improve Production Quantity per Unit of Energy: Case Study of a Japanese Manufacturing Company

Kenji Hirayama* and Yoshiyuki Nagasaka[†]

*Gimbal LLC, Hilton Plaza West, Ofice Tower 19th Floor, 2-2-2 Umeda,
Kita Ward, Osaka, OsakaPrefacture 531-0001, Japan
[†]Konan University, 8 Chome-9-1 Okamoto, Higashinada Ward
Kobe, Hyōgo Prefecture 658-0072, Japan

## 1. Introduction

Even small- and medium-sized enterprises (SMEs) cannot ignore their relationship with global environmental issues. In order to achieve sustainable development, it is recommended that a company takes environmental responsibility (Nagasaka, 2011). However, many SMEs are concerned that this approach to environmental issues can cause increase in costs.

The introduction of environmental management systems such as ISO14001 has led to the following comment. The company can achieve social responsibility and try for the reduction of the environmental load. However, the environmental performance increases and decreases by sales and production quantity. It is hard to say that an environmental load decreases uniformly. The expected cost curtailment effect is not provided (Endo, 2009).

In contrast, some companies have introduced ISO50001 (energy management system) because the reduction of the energy unit ratio contributes to significant improvement of productivity. In this chapter, production leveling as a means of environmental management has been considered through the case study of a medium-sized manufacturing company in Japan, KAAZ Corporation.

## 2. Reduction of Environmental Load through Reduction of Downtime

### 2.1 *Environmental management without additional cost*

Improving corporate performance seems to be the greatest motivation for SMEs to tackle environmental management. However, it is thought that SMEs are hesitant regarding investment if an additional cost is necessary for the action. This is because, in many cases, borrowing from financial institutions is necessary in order for SMEs to invest. However, it is thought that it is not easy to explain when investment in environmental management can achieve high ROI for a financial institution on borrowing it. Therefore, it is assumed that SMEs have a high level of interest in the action if environmental management is possible without an additional cost.

In general, numerous initiatives have been announced that realize environmental management through the introduction of state-of-the-art equipment and systems with low environmental impact. Replacing traditional lightbulbs with LED electric bulbs is an example of energy-saving investment.

If energy-saving production can only be achieved through reform of production control without additional cost, environmental management and, at the same time, the improvement of business performance of the company can be achieved. In other words, it is assumed that the company views environmental management positively if energy-saving production can be achieved without an additional cost.

### 2.2 *Relationship between production type and environmental load*

Production is classified into two different types. One that is produced mainly by a machine is referred to as "production made by machine work."

When one worker operates a number of automated machines to process a part, the parts are automatically processed by the machine, and the worker performs preparatory work for setup and monitoring while the machine is in operation. Specifically, in automated converting machinery such as the NC lathe, the operator makes a working program target every working part and plans the material for workings. Machining, which is the main operation, is automatically and repeatedly processed by the processing machine.

In this case, the converting operating machinery uses a significant amount of electricity. If the production per unit of energy when operating the automated converting machinery increases, it can be said that it is management aiming at energy saving. If the downtime of the processing machine during the operation time is minimized, it is assumed that the output per unit of electric power will increase, even if the amount of electric power per unit time is the same. That is, energy saving is achieved by minimizing the downtime.

Manual production is a type of production referred to as "production made by human work." Specifically, when a number of workers are assembling electric products using simple tools, the production amount per hour varies depending on the proficiency level of the workers, and the output is different depending on the increase or decrease in the number of workers. In the case of manufacturing based on human work, such as simple assembly, if the downtime within the operation time is minimized, even if the amount of electric power per hour is the same, the production per unit time will increase and energy-saving management can be achieved.

## 3. Issues and Countermeasures to Realize Production Leveling

### 3.1 *Issues*

Depending on the business conditions of the manufacturing industry, demand has the greatest increase and decrease in the year. When the production volume is high, the production required is generated by overtime or holiday work, but when the production volume is small, the work for the day ends before the working time, so downtime occurs. It is important to reduce the loss of overtime during times of high production volume and the loss of downtime when production volume is small.

Specifically, during the period of high production volume, overtime and the amount of loss due to overtime are calculated, efforts to reduce the loss amount are required, and in the period when the production amount is small, downtime within the operation time and efforts to reduce the loss amount are necessary.

The basis of production leveling is to realize day-by-day load leveling, that is, to make the amount of work per day constant. The first measure to achieve this is to level out production per day by changing the number of days of operation in relation to the monthly production volume. The next countermeasure is to increase the production volume by producing and stocking it as inventory at times when the shipment quantity is small. As inventory increases due to production leveling, cash flow worsens. The second method should be avoided. But, it is desirable to implement even the second one if production leveling is advantageous by evaluating over-time loss and down-time loss.

Based on the aforementioned scenarios, the following four approaches are suggested:

(1) Setting of efficiency standards and implementation of time manage-ment based on these standards.
(2) Calculation of loss of overtime and downtime.
(3) Setting and application of an "operation calendar" for each factory adjusted according to the balance between capacity and load.
(4) Planning and implementation of the stock production for leveling.

(1) and (2) are explained in detail in Sections 3.2 and 3.3.

## 3.2 *Setting of efficiency standards and implementation of time management based on these standards*

The efficiency standard is a productivity index authorized by the organiza-tion. For example, if five units of product A are produced per minute, the efficiency standard becomes five per minute. It should be authorized by the organization as the standard for business management. That is, the effi-ciency standard is a productivity index authorized by the organization.

Task instructions are updated every day based on the latest order receipt and shipping information, and the working time required to manufacture the instructed production volume is calculated based on the efficiency standard. For the required working time, overtime occurs when the number of held man-hours is small, and downtime occurs when the number of man-hours is large. In general, the company strictly manages overtime, but they do not correctly capture downtime within operating hours when the workload is small or take appropriate measures to eliminate downtime. Therefore, it is necessary to construct a time management mechanism based on the efficiency standards as follows:

(1) Set up reasonable "data-based efficiency standards."
(2) Create a work plan describing the start time and the completion time based on the efficiency standards and the number of workers.
(3) Calculate the actual downtime and the overtime losses, and the impact of such losses on performance.
(4) Calculate loss of downtime and overtime, and set up "a plan to minimize downtime and overtime."

## 3.3 *Accounting for loss of downtime and overtime*

Values clarified by calculation of downtime and downtime losses are important subjects of improvement activities. Since payment of allowance due to overtime is cached out, overtime hours are strictly managed, but "value of downtime loss" is not recognized and downtime is not considered. Downtime or overtime occurs every day. In particular, in the case of a manufacturing industry with high seasonal fluctuations, downtime and overtime occur throughout the year and losses are large. Such losses can be defined as follows and effectively utilized for business management (Hirayama, 2018).

The definition of downtime loss and overtime loss is shown in Fig. 1. Case (1) shows a case in which the workload is high, and overtime work

| | Regular operation hours | Overtime work hours |
|---|---|---|
| Case (1) | Normal working hours (A) | Overtime (B) |
| Case (2) | Working time calculated with efficiency standard (A) | Down-time (B) |

**Fig. 1.** The schematic view of downtime and overtime.

occurs. In cost accounting, a time charge is calculated by dividing the total cost of labor costs and "fixed expenses such as depreciation and rents" by the total working hours of A and B. Therefore, when the operating time is long as in Case (1), the time charge is reduced.

When calculating downtime and overtime losses, the total labor costs and fixed expenses such as depreciation and rents within the normal working hours are assigned to the normal working hours (A). The time charge in this case is defined as "absorption costing charge within normal working hours."

On the other hand, it can be considered that in overtime (B), which exceeds the normal working hours, production can only be achieved through incurring "additional costs", such as additional personnel expenses and additional electricity and fuel costs. Since the fixed expenses are not included in the time charge of overtime (B), it is lower than the time charge within the normal working hours. The time charge in this case is defined as "time charge of incremental cost."

In Case (2), the workload is small, and the downtime occurs within the normal working hours. There is a cost equivalent to "absorption costing charge within normal working hours" in the downtime hours, but there is no production volume.

Therefore, the loss of downtime loss and overtime loss is calculated as follows:

Downtime loss = "absorption costing charge within normal working hours"
× downtime
Overtime loss = "time charge of incremental cost" × overtime hours.

## 4. Examples of Improving Performance at the Same Time as Achieving Environmental Management

### 4.1 *Company profile*

KAAZ Corporation (KAAZ) is an agricultural machinery manufacturer with its head office and factory in Okayama, Okayama Prefecture. Its capital is 100 million yen and it employs around 100 people. FY2017 sales was 5.4 billion yen (FY2017 financial results). Its main products are agricultural machines such as brush cutters, lawn mowers, and so on as shown in Fig. 2.

**Fig. 2.** Products made by KAAZ Corporation (Brush Cutters, Lawn Mowers, and Air Launcher).

KAAZ adheres to "Made in Japan" as competitors transfer production overseas, especially to China, and 85% of sales is destined for export. Due to the collapse of the Lehman Brothers in September 2009 and the subsequent appreciation of the yen, the export environment of KAAZ deteriorated rapidly. The exchange rate was 170 yen/euro in 2008 but the euro weakened during the Lehman crisis and in 2012, the exchange rate was 100 yen/euro. The business results of KAAZ Corporation, which export finished goods to 42 countries around the world, rapidly worsened.

While improving performance is urgent, the strategy taken by KAAZ is the implementation of production leveling.

## 4.2 *Loss of downtime and overtime by monthly data*

There is significant seasonal fluctuation in sales of agricultural machinery. Therefore, it was assumed that the performance would improve by eliminating loss of downtime and overtime through the introduction of production leveling.

KAAZ has efficiency standards for the manufacture of each product, and the load man-hours required for production were calculated based on these standards. Table 1 shows the calculated downtime and overtime based on workload held and workload of FY2013 and FY2017. Total workload held indicates the total working hours of factory workers on the working day. The load shows the time required to make the planned monthly quantity.

For example, in FY2013, in July 2012, when the sales was less, the workload necessary for production was 2,907 hours. However, downtime of

**Table 1.**  Downtime and overtime (unit: hour).

|  | Month/ Year | Workload held (hr.) | Workload (hr.) | Downtime (hr.) | Overtime |
|---|---|---|---|---|---|
|  | 7/2012 | 7,030 | 2,907 | 4,123 |  |
|  | 8/2012 | 6,363 | 3,154 | 3,209 |  |
|  | 9/2012 | 6,473 | 2,475 | 3,998 |  |
|  | 10/2012 | 7,432 | 2,734 | 4,698 |  |
|  | 11/2012 | 7,070 | 3,763 | 3,307 |  |
| FY2013 | 12/2012 | 7,169 | 5,673 | 1,496 |  |
|  | 1/2013 | 7,082 | 6,427 | 655 |  |
|  | 2/2013 | 6,922 | 5,021 | 1,901 |  |
|  | 3/2013 | 6,852 | 5,900 | 952 |  |
|  | 4/2013 | 7,117 | 6,739 | 378 |  |
|  | 5/2013 | 7,021 | 9,201 |  | −2180 |
|  | 6/2013 | 6,960 | 11,438 |  | −4478 |
|  | **Total** | **83,491** | **65,431** | **24,718** | **−6658** |
|  | 7/2016 | 5,211 | 6,342 |  | −1131 |
|  | 8/2016 | 5,697 | 7,089 |  | −1392 |
|  | 9/2016 | 6,023 | 7,795 |  | −1772 |
|  | 10/2016 | 6,023 | 7,869 |  | −1846 |
|  | 11/2016 | 6,023 | 8,504 |  | −2481 |
| FY2017 | 12/2016 | 5,777 | 8,405 |  | −2628 |
|  | 1/2017 | 5,777 | 8,211 |  | −2434 |
|  | 2/2017 | 5,956 | 8,495 |  | −2539 |
|  | 3/2017 | 6,788 | 8,990 |  | −2202 |
|  | 4/2017 | 6,018 | 7,396 |  | −1378 |
|  | 5/2017 | 6,018 | 7,407 |  | −1389 |
|  | 6/2017 | 6,648 | 6,686 |  | −38 |
|  | **Total** | **71,959** | **93,189** | **0** | **−21230** |

4,123 hours (7,030–2,907) occurred in working hours because the workload held was actually 7,030 hours. In June 2013, the workload was 11,438 hours, but since the workload held was 6,960, a shortfall of 4,478 hours was covered using overtime. That is, this indicates that overtime has occurred.

In FY2017, five years after FY2013, the downtime disappears due to a reduction of the workload held and production leveling, and overtime hours occurred in all months. For example, in July 2016, the workload held was 5,211 hours, but the actual workload was 6,342 hours and the overtime was 1,131 hours.

## 4.3 *Calculation of loss of downtime and overtime*

Table 2 shows the loss of downtime and overtime in each period from FY2013 to FY2017. The time charge is calculated as the average of the fifth term; the charge for the loss of downtime is 3,968 yen/hour, and the charge for the loss of overtime is 2,233 yen/hour.

In FY2013, there was a combined total of 113 million yen in lost downtime and overtime, and a profit improvement of a maximum of 113 million yen is expected through production leveling. Therefore, KAAZ aimed to reduce downtime and overtime losses by implementing production leveling, and as a result attempted to achieve a maximum profit improvement of 113 million yen. As a result, downtime loss decreased from 98 million yen to zero yen and overtime loss increased from 15 million yen to 47 million yen. In total, profit improvement of 66 million yen was achieved compared to FY2013 and FY2017. As shown in Table 1, the time

**Table 2.** Calculation of loss of downtime and overtime.

| | | FY2013 | FY2014 | FY2015 | FY2016 | FY2017 | Difference between FY2017 and FY2013 |
|---|---|---|---|---|---|---|---|
| Time evaluation (hr.) | Downtime (hr.) | 24,718 | 816 | 0 | 0 | 0 | −24718 |
| | Overtime (hr.) | 6,658 | 9,230 | 25,290 | 23,860 | 21,230 | 14572 |
| | Total (hr.) | 31,376 | 10,046 | 25,290 | 23,860 | 21,230 | −10146 |
| Value evaluation (million yen) | Downtime loss (million yen) | 98 | 3 | 0 | 0 | 0 | −98 |
| | Overtime loss (million yen) | 15 | 21 | 6 | 53 | 47 | 33 |
| | Total (million yen) | 113 | 24 | 6 | 53 | 47 | −66 |

Charge of the downtime loss 3,968 Yen/Hour
Charge of the overtime work loss 2,233 Yen/Hour

held by FY2013 is 83,491 hours per year, but the time held by FY2017 is 71,959 hours, which is a decrease of 11,532 hours. It can be said that a profit improvement of about 58 million yen has been achieved by multiplying this decrease by the time charge of downtime loss (3,968 yen/ hour).

That is, when comparing FY2013 and FY2017, the total improvement of 124 (66 + 58) million yen, which is the reduction of downtime loss (66 million yen) and the reduction in holding time (58 million yen), is due to the implementation of production leveling.

## 4.4 *Realizing production leveling*

### (1) Achievement status of "daily production leveling"

In KAAZ, reform of production control was advanced with the aim of achieving daily production leveling. The progress is as shown in Table 3. The difference between the maximum and the minimum values of the production value per day for each month was used as a KPI, indicating that "daily production leveling" is progressing.

Table 3 shows the daily production value of FY2013 and FY2017. The production value per day is calculated as the production value of each month divided by the number of working days.

In parts processing of FY2013, the month with the smallest production value per day is July, with zero yen. The month with the largest number is March with 4.29 million yen. The difference of the largest number and the smallest number was compared in each period, and it was used as an index to measure the progress of "production leveling per day." For example, parts processing in FY2013 is 4.29 million yen, but it is reduced to 2.52 million yen in FY2017.

### (2) Achievement of "production leveling per day" of parts processing

Table 4 shows the status of "daily production leveling" of parts processing in each fiscal period.

Regarding the minimum value (MIN), there are months in FY2013 and FY2014 in which there was no production, but in FY2017 production was 4.07 million yen per day and it can be inferred that downtime is

**Table 3.** Daily production value of FY2013 and FY2017 (unit: million yen/day).

| | Month | Jul | Aug | Sep | Oct | Nov | Dec | Jan | Feb | Mar | Apr | May | Jun | Total | MIN (Minimum production amount) | MAX (Maximum production amount) | AVE (Average production amount) | MAX-MIN (Difference between MAX and MIN) |
|---|---|---|---|---|---|---|---|---|---|---|---|---|---|---|---|---|---|---|
| FY2013 | Parts processing | 0.00 | 0.94 | 0.50 | 0.21 | 0.61 | 3.48 | 4.11 | 3.71 | 4.29 | 3.46 | 1.27 | 3.75 | 2.21 | 0.00 | 4.29 | 2.19 | 4.29 |
| | Assembly processing | 9.21 | 7.83 | 4.31 | 6.82 | 7.52 | 11.49 | 10.04 | 8.26 | 10.83 | 9.71 | 16.54 | 18.43 | 10.24 | 4.31 | 18.43 | 10.08 | 14.12 |
| | Total | 9.21 | 8.77 | 4.81 | 7.03 | 8.13 | 14.97 | 14.15 | 11.97 | 15.12 | 13.18 | 17.81 | 22.18 | 12.46 | 4.81 | 22.18 | 12.28 | 17.37 |
| | Number of working days | 19 | 20 | 19 | 22 | 21 | 19 | 20 | 20 | 21 | 23 | 23 | 23 | 250 | | | | |
| FY2017 | Parts processing | 4.07 | 4.80 | 5.10 | 4.91 | 4.98 | 5.64 | 5.38 | 6.59 | 4.85 | 5.04 | 4.86 | 4.58 | 5.09 | 4.07 | 6.59 | 5.07 | 2.52 |
| | Assembly processing | 10.82 | 11.56 | 11.15 | 12.12 | 15.79 | 15.24 | 14.07 | 13.81 | 14.49 | 13.04 | 11.95 | 10.56 | 12.95 | 10.56 | 15.79 | 12.88 | 5.23 |
| | Total | 14.89 | 16.36 | 16.25 | 17.04 | 20.77 | 20.89 | 19.45 | 20.41 | 19.34 | 18.08 | 16.81 | 15.14 | 18.04 | 14.89 | 20.89 | 17.95 | 6.00 |
| | Number of working days | 16 | 19 | 20 | 20 | 20 | 20 | 20 | 22 | 25 | 22 | 22 | 21 | 247 | | | | |

K. Hirayama & Y. Nagasaka

**Table 4.** Achievement status of "production leveling per day" of parts processing (production value, million yen/day).

| Parts processing | FY2013 | FY2014 | FY2015 | FY2016 | FY2017 | FY2017/ FY2013 |
|---|---|---|---|---|---|---|
| MIN (Minimum production value) | 0.00 | 0.00 | 3.63 | 4.10 | 4.07 | — |
| MAX (Maximum production value) | 4.29 | 5.50 | 6.88 | 6.13 | 6.59 | 1.54 |
| AVE (Average production value) | 2.19 | 4.11 | 4.81 | 4.88 | 5.07 | 2.31 |
| MAX - MIN (Difference between MAX and MIN) | 4.29 | 5.50 | 3.24 | 2.03 | 2.52 | **0.59** |

decreasing. In addition, the maximum production value (MAX) is 1.54 times that of FY2017/FY2013, and the maximum value for daily production is high in FY2013. Furthermore, the average production value FY2017/FY2013 is 2.31, which means that the production volume per day is increasing. That is, with the achievement of "daily production leveling", the average value of daily production has significantly increased, and productivity has also increased. In parts processing, parts are processed using automated machines, and efforts to increase productivity by improving the performance of machines generally produce results. However, KAAZ did not invest in machinery renewal during this period. Therefore, it can be said that productivity has been increased by achieving "daily production leveling" rather than machine renewal. The difference (MAX − MIN) between the maximum and the minimum values of the daily production value for each period once increased in FY2014, but this is the result of production adjustment in FY2013.

The differences between maximum and minimum production value are reduced in FY2016 and FY2017. In addition, it is 0.59 for FY2017/ FY2013, indicating that daily production leveling is progressing.

## (3) Achievement status of "daily production leveling" of assembly processing

Table 5 shows the achievement status of "daily production leveling" in each fiscal period of assembly processing.

**Table 5.** Achievement status of "daily production leveling" of assembly processing (production value, million yen/day).

| Assembly processing | FY2013 | FY2014 | FY2015 | FY2016 | FY2017 | FY2017/ FY2013 |
|---|---|---|---|---|---|---|
| MIN (Minimum production value) | 4.31 | 6.96 | 5.45 | 7.33 | 10.56 | 2.45 |
| MAX (Maximum production value) | 18.43 | 17.68 | 19.20 | 17.00 | 15.79 | 0.86 |
| AVE (Average production value) | 10.08 | 10.67 | 12.29 | 13.32 | 12.88 | 1.28 |
| MAX - MIN (Difference between MAX and MIN) | 14.12 | 10.72 | 13.75 | 9.67 | 5.23 | 0.37 |

In terms of the minimum production value (MIN), it can be inferred that in FY2017 it is 2.45 times as compared with FY2013, and there is a decrease in downtime. In addition, the maximum production value (MAX) is 0.86 times larger than FY2017/FY2013, and the maximum production value for daily production is smaller after FY2013. Furthermore, the average production value in FY2017/FY2013 is 1.28 times, which means that the production value per day is increasing.

The difference (MAX - MIN) between the maximum and the minimum production value of the daily production value for each period is larger in FY2015, which is the result of production adjustment in FY2014.

The difference between the maximum production value and the minimum production value in FY2016 and FY2017 became small. In other words, leveling production has been achieved. As a result, "FY2017/FY2013" as an indicator for daily leveling production is 0.37, indicating that leveling production has been achieved even in five periods.

## 4.5 Relationship between achievement of daily production leveling and environmental management

### (1) Parts processing: capital investment-type production using machines

| Parts processing | | FY2013 | FY2014 | FY2015 | FY2016 | FY2017 | FY2017/FY2013 |
|---|---|---|---|---|---|---|---|
| Data | Amount of electricity consumed(kWh) | 798,128 | 1,081,320 | 1,149,399 | 1,177,865 | 1,246,213 | 1.56 |
| | Operating time(hr.) | 7,080 | 10,224 | 10,504 | 10,424 | 10,888 | 1.54 |
| | Production value(million yen) | 553 | 1,041 | 1,196 | 1,196 | 1,257 | 2.27 |
| KPI | Amount of electricity consumed(kWh)/ operating time(hr.) | 113 | 106 | 109 | 113 | 114 | 1.02 |
| | Production value/Amount of electricity consumed(kWh) | 0.00069 | 0.00096 | 0.00104 | 0.00102 | 0.00101 | 1.45 |
| | Production value/Operating time(hr.) | 0.08 | 0.10 | 0.11 | 0.11 | 0.12 | 1.48 |

| CO2 reduction | | FY2013 | FY2014 | FY2015 | FY2016 | FY2017 | Total |
|---|---|---|---|---|---|---|---|
| CO2 reduction | pre-improvement electricity consumption(kWh) | 798,128 | 1,500,656 | 1,725,491 | 1,725,413 | 1,812,769 | 7,562,457 |
| | Amount of electricity consumed(kWh) | 798,128 | 1,081,320 | 1,149,399 | 1,177,865 | 1,246,213 | 5,452,925 |
| | Reduced energy consumption (kWh) | 0 | -419,336 | -576,092 | -547,548 | -566,557 | -2,109,533 |
| | CO2 reduction(Ton) | 0 | -291 | -400 | -380 | -393 | -1,464 |

**Fig. 3.** Relationship between amount of electricity consumed, operating time, and production value.

Figure 3 shows the relationship between electricity consumed, operating time, and production value.

As KPIs, consider the following three indicators: (a) the electricity consumed per operating time, (b) the production value per amount of electricity consumed, and (c) the production value per operating time.

(a) The electricity consumed per operating time is 1.02 times greater in FY2017/FY2013, and no significant change is observed in the previous five fiscal periods. In the case of energy-saving investment, it appears that the electricity consumed per operating time will decrease, but since KAAZ did not invest in electricity savings during the previous five fiscal periods, it seems reasonable that there will be no change in the electricity consumed per operating time.

(b) The production value per unit of electric energy is 1.45 times greater in FY2017/FY2013. The fact that the production value is increasing even with the same amount of electricity consumption appears to be due to the fact that the downtime during the operation of the machine has decreased due to production leveling.

(c) Similarly, the production value per operating time is 1.48 times greater in FY2017/FY2013, and productivity also continues to increase after FY2014.

To summarize, the fact that the production value is increasing even with the same amount of electricity consumption is thought to be due to achieving production leveling, which has the effect of reducing the downtime while the machine is in operation.

In the case of capital investment-type production, even if "daily production leveling" is achieved, the amount of electricity consumed per hour does not change unless investment in power saving is carried out. Furthermore, the production value per unit of electricity consumed increases due to the fact that the downtime within the operating time is reduced by "daily production leveling." For the reasons stated herein, the production value per unit of electricity and the production value per operating time significantly increase at almost the same ratio. In the case of capital investment-type production, since the amount of electricity consumed in relation to the operation of facilities increases the cost, if the production value is increased, it can be said that production with less running time, that is, less electric energy constitutes environmentally friendly management.

Assuming that the production per unit of electricity consumed in FY2013 did not improve and parts processing continued with the same productivity, it becomes "pre-improvement electric power amount", as shown in Fig. 3.

By calculating the difference between the "pre-improvement electricity consumption" and the actual electric energy as "reduced electric energy", it becomes "reduced electric energy (kWh)" shown in Fig. 3. The amount of $CO_2$ reduction is based on the following calculation:

$$CO_2 \text{ emissions (kg} - CO_2) = \text{electricity usage (kWh)} \times CO_2 \text{ emission coefficient (kg} - CO_2/\text{kWh})$$

Based on data published by the Chugoku Electric Power Co., which supplies electricity to KAAZ, the $CO_2$ emission coefficient is 0.694 kg $- CO_2/$kWh. In FY2017, $CO_2$ emissions are reduced by 393 tons/year compared to FY2013. Assuming FY2013 as the base year, the cumulative $CO_2$ emission reduction amount for four years from FY2014 to FY2017 is 1,464 tons.

## (2) Assembly: Production based on human work

Figure 4 shows the relationship between the electricity consumed, the number of man-hours required for production, and the production value of the assembly.

| Assembly processing | | FY2013 | FY2014 | FY2015 | FY2016 | FY2017 | FY2017/ FY2013 |
|---|---|---|---|---|---|---|---|
| Data | Amount of electricity consumed(kWh) | 147,280 | 171,540 | 181,275 | 189,955 | 196,163 | 1.33 |
| | Operating time(hr.) | 48,215 | 31,008 | 41,646 | 41,906 | 45,395 | 0.94 |
| | Production value(million yen) | 2,561 | 2,712 | 3,062 | 3,285 | 3,198 | 1.25 |
| KPI | Amount of electricity consumed(kWh)/ operating time(hr.) | 3.05 | 5.53 | 4.35 | 4.53 | 4.32 | 1.41 |
| | Production value/Amount of electricity consumed(kWh) | 0.01739 | 0.01581 | 0.01689 | 0.01729 | 0.01630 | 0.94 |
| | Production value/Operating time(hr.) | 0.05 | 0.09 | 0.07 | 0.08 | 0.07 | 1.33 |
| CO2 reduction | | FY2013 | FY2014 | FY2015 | FY2016 | FY2017 | Total |
| CO2 reduction | pre-improvement electricity consumption(kWh) | 147,280 | 155,978 | 176,127 | 188,934 | 183,938 | 852,256 |
| | Amount of electricity consumed(kWh) | 147,280 | 171,540 | 181,275 | 189,955 | 196,163 | 886,213 |
| | Reduced energy consumption (kWh) | 0 | 15,562 | 5,148 | 1,021 | 12,226 | 33,957 |
| | CO2 reduction(Ton) | 0 | 11 | 4 | 1 | 8 | 24 |

**Fig. 4.** Relationship between electricity consumed, input man-hours, and production value.

As KPIs, consider the three indices: (a) the electricity consumed per input man-hour, (b) the production value per electricity consumed, and (c) the production value per input man-hour.

Assembly is human-centered production, and KPI compared with a worker's input man-hour is effective.

(a) The electricity consumed per input man-hour in FY2017 has increased to 1.41 times in FY2013. Assembly work is mainly manual work. Therefore, if the downtime decreases due to production leveling, it is reasonable that the electricity consumed per hour increases as the working density increases within working hours.

(b) For the above reasons, the production value per electricity consumed in FY2017 is 0.94 times compared to FY2013, and there is no significant difference in the index during the five fiscal periods.

(c) The production value per man-hour in FY2017 is 1.33 times in FY2013, indicating that productivity is improving. If the same production value is achieved, it can be said that this constitutes environmentally friendly management to ensure production with less electric energy and fewer man-hours, but in the case of manual work such as assembly, the production value per unit of electricity consumed does not change.

Assembly work is mainly manual work, so it would be reasonable for the production value to increase within the working hours if the working density per hour rises due to "daily production leveling." Since the worker is the largest cost factor in assembly, if the production value per man-hour increases, the cost will decrease and contribute to improvement in performance.

Reduction in electricity consumption and $CO_2$ emissions reduction amount are calculated in the same way as for parts production. In FY2017, $CO_2$ emissions are increasing (8 tons/year) compared to when there is no improvement in production leveling. Taking FY2013 as the base year, the cumulative $CO_2$ emissions of FY2014–FY2017 increased by 24 tons over the four years. That is, in manual assembly work, $CO_2$ emissions will increase as work density increases through "daily production leveling."

## 5. Improvement of Financial Performance through "Production Leveling"

As shown in Table 6, the financial performance of KAAZ is rapidly improving.

Evaluate improvement of business results by "daily leveling production" by gross profit margin. The gross–margin ratio increased to 1.70 in FY2017/ FY2013. KAAZ made efforts to implement "daily production leveling" with the aim of improving financial performance, and as a result, the production value per unit of electricity consumed and the production value per man-hour have greatly improved. As a result, the gross profit margin is increasing every year, and realization of "daily leveling production" appears to make a significant contribution to business results. In the case of KAAZ, it is possible to evaluate this by eliminating the factors caused by the increase and decrease in sales, by aiming for improvement in performance through improving production control without aiming to improve performance by

Table 6. KAAZ's financial performance trends.

| Financial performance trends | FY2013 | FY2014 | FY2015 | FY2016 | FY2017 | FY2017/ FY2013 |
|---|---|---|---|---|---|---|
| Sales amount (million yen) | 5,512 | 5,457 | 5,331 | 5,016 | 5,391 | 0.98 |
| Gross profit margin (million yen) | 586 | 794 | 883 | 870 | 976 | 1.67 |
| Gross-margin ratio | 10.6% | 14.6% | 16.6% | 17.3% | 18.1% | 1.70 |

sales growth. As previously mentioned, since KAAZ did not conduct rationalization investment during five fiscal periods, it can be seen that performance is greatly improved by improving "daily leveling production."

## 6. Summary

Through examples of efforts to improve performance, it was proved that achievement of "daily production leveling" can simultaneously achieve both performance improvement and environmental impact reduction. The significance of this is that what was theoretically perceived could be realized in the actual challenge of management, and as a result, many companies are expected to become flexible in order to achieve both comprehensive performance improvement and environmental management. That is, it is expected that managers who believe that investing in environmental management show that such management can be realized by improving production control such as "daily production leveling."

In the future, it is necessary to present a number of case examples that demonstrate improvement in performance while realizing production with low environmental load by improving production control.

## References

Endo, M. (2009). Introduction check factor of environmental management in SMEs — Focused on mental aspect in Top management. *Research Bulletin of the Kyushu Institute of Information Sciences 11*, 85–96 (in Japanese).

Hirayama, K. (2018). *A challenge to common value creation — Local bank to win, the manufacturing industry to revive*. KINZAI (in Japanese), ISBN-10: 4322132561

Nagasaka, Y. (2011). Issue of SCM for Japanese companies and their efforts toward green logistics. In Monden, Y. (ed.) *Management of an Inter-Firm Network*, World Scientific, pp. 155–169.

# Index

action controls, 136
action research, 113, 122, 123, 125, 126
actions controls, 132
advertising costs, 195
agency theory, 153–156, 170
annual capital cost, 210
Asian Productivity Organization (APO), 75
auditors, 177

balance sheet, 209
beliefs system, 34
big data, 198
board of directors, 35
boundary system, 34

Canon, 71
capital investment-type production, 235
capital structure, 176
case study, 96, 97
CIfE, 208
$CO_2$ emission, 72, 76
cognitive legitimacy, 53, 54, 60, 61
collaborative filtering, 198
communication, 30

compatibility, 85
complexity, 85
contribution, 190, 194
corporate environmental management, 131
corporate governance, 34, 173
corporate social responsibility (CSR), 33, 167
corporate value, 121
cost accounting, 70
cost reduction, 71, 75
cost reduction effect, 207
cost reduction effect analysis, 204
critical mass, 191
cultural controls, 132, 136
cycle time system, 117

daily leveling production, 237
daily production leveling, 230, 232
delivery costs, 195
developability, 86, 89
diagnostic control system, 34
diffusion theory, 84
direct network effect, 190
diversified business, 193
downtime loss, 226, 230

economic behavior principle, 99
economic effect, 203
ecosystem, 77
efficiency standard, 224, 225
emotion, 95
energy cost, 73
energy-saving management, 223
Enterprise Resource Planning (ERP), 67
environmental communication, 20,
    21, 24
environmental effect, 204
environmental load index, 213
environmental load reduction, 218
environmentally conscious capital
    investment, 204
environmental management, 203, 221,
    238
environmental management
    accounting, 212
environmental management control
    systems (EMCSs), 16, 132
environmental management systems
    (EMSs), 131
environmental performance, 178

foreign investors, 38

German MFCA, 65, 67
Global Reporting Initiative (GRI), 49,
    168
Green Productivity Program, 75
GRI standards, 179

holding time, 230
human-centered production, 236

imperfect competition market, 191
incentive payments, 194
incentives, 190

indirect network effect, 190, 192
inputs, 214
Institut für Management und Umwelt
    (IMU), 65, 66
institutional investors, 38
institutional theory, 153, 154
insufficient budget, 86
integration, 3
interactive control system, 34
internal profit rate, 212
International Integrated Reporting
    Council (IIRC), 49
interruption of knowledge, 86
invested capital, 209
investment in the sales management,
    197
IRR, 208
ISO 14000 family, 81
ISO 14001, 132, 146
ISO 14051, 65
ISO 26000, 56
ISO: International Organization for
    Standardization, 71

Japanese MFCA, 65, 68, 69
Japan Industrial Standards Committee
    (JISC), 71
J-Cost, 117, 118
Just-in-Time, 115

KAAZ Corporation, 226
kaizen, 72
knowledge interruptions, 90
KPI, 3, 234

lean accounting, 117
Lean Management, 72
legitimacy theory, 153, 154, 156, 160,
    170

levers of control (LOC), 33
life cycle assessment (LCA), 72
loss of overtime, 224

Malaysia Productivity Corporation
(MPC), 76
management control, 17
management control systems (MCSs),
  33
manufacturing cost, 206
manufacturing industry, 223
mass balance, 70, 71
material and resource flows, 78
material flow chart, 70, 71
material flow cost accounting
  (MFCA), 65, 81, 82, 113, 212
material flow model, 213
material flows and stocks, 69
material flow time costing (MFTC),
  113, 118
material loss, 70, 71, 74, 76, 212
Matsushita Electric Industrial
  (Panasonic), 71
maximum production value, 233
media, 178
mesoscopic model, 122
METI, 68
MFCA design, 84
MFCA mass data, 75
minimum production value, 233
moral legitimacy, 53, 54, 60, 61

negative product, 71, 215
negative product ratio, 74
new Kaizen tool, 69
Nippon Paint, 71
Nitto Denko, 71
non-fee paying customers, 192
non-financial reporting, 150, 155, 157

NPV, 208
numerical examples, 218

observability, 85
Öko-Controlling (eco-controlling), 18
operating profit, 211
Oracle, 67
outputs, 214
outside directors, 38
Overtime loss, 226
Ownership structure, 176

perceived attributes of innovation, 85
personnel controls, 132, 136
platform, 189
policy, 89
polite communication, 31
pollution reduction, 137, 144
positive product, 71, 217
positive product rate, 217
practice theory, 100
pragmatic legitimacy, 53, 60
production leveling, 222, 224, 227,
  229
profitability, 172
profit potential, 117
proportion of waste, 218

quality circle (QC), 68
quantity centers, 71
quantity flow, 212
questionnaire, 84

ratio of material loss, 217
reduction rate, 207
relative advantage, 85
religion, 157, 158, 161
resistance, 86
resource efficiency, 137, 144

result controls, 132, 134
risk spreading, 193

SAP, 67
Schatzki, T., 100
sensitivity, 31
small- and medium-sized enterprises
     (SMEs), 102, 221
social and environmental reporting,
     149, 159, 160
social costs and benefits, 77
Sony EMCS, 71
stakeholder influence, 136
stakeholder theory, 153, 154, 156,
     160, 170
steel company, 203
structural equation modeling (SEM),
     42
subscription fee, 192, 195
sunk cost, 192
sustainability, 127
sustainability management, 81
sustainability management control
     systems (SMCSs), 33

sustainability reporting, 167
sustainability strategy, 4
sustainable economy, 75
sustainable management, 131
system cost, 68, 72
system investment costs, 195

Tanabe-Seiyaku, 71
tax rate, 211
text analysis, 50
text mining, 50, 52, 55, 60, 61
Total Productive Maintenance (TPM),
     68
Toyota Production System (TPS), 113
traditional cost accounting, 215
two-sided market, 189

Volkswagen AG, 79

WACC, 118, 120, 121, 126
waste products, 82
waste treatment cost, 75
water input cost, 73
working hours, 228

CPSIA information can be obtained
at www.ICGtesting.com
Printed in the USA
JSHW020712161019
1952JS00001B/5

9 789811 200182